# MOUTHS OF RAIN

D1569902

# MOUTHS OF RAIN

## AN ANTHOLOGY OF
## BLACK LESBIAN THOUGHT

Edited by

# BRIONA SIMONE JONES

NEW YORK
LONDON

© 2021 by The New Press
All rights reserved.
No part of this book may be reproduced, in any form, without written permission from the publisher.

Permissions information can be found on pages 361–363.

Requests for permission to reproduce selections from this book should be made through our website: https://thenewpress.com/contact.

Published in the United States by The New Press, New York, 2021
Distributed by Two Rivers Distribution

ISBN 978-1-62097-576-3 (pb)
ISBN 978-1-62097-625-8 (ebook)
CIP data is available

The New Press publishes books that promote and enrich public discussion and understanding of the issues vital to our democracy and to a more equitable world. These books are made possible by the enthusiasm of our readers; the support of a committed group of donors, large and small; the collaboration of our many partners in the independent media and the not-for-profit sector; booksellers, who often hand-sell New Press books; librarians; and above all by our authors.

www.thenewpress.com

*Book design and composition by Bookbright Media*
*This book was set in Bembo, Lato, and Gotham*

Cover photograph by TCHHNNH (tochihannah)

Printed in the United States of America

*Art serves many purposes; it can heal, educate, entertain, and challenge.
Art is a tool for speaking out because it has the ability to transform people.*

—Andrea Jenkins

Kaladaa Crowell, Brandi Mells, Shanta Myers, Kerrice Lewis, Crystal Jackson, Britney Cosby

#SayHerName

# Contents

# Foreword: We Won't Stop the Rain
## Cheryl Clarke

There is no better gift, as I enter this third decade of the twenty-first century, than to hold *Mouths of Rain* to my breast. Editor Briona Simone Jones places it so confidently and forthrightly before me—this "florilegium" of Black lesbian feminist writing. It is various, sophisticated, and timely. This collection, spanning vintage to millennial Black lesbian feminist writers, answers affirmatively that those of us who write as Black lesbians today owe our voices to writers like Mamie Burrill, Alice Dunbar-Nelson, Angelina Weld Grimké, and Pauli Murray, and our boldness to blues-women songwriters like Lucille Bogan and Ma Rainey, because they put out the *word* with songs like "B.D. Woman's Blues" and "Prove It On Me": "Went out last night with a crowd of my friends, / They must've been women, 'cause I don't like no mens" (Rainey).

There are vital texts here: excerpts from "Introductions" of preceding anthologies of Black lesbian writing, theoretical and political texts, and cross-generational poetry, short fiction, interviews, and never-before-published texts—as I said, florilegium.

Jones regales us with the work of New Negro Renaissance, pre–World War II, Boomer, Gen X, and Millennial dykes, queer women, butches, femmes, and lesbians. But I want to shout out to some friends of my generation with whom I grew into my lesbianism, who are in this collection: Cheryl Boyce-Taylor, Alexis De Veaux, Jewelle Gomez, Akasha Gloria Hull, Michelle Parkerson, Kate Rushin, Beverly Smith, and Barbara Smith.

Jones gives us five guideposts—"rigid as mountains" ("Love Poem")— of Black lesbian writing: "Uses of the Erotic," "Interlocking Oppressions and Identity Politics," "Coming Out and Stepping Into," "The Sacred," and "Radical Futurities."

Unabashedly and unapologetically, Jones puts sexuality right up front, where it belongs, in the first part—lest we forget all the struggle in which we've engaged and still engage to sleep with women. Audre Lorde's "Love Poem" appears here and is the inspiration for the book's title. Says Lorde, "My hips . . . carved out by the *mouth of rain*." Lorde's generation of Black lesbian writers showed us how to talk *and* write about sex.

In her 1976 "Democratic National Convention Keynote Address" (Part V, "Radical Futurities"), the late Barbara Jordan describes Americans as still "a people in search of our future." If she were giving this address today, perhaps Barbara Jordan would be able to be an "out" lesbian congressperson.

I am happy to see the poetry of the late Terri Jewell, who left us too, too soon, visited here. I am reminded of how remarkable her verse is.

I'm happy to see Canadian Dionne Brand's wry and artful poetry included in *Mouths of Rain* (Part III, "Coming Out and Stepping Into").

It is interesting how Alexis Pauline Gumbs (Part V, "Radical Futurities") and the late Michelle Cliff (Part III, "Coming Out and Stepping Into") both ruminate on the meaning of the word "survival." While Gumbs defines "survival" as "our living in the context of what we have overcome," Cliff in her early "Notes on Speechlessness" opines that it is "deciding not to be speechless. . . . nothing more or less than seeking my own language. This may be what women will do." Women writers, Black lesbian feminist writers, no less, and a hell of a lot more, have changed language. And like Janie Starks would declare to her abusive second husband, so too do we proclaim to "white heteropatriarchy": "Ah'll change jez ez many words ez Ah Durn please" (*Their Eyes Were Watching God*).

Treasure Alice Walker's surprising and previously unpublished poem "Can It Be?" (Part I, "Uses of the Erotic"), whose speaker's hands cry out to her beloved:

> *Give us*
> *our proper work*
> *. . . the work of*
> *devotion.*

Diverse complements of writers in each section make for rich conversations of intersectionality, hip-hop, Black deviance as Black resistance, Black trans lesbianism, Black lesbian fiction, poetry, essay, theory, and, as Bettina Love enounces, "a *ratchet* methodological perspective for research that studies the unique challenges of Black queer youth . . ." (Part V, "Radical Futurities"). I could use some *ratchet*.

From Audre Lorde's interview of Anita Cornwell (Part II, "Interlocking Oppressions and Identity Politics"), published in 1983, and Ann Allen Shockley's story "A Meeting of the Sapphic Daughters"—both authors in their nineties now—to "Wolfpack," by Mecca Jamilah Sullivan, a gripping story based on a true 2006 incident, to Cathy Cohen's crucial article, "Deviance as Resistance" (Part V, "Radical Futurities"), to the notorious and hilarious "Suzie Q" by transman Red Jordan Arobateau, to the divinations of Alexis De Veaux's "Interspecies" (Part IV, "The Sacred")—as always, exploring new ground—and the forecasting of Alexis Pauline Gumbs, and the exquisite voice of Cheryl Boyce-Taylor, to inventive and innovative younger poets Arisa White (Part IV, "The Sacred") and Kai Davis (Part II, "Interlocking Oppressions and Identity Politics"), and essayist Kaila Story, who pays smart tribute to the "resistive" culture of Black femmes: these artfully chosen selections elucidate the ways sexuality, race, and gender mesh and mingle across the "resistive" and restive topography of the Black lesbian body, and so much more.

I will take a lesson from the late Toni Cade Bambara's playbook. When she wrote her brilliant and gracious "Foreword" to Cherríe Moraga and Gloria Anzaldúa's iconic *This Bridge Called My Back: Writings By Radical Women of Color*, she asserted in a Dinah Washington tone, "Quite frankly, *This Bridge* needs no Foreword. It is the Afterward that'll count."

Will we continue the "Afterward" as Black lesbian feminist writers? What will be our survival as Black lesbian, queer, trans feminist writers?

A space on my anthology shelf awaits *Mouths of Rain* next to *The Book of American Negro Poetry, The Black Woman: An Anthology, Conditions Five: The Black Women's Issue, This Bridge Called My Back: Writings By Radical Women of Color, Home Girls: A Black Feminist Anthology, Other Countries: Black Gay Voices, A First Volume*, and *In The Life: A Black Gay Anthology*. Welcome to the shelf, *Mouths of Rain*.

# Mouths of Rain: Be Opened
## Alexis Pauline Gumbs

In Anguilla they say that my grandmother knew how to control the rain. No one ever told me that she had those powers while she was alive, but on the way to her funeral the rain stopped just in time for us to get out of the cars and walk into one of the several local churches where my grandmother Lydia organized. That's when my Aunt Una said it: "That's mommy telling us she's with us; you know, everyone said she could control the rain."

I would have loved to ask my grandmother whether she was Storm from the X-Men. But all I have are archival materials that I piece together as a kind of evidence. Yes. My grandmother was the founder of the Anguilla Beautification Society, a group of people committed to growing flowers on a desert island. Yes. My grandfather, who often lived apart from my grandmother, would write letters asking her to send rain. And sometimes he included graphs of the local water table, so it seems he meant it quite literally. When it was time to go through my grandmother's jewelry and divide it among granddaughters, the necklace that spoke to me was a large turquoise stone, evidence of gathered elements, used in Navajo culture to invite rain. I now wear it almost every day. All that is to say, I can say yes. My grandmother had a special relationship to rain. Or maybe her water power was a community-held metaphor. My grandmother had that kind of impact, like water in the desert. She nourished the communities where she was planted. She founded hospitals and service organizations; she was involved in all the churches because that was where the people were organized. She even designed the flag during the Anguillian Revolution in 1967. Three dolphins swimming in a circle. Like water nourishing the ground, she made the impossible bloom. And in the years after my grandmother's death, Anguilla has become so lush and green, you would almost never know it had ever been a desert island. So yes. I have my own reasons to believe in the power of rain.

It was on that same island, Anguilla, vacationing with the scholar and activist Gloria Joseph, that poet, theorist, and icon Audre Lorde began to imagine a new form of fertility for herself. According to biographer Alexis De Veaux (an icon in her own right, also featured in this book), Lorde's experience in Anguilla inspired her to make a decision that would add years to her life—to move full-time to the Caribbean. Lorde had imagined the Caribbean as a mythical ancestral home because her parents were from Grenada and Barbados, but her time collaborating with the Women's Coalition in St. Croix and visiting Anguilla helped her decide that living in the Caribbean was practical for her physical health and peace of mind. The decision to live in the Caribbean was also a decision to make roots with another Black woman, Gloria Joseph, another form of homecoming that watered the last years of her life.

Now Anguilla calls herself "rainbow city" and the tourist board markets the country as an island of rainbows. I am almost 100 percent sure that no one on the Anguillian tourist board was inspired by the rainbow symbols of the gay pride flag. Rainbows, which one can see frequently in Anguilla, come from the fact that Anguilla has become a place with short rain showers followed by sun, the wind-propelled variance resulting in prismatic reflection; sunshowers lead to rainbows. Of course, as Audre Lorde would learn in 1989 in St. Croix, too much rain and wind in the Caribbean, the ferocity of the still outraged winds of the transatlantic slave trade routes, can result in devastating hurricanes, and now because of climate change more frequently they *do*. In 2017, Anguilla experienced the most destructive hurricane in local history.

Oya, the Yoruba goddess of the storm, of change, is also the keeper of the graveyard, the ancestral connector, the helix. Audre Lorde learned from a priest late in her life that she was a daughter of Oya. The hurricane is also represented in Orisha iconography by the rainbow. Was my grandmother a representative of Oya? Family lore suggests she was definitely in touch with her rage, and she was undoubtedly a change maker in her community.

What does it mean for us, readers of this book, writers in what Briona Simone Jones calls and claims as an expansive Black lesbian literary tradition, to claim an intimate relationship with rain at a time of climate change and wildfires, in a time thirsty for ancestral remembrance and change? Is there a relationship to the legacy of this tradition of women nourishing each other and ourselves, often in spaces that seem hostile to the growth of our love and the healing change our planet needs right now? And is it possible?

Let me tell you another story. Or another part of the same story. Over 150 years ago, after a year of organized intelligence, Harriet Tubman led what may have been the most successful uprising of enslaved Africans in North American history. In the midst of the Civil War, about eight hundred enslaved people stole themselves to freedom, burned down thirty-six plantation buildings, and flooded the rice fields of the South Carolina plantation owners who were bankrolling the Confederate effort. The night of that successful mission, called the Combahee River Raid, there was a fierce storm. In a transcribed letter, Tubman describes the sounds of the thunder and the rain, and the songs she sang to let the multitude know to get in the Union Army river boats she had waiting. The next day, Tubman made her first public speech documented in a newspaper. This uprising was the first act against slavery that she could publicly take credit for because it happened in the context of the Civil War and with the support of those most radical members of the Union Army who had ridden with John Brown. This successful strategic influx of power into the Union effort and attack on the Confederacy where it hurt the most was decisive in the Union victory in the Civil War and the de facto end of slavery in the United States.

In the mid-1970s, the members of what was at the time the Boston Chapter of the National Black Feminist Organization decided to create their own organization because they felt the National Black Feminist Organization was lacking in the analysis they needed around homophobia and capitalism. They named their organization the Combahee River Collective because they were inspired by the collective action that Harriet Tubman orchestrated for Black freedom and they saw their work as Black feminist socialist lesbians as a contribution to the freedom of all Black people. Though by the time I was born the Combahee River Collective was no longer an organization, their Black Feminist Statement remains one of the foundational documents of contemporary Black feminism.

Weeks before I turned thirty years old, my partner, Sangodare, and I made our own trip to the Combahee River, the spot where it now flows under the Harriet Tubman Bridge. It wasn't until we were already on the road that we realized we were traveling to the Combahee exactly 150 years after Harriet Tubman had come to the area to start preparing for her mission. And you won't believe what happened: three dolphins swam under the bridge, circled each other in the exact formation of the flag my grandmother designed, and swam out to sea. I stood there in my white dress, with my jar of Combahee River water and my grandmother's turquoise necklace on my heart, and decided with my partner that one year later we had to come back and bring more Black feminists in the legacy of Harriet Tubman and the Combahee River Collective to honor the 150-year anniversary of this collective victory that still reverberates.

So we came back, twenty-one Black feminists dressed in white, most of us queer. With us was an elder of ours who was mentored by the members of the Combahee River Collective. Demita Frazier, one of the three co-authors of the Combahee River Collective Statement, advised us on our journey and told us that our pilgrimage inspired her to begin renewed work on her much anticipated memoir. On the sunny morning of June 3, we sang, we chanted quotations from the Combahee River Collective Statement like "Black women are inherently valuable" and Harriet Tubman's mantra, "My people are free." We recited Tubman's transcribed letter about the storm that night and imagined what the fleeing multitude might have said at the moment of action. We knew in that moment that what it meant to love Black women was time travel and study, reverence and ceremony. It required all of who we were and who we could become. We knew we had to love the women we were and the women of our lineages, our grandmothers and our great grandmothers, the women we never got to hold, the people coming after us and ourselves and the bridge and an invitation to all of it. And as we fully brought our spirits to that moment in the midst of a sunny day, the sky suddenly opened up and rain fell into our open mouths.

So is it possible for a Black queer relationship to rain to have a tangible impact on the world we find before us? Yes. It is possible. Yes, we can water our decisions with the words of the writers in this book. Yes. The words can nourish the futures we deserve. As you read this book, know that you are in a sacred place dedicated with the words and lives of people who believed and believe now that love can change everything, even the weather. Allow yourself to be opened, to be grateful, to be free.

# Introduction: No Hand, No Gaze*

T his collection is an offering. In it, I aspire to trace the long history of love between Black women because I have come to recognize that our love stories have been buried underneath our activism. But our love, too, is both personal and political. *Mouths of Rain* aspires to tell a deep and ancient history of eroticism from the purview of the poet, blues woman, essayist, and critic. *Mouths of Rain* aspires to demonstrate how life can be made anew if we dare to survive. Black lesbians have fully embodied new ways of being, teaching us how to expand our own expectations of the possible. Love and living are sacred to Black lesbians. Their words outline a hope and a future. If you need a reason to survive or a litany, *Mouths of Rain* is communion, mantra, and daily bread.

*Mouths of Rain* was conceived because books like *The Black Woman: An Anthology*, *Midnight Birds: Stories of Contemporary Black Women Writers*, *Words of Fire: An Anthology of African-American Feminist Thought*, *Afrekete: An Anthology of Black Lesbian Writing*, *does your mama know?: An Anthology of Black Lesbian Coming Out Stories* lived to tell the tale. These anthologies functioned as archives, and reading them was a sign that I could live to speak, too. *When I met my first Black lesbian living a full life, I was eighteen, a freshman in college; small town girl with big dreams. Environmental Science was an 8 a.m. class, but G stumbled in like ten minutes late. Her presence commanded the room. She was thriving in this space and loving in this world. In retrospect, this moment was a first encounter that changed my life. I think we all need models of how to be, who to be, where to be. G was that for me.*

We were introduced to the brilliance of Zora Neale Hurston because Alice Walker was curious. Walker was in search of models, of paradigms, of points of reference, and connection. She helped move Hurston from the periphery to the center. Because Toni Morrison wrote the books that she wanted to

* Many thanks to Xhercis for her guidance throughout my revision process. Thank you for your careful eye and precise words.

read and Alice Walker writes all the things she should have been able to read, *Mouths of Rain* is compiled in the same spirit. *Mouths of Rain* is evidence of what Alice Walker dreamt to fruition when she wrote "Saving the Life That Is Your Own: The Importance of Models in the Artist's Life." Anthologies by and about Black women have been my perfect models and greatest gifts. *Mouths of Rain* is a companion to your words of fire, an intergenerational call and response. When I met with Beverly Guy-Sheftall almost three years ago, I intended to discuss my dissertation project, but I left with a larger perspective and a dream come to pass. She suggested that I do the job of archiving Black lesbian life, offering her name as the subject line, a bridge for me to cross over and chart a new path. It was not about Black lesbian life mattering, it was about creating conditions for Black lesbian life to live. Beverly did that for me, and for us.

As we stand in the center of rampant anti–Blackness and transphobia, Black lesbians model how to love what is not seen as beautiful and precious. Black lesbians teach us how to love that which is most despised and undervalued. And they do it gloriously, in the face of opposition. Black lesbians develop new modes of kinship and intimacy. It matters in this moment we are facing, that we turn to Black lesbian models to learn how to shift and shape into beings that love. So when you come to this book, you are entering into a world of Black lesbian dreams, a world where we experience a larger kind of freedom, an expansive kind of love.

*Mouths of Rain* is a love poem. When the earth spoke to me, I was moved to compose a collection of love letters between Black women. I want to account for the tender, the sweet, the rebirth, and the radical. These are futures as imagined by Black women who outgrew the margins of error that placed them on the outside. Feel these words in your mouth, when you dare to speak about who you love, how you love, and why you love. Feel these words in your throat, when silence can no longer be held there. In your times of needed intimacy, read this book, and know that you are kept. In the age of COVID-19, when community and proximity are distant lovers, believe that words can meet needs and offer comfort.

Each section begins with a North Star because this book is evidence of my ancestors' wildest dreams. Harriet did so I could, and here *we* are. The North Stars serve as guiding lights throughout each section of this anthology. When you read these epigraphs, keep what they reveal.

*Mouths of Rain* begins with **the erotic** to underscore the necessity of its vitality as a life force. Audre Lorde poeticized about this resource within each of us, underscoring how it undergirds our loving, living, and doing. Activism is not devoid of eroticism. A plurality of being is what Black lesbians offer to the world, and this plurality lends itself to full recognition of an integrated analysis. When Black lesbians theorize about **interlocking oppressions** and **identity politics**, the poetic, political, and intersection of many crossroads gather. Black lesbians articulate the complexity of embodying a multiplicitous self, reaching many home truths in their lives and in their writings, giving readers a glimpse into what it means to model wholeness; a challenge against dismemberment, distortion, and absence.

In their writings, Black lesbians **come out** and **step into** a new way of being, giving credence to the all too familiar territory of identifying as Black *and* lesbian, while also underscoring that identity is praxis, too:

> I name myself "lesbian" because this culture oppresses, silences, and destroys lesbians, even lesbians who don't call themselves "lesbians." I name myself "lesbian" because I want to be visible to other Black lesbians. I name myself "lesbian" because I do not subscribe to predatory/institutionalized heterosexuality. I name myself "lesbian" because I want to be with women (and they don't all have to call themselves "lesbians"). I name myself "lesbian" because it is part of my vision. I name myself "lesbian" because being woman-identified has kept me sane. I call myself "Black," too, because Black is a part of my aesthetic, my politics, my vision, my sanity (Cheryl Clarke, "New Notes On Lesbianism" 85–86).

The power of naming and the inseparability of Blackness and lesbianism are indeed two parts of the same whole. There is fluidity in Black lesbianism, and these coming-out stories underscore just that. Black lesbian is a political posturing; the name is a bridge, a move towards coalition; the name symbolizes shared intimacy and reciprocity; the name establishes connection between other bodies—even bodies that don't share this same name; the name is about futurity—both imagined and realized; the name is indivisible, and resistant to hierarchy; the name is an aesthetic—a pattern, a behavior, a sensory thing; a touch—an art, too, that resists constraining definitions, but instead constantly reinvents and reimagines itself. *I became a Black lesbian after falling in love. For me, becoming is this active thing; I became accountable to myself and who I knew I needed to be. Becoming was a revival. I was strengthened and my conditions were improved after making a deliberate choice to live life on full.*

**The sacred** has always been an integral part of Black lesbianism. Black lesbians call us to read about the sacred and build our temple within and between these pages. Black lesbians have reconstructed and redefined spirituality, memory, afterlife, conjure, and ritual. Whether through praxis, prayer, supplication, or the convergence of all three, the connection to the divine has remained salient. The sacred, as typified in Black lesbian writing, demonstrates that sexual intimacy is daily bread; that speculative fiction has spiritual underpinnings; that god could never be understood through the confines of gender; that our relations to land are sacred connections as our relations to each other. The sacred carries the Black lesbian and sustains Black lesbian life—it imbues our politics, it is our litany for survival, it is sexual, emotional, spiritual, ancestral, present, future, and after.

A place beyond captivity has been imagined, desired, sought after, and contested for the Black lesbian. **Radical futures** are imagined through Black lesbian feminist thinkers who challenge myriad angles of oppression like imperialism, capitalism, racism, sexism, and homophobia. Black lesbians construct a new politic; one wherein coalitional politics and ending all forms of oppression for everyone are at the forefront of their liberatory discourses and practices. This section re-remembers that there is no hierarchy of oppression, that survival is sacred, and not considered to be that middle ground between prosperity and death.

You see, to be Black and lesbian is a capacious thing—a branch of knowledge; an interpretation; a body and flesh, too. Black lesbian is they, she, his, mine, and yours. Black lesbians define themselves for themselves—meaning that, for example, Audre Lorde's marriage with a gay man, which facilitated the birth of her two children, did not occlude the possibility of her self-definition as a lesbian. It is the porosity of Black lesbianism that has expanded Black Feminism, decolonization, abolition, mothering, and spiritual praxis. They teach us how to love within difference and contradiction.

*Mouths of Rain* invites readers to assess the life that has been made possible because Black lesbian thinkers insisted that a life and politic(s) be constructed on the basis of plurality and generosity. And so, *Mouths of Rain* is an offering to the Black lesbians who named themselves, taking everything that came with being in the life. *Mouths of Rain* is an offering to the Black lesbians who could not name themselves, who named themselves and died because of it. *Mouths of Rain* is an offering to the Black lesbians who have yet to be called or named.

I am honored and privileged to present the work of generations of women who speak truth and live their truth through lyric, poetic, word, essay, and speech. My deepest desire is that *Mouths of Rain* meets its reader wherever they are in a journey of self-definition and self-discovery. Perhaps, this book is an implicit gesture at examining Black lesbianism as an ontology, epistemology, philosophy, hermeneutic, and haptic. An intimacy, a practice, an ethics of care. A community lover and friend. The history is vast and our possibilities are endless. Let this text be a way in and a way through. A blueprint, a paradigm, a roadmap, a bridge, an opening, a river, a north star, the ocean crossing home.

P.S.

# I Am Lustful for My Own Name

I came out as a Black lesbian at the age of twenty-one. Loving a Black woman felt like returning home; there was something about feeling kept and being seen that felt familiar. Love provided me with confidence and courage.

Literature offered a different portal into my Black lesbianism. Black lesbian words were a reintroduction to my body. In isolation, I was searching for company. I was always looking for models on *how* to be, tangible examples of how to live this life. These stories felt like and offered community when close proximity wasn't possible. When I read my first poem by Audre Lorde, "A Litany For Survival," I learned how to ritualize survival and care for myself. I remember swallowing my words whole but this poem broke apart and placed back together something within me. Lorde taught me how poetry is daily bread, because Black lesbians know that ebbs and flows are constant. They also know that if fear is inevitable, the audacity to choose must be, too. Here is me being deliberate and afraid of nothing.

Briona Simone Jones
Atlanta, Georgia

# PART I

# USES OF THE EROTIC

## 1909-2020

I went out last night with a crowd of my friends,
It must've been women, 'cause I don't like no men.
Wear my clothes just like a fan,
Talk to the gals just like any old man.

Ma Rainey

I plainly want[ed] to advance Audre Lorde's thesis in her piece "Uses of the Erotic" by promoting the concept of lesbian sex, which itself is poetry—it is without beginning, middle, and end.

Cheryl Clarke

The butch goes down, licking her; the tip of her tongue flicking, probing, gently pushing the folds of the labia back with her fingers. Smooth, grainy, that female smell in her nostrils, mouth sucking, tongue alternately seeking out that hood-shaped spot, and the pearl emerges. The femme's clitoris becomes hard. The butch's tongue moves faster, harder in that most loving of physical acts. The femme moans as she lays back on the bed, her body goes taut, fingers alternately grasping the butch's hair and the sheet of the bed at either side. The butch alternately sucks and licks the woman's vagina, concentrating on the clitoris, then the woman puts her whole mouth against her woman's sex, sucking, while reaching up and fondling her breasts at the same time. The smell of their own strong sexuality. Then her mouth pulls away while her hand reaches down to manipulate the pearl tongue between the woman's legs, mouth sucking the nipple of one breast and wrapping her arms around her body to play with the woman's other nipple. Gently she push her fingers into her mate's pussy, thrusting a little ways, one finger in and out, then, as the vagina gets bigger, two, then three fingers; at the same time alternately kissing the femme's mouth or sucking her nipple. The love partner moans, arms wrapped around her lover's body, arching her back. The butch slides down the femme's raptured body and goes down, again sucking her clitoris, while her fingers move in and out of her vagina at the same time. The femme climaxes, moaning, her body hot, shuddering in short jerks, a sob deep in her throat.

Now the butch stands over her mate at the side of the bed. The femme caresses the masculine woman's thighs. Carefully she moves back the skin of her labia with her fingers and tentatively flicks the tip of her tongue, exploring, tasting, seeking the clitoris. She cups her hands around the butch's buttocks, pulling the butch to her, till her fuzzy head is buried in pubic hair and she gets the woman's sex in her whole mouth, sucking, and the butch's hips thrusting so that her sex goes up and down on the woman's lips in short jerks. But she doesn't come that way; instead, she gently pushes her mate back on the bed. The femme spreads her legs for her, slowly sliding up around her body, as she gets between them, the butch's pussy against the femme's, and pumps fast 'till the heat builds up inside to a climax, pounding to a finish, a huge explosion like her whole body sobbing, or breathing. Hearts still beating, totally relaxed, they lie beside each other. Then, they repeat this procedure for at least one more go 'round, but probably two. Three orgasms each, in other ways, maybe 69. The two of them sharing. They are both starved for a woman; it's been such a long time. The beginning of a good thing.

**Red Jordan Arobateau**

## Alice Ruth Moore Dunbar-Nelson
# You! Inez!

Orange gleams athwart a crimson soul
Lambent flames; purple passion lurks
In your dusk eyes.
Red mouth; flower soft,
Your soul leaps up—and flashes
Star-like, white, flame-hot.
Curving arms, encircling a world of love,
You! Stirring the depths of passionate desire!

# Alice Walker
## Can It Be?

Can it be that I am dying
after all
even though I am happy
and you say you love me?

Can it be that I am weeping
after all
though your arms reach
to hold me
and my mouth is
imprinted
with your kiss?

All day long I languish
about my house
eating &
sleeping.
Washing travel
and misunderstandings
from my locs.

Every thought
is of you.
Of your vivid dark
eyes
and how they pin me
to my soul.
Of your gentle mouth
and how its nearness

to mine
brings breath
leaping
to my throat.
Of your wilderness
of hair
now lost
territory
to my exploring
fingertips.

O' woman
your body is as sacred to me
as the earth.
The black of it
so secret
so sweet &
so mysterious
the brown of it
so velvet &
so lush.

My eyes and hands
and tongue
are weak
with wanting you.
Washing dishes
sweeping a room
writing a letter
they call
to you.
Give us

our proper work
they cry: the work of
devotion.

My mind curls
around your bed
while you sleep.
My thoughts fly, like angels,
about your forehead
when you rise, at last,
and beckon to your dogs.

There is no exhaustion
like that of passion.
I feel as though my heart
has nearly expired
on our mutual rack
of bliss.

And so, Beloved, I suffer.
Constructing mountains
of reasons

to separate from you
out of molehills
of memory.
A cross word. A cross
look.
But I know
in my heart
that it is only love
and I have loved
beyond capacity

and now
fatigue has
laid me low
and caused me
to think of dying
and caused me
to weep.

I wonder if
like here
the rain is falling gently
where you are?
If the bright green spring is everywhere
and everywhere seems to be on fire?
If the stiff wind
as you walk the dogs
blows the freshness of new
beginnings
into your soul?
If you are making music?
If you are happy?

If you miss me
as I you?

# Angelina Weld Grimké
# A Mona Lisa

I should like to creep
Through the long brown grasses
    That are your lashes;
I should like to poise
    On the very brink
Of the leaf-brown pools
    That are your shadowed eyes;
I should like to cleave
    Without sound,
Their glimmering waters,
    Their unrippled waters,
I should like to sink down
    And down
      And down. . . .
        And deeply drown.


2


Would I be more than a bubble breaking?
    Or an ever-widening circle?
    Ceasing at the marge?
Would my white bones
    Be the only white bones
Wavering back and forth, back and forth
    In their depths?

# Audre Lorde
# Love Poem

Speak earth and bless me with what is richest
make sky flow honey out of my hips
rigid as mountains
spread over a valley
carved out by the mouth of rain.

And I knew when I entered her I was
high wind in her forests hollow
fingers whispering sound
honey flowed
from the split cup
impaled on a lance of tongues
on the tips of her breasts on her navel
and my breath
howling into her entrances
through lungs of pain.

Greedy as herring-gulls
or a child
I swing out over the earth
over and over
again.

# Audre Lorde
## Woman

I dream of a place between your breasts
to build my house like a haven
where I plant crops
in your body
an endless harvest
where the commonest rock
is moonstone and ebony opal
giving milk to all of my hungers
and your night comes down upon me
like a nurturing rain.

# Audre Lorde
# Uses of the Erotic: The Erotic as Power

There are many kinds of power, used and unused, acknowledged or otherwise. The erotic is a resource within each of us that lies in a deeply female and spiritual plane, firmly rooted in the power of our unexpressed or unrecognized feeling. In order to perpetuate itself, every oppression must corrupt or distort those various sources of power within the culture of the oppressed that can provide energy for change. For women, this has meant a suppression of the erotic as a considered source of power and information within our lives.

We have been taught to suspect this resource, vilified, abused, and devalued within Western society. On the one hand, the superficially erotic has been encouraged as a sign of female inferiority; on the other hand, women have been made to suffer and to feel both contemptible and suspect by virtue of its existence.

It is a short step from there to the false belief that only by the suppression of the erotic within our lives and consciousness can women be truly strong. But that strength is illusory, for it is fashioned within the context of male models of power.

As women, we have come to distrust that power which rises from our deepest and non-rational knowledge. We have been warned against it all our lives by the male world, which values this depth of feeling enough to keep women around in order to exercise it in the service of men, but which fears this same depth too much to examine the possibility of it within themselves. So women are maintained at a distant/inferior position to be psychically milked, much the same way ants maintain colonies of aphids to provide a life-giving substance for their masters.

But the erotic offers a well of replenishing and provocative force to the woman who does not fear its revelation, nor succumb to the belief that sensation is enough.

The erotic has often been misnamed by men and used against women. It has been made into the confused, the trivial, the psychotic, the plasticized sensation. For this reason, we have often turned away from the exploration and consideration of the erotic as a source of power and information, confusing it with its opposite, the pornographic. But pornography is a direct denial of the power of the erotic, for it represents the suppression of true feeling. Pornography emphasizes sensation without feeling.

The erotic is a measure between the beginnings of our sense of self and the chaos of our strongest feelings. It is an internal sense of satisfaction to which, once we have experienced it, we know we can aspire. For having experienced the fullness of this depth of feeling and recognizing its power, in honor and self-respect we can require no less of ourselves.

It is never easy to demand the most from ourselves, from our lives, from our work. To encourage excellence is to go beyond the encouraged mediocrity of our society, is to encourage excellence. But giving in to the fear of feeling and working to capacity is a luxury only the unintentional can afford, and the unintentional are those who do not wish to guide their own destinies.

This internal requirement toward excellence which we learn from the erotic must not be misconstrued as demanding the impossible from ourselves nor from others. Such a demand incapacitates everyone in the process. For the erotic is not a question only of what we do; it is a question of how acutely and fully we can feel in the doing. Once we know the extent to which we are capable of feeling that sense of satisfaction and completion, we can then observe which of our various life endeavors brings us closest to that fullness.

The aim of each thing which we do is to make our lives and the lives of our children richer and more possible. Within the celebration of the erotic in all our endeavors, my work becomes a conscious decision—a longed-for bed which I enter gratefully and from which I rise up empowered.

Of course, women so empowered are dangerous. So we are taught to separate the erotic demand from most vital areas of our lives other than sex. And the lack of concern for the erotic root and satisfactions of our work is felt in our disaffection from so much of what we do. For instance, how often do we truly love our work even at its most difficult?

The principal horror of any system which defines the good in terms of profit rather than in terms of human need, or which defines human need to the exclusion of the psychic and emotional components of that need—the principal horror of such a system is that it robs our work of its erotic value, its erotic power and life appeal and fulfillment. Such a system reduces work to a travesty of necessities, a duty by which we earn bread or oblivion for ourselves and those we love. But this is tantamount to blinding a painter and then telling her to improve her work, and to enjoy the act of painting. It is not only next to impossible; it is also profoundly cruel.

As women, we need to examine the ways in which our world can be truly different. I am speaking here of the necessity for reassessing the quality of all the aspects of our lives and of our work, and of how we move toward and through them.

The very word *erotic* comes from the Greek word *eros*, the personification of love in all its aspects—born of Chaos, and personifying creative power and harmony. When I speak of the erotic, then, I speak of it as an assertion of the lifeforce of women; of that creative energy empowered, the knowledge and use of which we are now reclaiming in our language, our history, our dancing, our loving, our work, our lives.

There are frequent attempts to equate pornography and eroticism, two diametrically opposed uses of the sexual. Because of these attempts, it has become fashionable to separate the spiritual (psychic and emotional) from the political, to see them as contradictory or antithetical. "What do you mean, a poetic revolutionary, a meditating gunrunner?" In the same way, we have attempted to separate the spiritual and the erotic, thereby reducing the spiritual to a world of flattened affect, a world of the ascetic who aspires to feel nothing. But nothing is farther from the truth. For the ascetic position is one of the highest fear, the gravest immobility. The severe abstinence of the ascetic becomes the ruling obsession. And it is one not of self-discipline but of self-abnegation.

The dichotomy between the spiritual and the political is also false, resulting from an incomplete attention to our erotic knowledge. For the bridge which connects them is formed by the erotic—the sensual—those physical, emotional, and psychic expressions of what is deepest and strongest and richest within each of us, being shared: the passions of love, in its deepest meanings.

Beyond the superficial, the considered phrase, "It feels right to me," acknowledges the strength of the erotic into a true knowledge, for what that means is the first and most powerful guiding light toward any understanding. And understanding is a handmaiden which can only wait upon, or clarify, that knowledge, deeply born. The erotic is the nurturer or nursemaid of all our deepest knowledge.

The erotic functions for me in several ways, and the first is in providing the power which comes from sharing deeply any pursuit with another person. The sharing of joy, whether physical, emotional, psychic, or intellectual, forms a bridge between the sharers which can be the basis for understanding much of what is not shared between them, and lessens the threat of their difference.

Another important way in which the erotic connection functions is the open and fearless underlining of my capacity for joy. In the way my body stretches to music and opens into response, hearkening to its deepest rhythms, so every level upon which I sense also opens to the erotically satisfying experience, whether it is dancing, building a bookcase, writing a poem, examining an idea.

That self-connection shared is a measure of the joy which I know myself to be capable of feeling, a reminder of my capacity for feeling. And that deep and irreplaceable knowledge of my capacity for joy comes to demand from all of my life that it be lived within the knowledge that such satisfaction is possible, and does not have to be called marriage, nor god, nor an afterlife.

This is one reason why the erotic is so feared, and so often relegated to the bedroom alone, when it is recognized at all. For once we begin to feel deeply all the aspects of our lives, we begin to demand from ourselves and from our life-pursuits that they feel in accordance with that joy which we know ourselves to be capable of. Our erotic knowledge empowers us, becomes a lens through which we scrutinize all aspects of our existence, forcing us to evaluate those aspects honestly in terms of their relative meaning within our lives. And this is a grave responsibility, projected from within each of us, not to settle for the convenient, the shoddy, the conventionally expected, nor the merely safe.

During World War II, we bought sealed plastic packets of white, uncolored margarine, with a tiny, intense pellet of yellow coloring perched like a topaz just inside the clear skin of the bag. We would leave the margarine out for a while to soften, and then we would pinch the little pellet to break it inside the bag, releasing the rich yellowness into the soft pale mass of margarine. Then, taking it carefully between our fingers, we would knead it gently back and forth, over and over, until the color had spread throughout the whole pound bag of margarine, thoroughly coloring it.

I find the erotic such a kernel within myself. When released from its intense and constrained pellet, it flows through and colors my life with a kind of energy that heightens and sensitizes and strengthens all my experience.

We have been raised to fear the yes within ourselves, our deepest cravings. But, once recognized, those which do not enhance our future lose their power and can be altered. The fear of our desires keeps them suspect and indiscriminately powerful, for to suppress any truth is to give it strength beyond endurance. The fear that we cannot grow beyond whatever distortions we may find within ourselves keeps us docile and loyal and obedient, externally defined, and leads us to accept many facets of our oppression as women.

When we live outside ourselves, and by that I mean on external directives only rather than from our internal knowledge and needs, when we live away from those erotic guides from within ourselves, then our lives are limited by external and alien forms, and we conform to the needs of a structure that is not based on human need, let alone an individual's. But when we begin to live from within outward, in touch with the power of the erotic within ourselves, and allowing that power to inform and illuminate our actions upon the world around us, then we begin to be responsible to ourselves in the deepest sense. For as we begin to recognize our deepest feelings, we begin to give up, of necessity, being satisfied with suffering and self-negation, and with the numbness which so often seems like their only alternative in our society. Our acts against oppression become integral with self, motivated and empowered from within.

In touch with the erotic, I become less willing to accept powerlessness, or those other supplied states of being which are not native to me, such as resignation, despair, self-effacement, depression, self-denial.

And yes, there is a hierarchy. There is a difference between painting a back fence and writing a poem, but only one of quantity. And there is, for me, no difference between writing a good poem and moving into sunlight against the body of a woman I love.

This brings me to the last consideration of the erotic. To share the power of each other's feelings is different from using another's feelings as we would use a Kleenex. When we look the other way from our experience, erotic or otherwise, we use rather than share the feelings of those others who participate in the experience with us. And use without consent of the used is abuse.

In order to be utilized, our erotic feelings must be recognized. The need for sharing deep feeling is a human need. But within the European-American tradition, this need is satisfied by certain proscribed erotic comings-together. These occasions are almost always characterized by a simultaneous looking away, a pretense of calling them something else, whether a religion, a fit, mob violence, or even playing doctor. And this misnaming of the need and the deed give rise to that distortion which results in pornography and obscenity—the abuse of feeling.

When we look away from the importance of the erotic in the development and sustenance of our power, or when we look away from ourselves as we satisfy our erotic needs in concert with others, we use each other as objects of satisfaction rather than share our joy in the satisfying, rather than make connection with our similarities and our differences. To refuse to be conscious of what we are feeling at any time, however comfortable that might seem, is to deny a large part of the experience, and to allow ourselves to be reduced to the pornographic, the abused, and the absurd.

The erotic cannot be felt secondhand. As a Black lesbian feminist, I have a particular feeling, knowledge, and understanding for those sisters with whom I have danced hard, played, or even fought. This deep participation has often been the forerunner for joint concerted actions not possible before.

But this erotic charge is not easily shared by women who continue to operate under an exclusively European-American male tradition. I know it was not available to me when I was trying to adapt my consciousness to this mode of living and sensation.

Only now, I find more and more women-identified women brave enough to risk sharing the erotic's electrical charge without having to look away, and without distorting the enormously powerful and creative nature of that exchange. Recognizing the power of the erotic within our lives can give us the energy to pursue genuine change within our world, rather than merely settling for a shift of characters in the same weary drama.

For not only do we touch our most profoundly creative source, but we do that which is female and self-affirming in the face of a racist, patriarchal, and anti-erotic society.

## Cheryl Clarke
# Kittatinny

*I wanna love you and treat you right, love and treat you right.*
Bob Marley

Kittatinny Tunnel in that holy place you let me hit
I push on toward your darker part.
I'll take you there and mean it.

In my car, by the road, in a tent, in a pit
stop, and practice a funkier art,
Kittatinny Tunnel of that holy place you let me hit.

Shout, cry, promise, beg, cajole, go limp, or spit
on me with dirty words to test my heart.
I'll take you there and mean it.

Crawl from me, pitch a fit,
stand, hug the wall, bend, and direct me part
and penetrate Kittatinny, that holy place you let me hit.

And take it, take it, take it.
Call it bitch, whore, slave, tart.
I'll take you there and mean it.

Tribad, dildo, lick your clit-
oris. Come, pee, shit, or fart,
I'll take you there and mean it,
Kittatinny Tunnel of that holy place you let me hit.

## Lucille Bogan
# B.D. Woman's Blues

Comin' a time, B.D. women ain't gonna need no men
Comin' a time, B.D. women ain't gonna need no men
Oh the way they treat us is a lowdown and dirty sin

B.D. women, you sure can't understand
B.D. women, you sure can't understand
They got a head like a sweet angel and they walk just
like a natural man

B.D. women, they all done learnt their plan
B.D. women, they all done learnt their plan
They can lay their jive just like a natural man

B.D. women, B.D. women, you know they sure is rough
B.D. women, B.D. women, you know they sure is rough
They all drink up plenty whiskey and they sure will strut
their stuff

B.D. women, you know they work and make their dough
B.D. women, you know they work and make their dough
And when they get ready to spend it, they know they
have to go

# Michelle Parkerson
# Finer with Time

For Avon, it was the ritual of the thing. Once a month (usually on a Tuesday, sometimes on a Thursday after her day job), the custom was kept. A foraging through silk pajamas and banlon socks . . . Pulling the purple velvet box from her bottom drawer, Avon always held that same self-satisfied expression. Inspecting the precious contents, she felt a spell of power and respect like a wizard surveying his wands.

Now there were ten, all told—ten dildos of unusual shape and rare color. Each selected with time and meticulous care over the years. Avon fondly recalled the pleasures she had given (pleasures she had had) with her "love toys"—that's what she called 'em.

And at her age, she had memories full of pleasure. Like Delores. She took a liking to the turquoise one. And Frankie back in '68 (only butch she ever turned out). She favored your double-headed model, The Dyke Delight.

"Ain't a straight bone in this body," Avon would say, caressing a drink with a fistful of rings, head full of jheri curl. Far as she knew, she'd been butch all her life. And she still cut an imposing figure at the bar, or on the street, where her he/she handsomeness conjured confusion, provoked fear, obscenities, prompted winks from women passing by.

Long before all this "gay" business, years of brushes with the police, years of livin' as a bulldagga, had forged her bravado and sharpened her reflexes. She wore her womanloving ways as flagrantly as her suits. Such well-tailored armor encased the tenderest heart. Way Avon figured it, God had designed her for the fine art of fucking women. She took it as a calling, spent years perfecting her craft.

Avon reverently slipped her keepsakes back in their place of honor. Lord knows her "love toys" never grew old . . .

Well, tonight she was celebrating another birthday, her sixty-sixth, and there were two very lovely surprises in store. There was Helen, an incurable femme, but a friend and constant lover for forty years. And Miss Mika, a pretty young thang Avon met at a club. That girl was hot for Avon's dark, ancient allure.

Lord knows she loved the pleasure of Mika cooing again, again, "Baby, you fine." But she loved it even better when Helen—opening her sex, wetness waiting—whispered, "Baby, you get *finer* with time!"

Was only natural. Avon had always been a woman's woman. Always.

# Monica Arac de Nyeko
# Jambula Tree

I heard of your return home from Mama Atim, our next door neighbor. You remember her, don't you? We used to talk about her on our way to school, hand in hand, jumping, skipping, or playing run-and-catch-me. That woman's mouth worked at words like ants on a cob of maize. Ai! Everyone knows her quack-quack-quack mouth. But people are still left wordless by just how much she can shoot at and wreck things with her machine-gun mouth. We nicknamed her "lecturer." The woman speaks with the certainty of a lecturer at her podium claiming an uncontested mastery of her subject.

I bet you are wondering how she got to know of your return. I could attempt a few guesses. Either way, it would not matter. I would be breaking a promise. I hate that. We made that promise never to mind her or be moved by her. We said that after that night. The one night no one could make us forget. You left without saying goodbye after that. You had to, I reasoned. Perhaps it was good for both of us. Maybe things could die down that way. Things never did die down. Our names became forever associated with the forbidden. Shame.

Anyango—Sanyu.

My mother has gotten over that night. It took a while, but she did. Maybe it is time for your mother to do the same. She should start to hold her head high and scatter dust at the women who laugh after her when she passes by their houses.

Nakawa Housing Estates has never changed. Mr. Wangolo, our SST teacher, once said those houses were just planned slums with people with broken dreams and unplanned families for neighbors. Nakawa is still over one thousand families on an acre of land they call an estate. Most of the women don't work. Like Mama Atim they sit and talk, talk, talk and wait for their husbands to bring home a kilo of offal. Those are the kind of women we did not want to become. They bleached their skins with Mekako skin-lightening soap till they became tender and pale like a sun-scorched baby. They took

22

over their children's *dool* and *kwepena* catfights till the local councilor had
to be called for arbitration. Then they did not talk to each other for a year.
Nakawa's women laugh at each other for wearing the cheapest sandals on sale
by the hawkers. Sanyu, those women know every love charm by heart and
every ju-ju man's shrine because they need them to conjure up their husbands' love and penises from drinking places with smoking pipes filled with
dried hen's throat artery. These women know that an even number is a bad
sign as they watch the cowry shells and coffee beans fall onto cowhide when
consulting the spirits about their husbands' fidelity.

That's what we fought against when we walked to school each day. Me
and you hand in hand, toward school, running away from Nakawa Housing
Estates' drifting tide, which threatened to engulf us and turn us into noisy,
gossiping, and frightening housewives. You said it yourself, we could be anything. Anything coming from your mouth was seasoned and alive. You said
it to me, as we sat on a mango tree branch. We were not allowed to climb
trees, but we did, and there, inside the green branches, you said—we can be
anything. You asked us to pause for a moment to make a wish. I was a nurse
in a white dress. I did not frighten children with big injections. You wished
for nothing. You just made a wish that you would not become what your
father wanted you to be—an engineer, making building plans, for his man-
sion, for his office, for his railway village. The one he dreamt about when he
went to bed at night.

Sanyu, after all these years, I still imagine shame trailing after me, tagged
onto the hem of my skirt. Other times, I see it, floating into your dreams
across the desert and water, to remind you of what lines we crossed. The
things we should not have done when the brightness of Mama Atim's torch
shone upon us—naked. How did she know exactly when to flash the light?
Perhaps asking that question is a futile quest for answers. I won't get any! Perhaps it is as simple as accepting that the woman knows everything. I swear if
you slept with a crocodile under the ocean, she would know. She is the only
one who knows firsthand whose husband is sleeping with whose daughter at
the estate, inside those one-bedroomed houses. She knows whose son was
caught inside the fences at Lugogo Show Grounds, the fancy trade fair center

just across Jinja Road, the main road which meanders its way underneath the estate. Mama Atim knows who is soon dying from gonorrhoea, who got it from someone, who got it from so-and-so who in turn got it from the soldiers who used to guard Lugogo Show Grounds, two years ago.

You remember those soldiers, don't you? The way they sat in the sun with their green uniforms and guns hanging carelessly at their shoulders. With them the AK-47 looked almost harmless—an object that was meant to be held close to the body—black ornament. They whistled after young girls in tight miniskirts that held onto their bums. At night, they drank Nile Lager, tonto, Mobuku, and sang harambe, Soukous, or Chaka Chaka songs.

> Eh moto nawaka mama, Eh moto nawaka,
> I newaka tororo, Nawaka moto
> Nawaka moto, Nawaka moto

> *Eh fire, burns mama, Eh fire, burns*
> *It is burning in Tororo, It is burning*
> *It is burning, It is burning*

Mama Atim never did pass anywhere near where they had camped in their green tents. She twisted her mouth when she talked about them. What were soldiers doing guarding Lugogo? she asked. Was it a front line? Mama Atim was terrified of soldiers. We never did find out why they instilled such fear in her. Either way, it did not matter. Her fear became a secret weapon we used as we imagined ourselves being like goddesses dictating her fate. In our goddess hands, we turned her into an effigy and had soldiers pelt her with stones. We imagined that pelting stones from a soldier was just enough to scare her into *susuing* in her XXL mother's union panties. The ones she got a tailor to hem for her, from leftover materials from her children's nappies. How we wished those materials were green, so that she would see soldiers and stones in between her thighs every time she wore her green soldier color, stone pelting color, and AK-47 color.

We got used to the sight of green soldiers perched in our football fields.

This was the new order. Soldiers doing policemen's work! No questions, Uganda, *yetu, hakuna matata*. How strange it was, freedom in forbidden colors. Deep green—the color of the morning when the dew dries on leaves to announce the arrival of shame and dirt. And everything suddenly seems so uncovered, so exposed, so naked.

Anyango–Sanyu.

Mama Atim tells me you have chosen to come back home, to Nakawa Housing Estates. She says you refuse to live in those areas on the bigger hills and terraced roads in Kololo. You are coming to us and to Nakawa Housing Estates, and to our many houses lined one after another on a small hill overlooking the market and Jinja Road, the football field and Lugogo Show Grounds. Sanyu, you have chosen to come here to children running on the red earth, in the morning shouting and yelling as they play *kwepena* and *dool*—familiar and stocked with memory and history. You return to dirt roads filled with thick brown mud on a rainy day, pools of water in every pothole and the sweet fresh smell of rain on hard soil. Sanyu, you have come back to find Mama Atim.

Mama Atim still waits for her husband to bring the food she is to cook each night. We used to say, after having nine sons and one daughter, she should try to take care of them. Why doesn't she try to find a job in the industrial area like many other women around the estate? Throw her hips and two large buttocks around and play at entrepreneurship. Why doesn't she borrow a little *entandikwa* from the micro-finance unions so she can buy at least a bale of secondhand clothes at Owino market, where she can retail them at Nakawa market? Secondhand clothes are in vogue, for sure. The Tommy Hilfiger and Versace labels are the "in thing" for the young boys and girls who like to hang around the estate at night. Secondhand clothes never stay on the clothes hangers too long; like water during a drought, they sell quickly.

Mummy used to say those secondhand clothes were stripped off corpses in London. That is why they had slogans written on them such as—YOU WENT TO LONDON AND ALL YOU BROUGHT ME WAS THIS LOUSY T-SHIRT! When Mummy talked of London, we listened with our mouths open. She had travelled there not once, not twice, but three times to visit her sister. Each time she came back with her suitcase filled up with stories. When her sister died, Mummy's trips stopped like that bright sparkle in her eye and the Queen Elizabeth stories, which she lost the urge to retell again and again. By that time we were grown. You were long gone to a different place, a different time, and to a new memory. By then, we had grown into two big girls with four large breasts and buttocks like pumpkins and we knew that the stories were not true. Mummy had been to Tanzania—just a boat trip away on Lake Victoria, not London. No Queen Elizabeth.

Mama Atim says you are tired of London. You cannot bear it anymore. London is cold. London is a monster which gives no jobs. London is no cozy exile for the banished. London is no refuge for the immoral. Mama Atim says this word *immoral* to me—slowly and emphatically in Jhapadhola, so it can sink into my head. She wants me to hear the word in every breath, sniff it in every scent so it can haunt me like that day I first touched you. Like the day you first touched me. Mine was a cold unsure hand placed over your right breast. Yours was a cold scared hand, which held my waist and pressed it closer to you, under the jambula tree in front of her house. Mama Atim says you are returning on the wings of a metallic bird—Kenya Airways.

You will land in the hot Kampala heat, which bites at the skin like it has a quarrel with everyone. Your mother does not talk to me or my mother. Mama Atim cooks her kilo of offal, which she talks about for one week until the next time she cooks the next kilo again, bending over her charcoal stove, her large and long breasts watching over her saucepan like cow udders in space. When someone passes by, she stops cooking. You can hear her whisper. Perhaps that's the source of her gonorrhoea and Lugogo Show Ground stories. Mama Atim commands the world to her kitchen like her nine sons and one daughter. None of them have amounted to anything. The way their mother talks about me and you, Sanyu, after all these years, you would think her sons are priests. You would think at least one of them got a diploma and a low-paying job at a government ministry. You would think one of them could at least bring home a respectable wife. But *wapi!* their wives are like used bicycles, ridden and exhausted by the entire estate's manhood. They say the monkey which is behind should not laugh at the other monkey's tail. Mama Atim laughs with her teeth out and on display like cowries. She laughs loudest and forgets that she, of all people, has no right to urinate at or lecture the entire estate on the gospel according to St. Morality.

Sometimes I wonder how much you have changed. How have you grown? You were much taller than I. Your eyes looked stern, created an air about you—one that made kids stop for a while, unsure if they should trample all over you or take time to see for sure if your eyes would validate their preconceived fears. After they had finally studied, analyzed, added, multiplied, and subtracted you, they knew you were for real.

When the bigger kids tried to bully me, you stood tall and dared them to lay a finger on me. Just a finger, you said, grinding your teeth like they were aluminum. They knew you did not mince words and that your anger was worse than a teacher's bamboo whipping. Your anger and rage coiled itself like a python around anyone who dared, anyone who challenged. And that's how you fought, with your teeth and hands but mostly with your feet. You coiled them around Juma when he knocked my tooth out for refusing to let him have his way at the water tap when he tried to cheat me out of my turn at the tap.

I wore my deep dark green uniform. At lunch times the lines could be long and boys always jumped the queue. Juma got me just as I put my water container to get some drinking water after lunch. He pushed me away. He was strong, Sanyu. One push like that and I fell down. When I got up, I left my tooth on the ground and rose up with only blood on the green; deep green, the color of the morning when the dew dries off leaves.

You were standing a distance. You were not watching. But it did not take you too long to know what was going on. You pushed your way through the crowd and before the teachers could hear the commotion going on, you had your legs coiled around Juma. I don't know how you do it, Sanyu. He could not move.

Juma, passed out? Hahahahahahaha!

I know a lot of pupils who would be pleased with that. Finally his big boy muscles had been crushed, to sand, to earth, and to paste. The thought of that tasted sweet and salty like grasshoppers seasoned with onion and *kamulari*—red, red-hot pepper.

Mr. Wangolo came with his hand-on-the-knee limp and a big bamboo cane. It was yellow and must have been freshly broken off from the mother bamboos just outside the school that morning. He pulled and threatened you with indefinite expulsion before you let big sand-earth-paste Juma go. Both you and Juma got off with a two-week suspension. It was explicitly stated in the school rules that no one should fight. You had broken the rules. But that was the lesser of the rules that you broke. That I broke. That we broke.

Much later, at home, your mother was so angry. On our way home, you had said we should not say how the fight started. We should just say he hit you and you hit him back. Your house was two blocks from ours, and the school was the nearest primary school to the estate. Most of the kids in the neighborhood studied at Nakawa Katale Primary School alright, but everyone knew we were great friends. When your mother came and knocked upon our door, my mother had just put the onions on the charcoal stove to fry the goat's meat.

Mummy bought goat's meat when she had just got her salary. The end of month was always goat's meat and maybe some rice if she was in a good mood. Mummy's food smelt good. When she cooked, she joked about it. Mummy said if Papa had any sense in his head, he would not have left her with three kids to raise on her own to settle for that slut he called a wife. Mummy said Papa's new wife could not cook and that she was young enough to be his daughter. They had to do a caesarean on her when she gave birth to her first son. What did he expect? That those wasp hips could let a baby's head pass through them?

When she talked of Papa, she had that voice. Not a "hate voice" and not a "like voice," but the kind of voice she would use to open the door for him and tell him welcome back even after all these years when he never sent us a single cent to buy food, books, soap, or Christmas clothes. My papa is not like your papa, Sanyu. Your papa works at the Ministry of Transport. He manages the Ugandan railways, which is why he wants you to engineer a railway village for him. You say he has gotten so intoxicated with the railways that every time he talks of it, he rubs his palms together like he is think-ing of the best ever memory in his life. Your father has a lot of money. Most of the teachers knew him at school. The kids had heard about him. Perhaps that is why your stern and blank expression was interpreted with slight over-tones. They viewed you with a mixture of fear and awe; a rich man's child.

Sometimes Mummy spoke about your family with slight ridicule. She said no one with money lived in Nakawa Housing Estates of all places. If your family had so much money, why did you not go to live in Muyenga, Kololo, and Kansanga with your Mercedes Benz lot? But you had new shoes every term. You had two new green uniforms every term. Sanyu, your name was never called out aloud by teachers, like the rest of us whose parents had not paid school tuition on time and we had to be sent back home with circulars.

Dear Parent,

This is to remind you that unless this term's school fees are paid out in full, you daughter/son . . . will not be allowed to sit for end of term exams . . .

Blah blah blah . . .

Mummy always got those letters and bit her lip as if she had just heard that her house had burnt down. That's when she started staring at the ceiling with her eyes transfixed on one particular spot on the brown tiles.

On such days, she went searching through her old maroon suitcase. It was from another time. It was the kind that was not sold in shops anymore. It had lost its glitter, and I wished she never brought it out to dry in the sun. It would be less embarrassing if she brought out the other ones she used for her Tanzania trips. At least those ones looked like the ones your mother brought out to dry in the sun when she did her weekly house cleaning. That suitcase had all Mummy's letters—the ones Papa had written her when, as she said, her breasts were firm like green mangoes. Against a kerosene lamp, she read aloud the letters, reliving every moment, every word, and every promise.

*I will never leave you. You are mine forever. Stars are for the sky, you are for me. Hello my sweet supernatural colours of the rainbow. You are the only bee on my flower. If loving you is a crime I am the biggest criminal in the world.*

Mummy read them out aloud and laughed as she read the words in each piece of stained paper. She had stored them in their original airmail envelopes with the green and blue decorations. Sometimes Papa had written to her in aerogramme. Those were opened with the keenest skill to keep them neat and almost new. He was a prolific letter writer, my papa, with a neat handwriting. I know this because oftentimes I opened her case of memories. I never did get as far as opening any letter to read; it would have been trespassing. It did not feel right, even if Mummy had never scolded me from reading her "To Josephine Athieno Best" letters.

I hated to see her like that. She was now a copy typist at Ramja Securities. Her salary was not much, but she managed to survive on it, somehow, somehow. There were people who spoke of her beauty as if she did not deserve being husbandless. They said with some pity, "Oh, and she has a long ringed neck, her eyes are large and sad. The woman has a voice, soft, kind, and patient. How could the man leave her?" Mummy might have been sad sometimes, but she did not deserve any pity. She lived her life like her own fingernails and temperament: so calm, so sober and level-headed, except of course when it came to reading those Papa letters by the lantern lamp.

I told you about all this, Sanyu. How I wished she could be always happy, like your mother, who went to the market and came back with two large boys carrying her load because she had shopped too much for your papa, for you, for your happy family. I did not tell you, but sometimes I stalked her as she made her way to buy things from the noisy market. She never saw me. There were simply too many people. From a distance, she pointed at things, fruit ripe like they had been waiting to be bought by her all along. Your mother went from market stall to market stall, flashing her white Colgate smile and her dimpled cheeks. Sometimes I wished I were like you, with a mother who bought happiness from the market. She looked like someone who summoned joy at her feet and it fell in salutation, humbly, like the *kabaka* subjects who lay prostate before him.

When I went to your house to do homework, I watched her cook. Her hand stirred groundnut soup. I must admit, Mummy told me never to eat at other people's homes. It would make us appear poor and me rather greedy. I often left your home when the food was just about ready. Your mother said, in her summon-joy-voice: "Supper is ready. Please eat." But I, feigning time-consciousness, always said, "I have to run home, Mummy will be worried." At such times, your father sat in the bedroom. He never came out from that room. Everyday, like a ritual, he came home straight from work.

"A perfect husband," Mummy said more times than I can count.

"I hate him," you said more times than I could count. It was not what he didn't do, you said. It was what he did. Those touches, his touches, you said. And you could not tell your mother. She would not believe you. She never did.

Like that time she came home after the day you taught Juma a good lesson for messing around with me. She spoke to my mother in her voice which sounded like breaking china.

"She is not telling me everything. How can the boy beat her over nothing? At the school tap? These two must know. That is why I am here. To get to the bottom of this! Right now!"

She said this again and again, and Mummy called me from the kitchen, where I had escaped just when I saw her knock on our back door holding your hands in hers and pulling you behind her like a goat!

"Anyango, Anyangooooo," Mummy called out.

I came out, avoiding your eyes. Standing with my hands held in front of me with the same kind of embarrassment and fear that overwhelmed me each time I heard my name called by a teacher for school fees default.

They talked for hours. I was terrified, which was why I almost told the truth. You started very quickly and repeated the story we had on our way home. Your mother asked, "What was Anyango going to say again?" I repeated what you had just said, and your mother said, "I know they are both lying. I will get to the bottom of this at school in two weeks' time when I report back with her." And she did. You got a flogging that left you unable to sit down on your bum for a week.

When you left our house that day, they talked in low voices. They had
sent us outside to be bitten by mosquitoes for a bit. When they called us back
in, they said nothing. Your mother held your hand again, goat style. If Juma
had seen you being pulled like that, he would have had a laugh one hundred
times the size of your trodden-upon confidence. You never looked back. You
avoided looking at me for a while after that. Mummy had a list of don'ts after
that for me too. They were many. Don't walk back home with Sanyu after
school. Don't pass by their home each morning to pick her up. Don't sit next
to her in class. Don't borrow her text books. I will buy you your own. Don't
even talk to her. Don't, don't, don't do anymore Sanyu.

It was like that, but not for long. After we started to talk again and look
each other in the eyes, our parents seemed not to notice, which is why our
secondary school applications went largely unnoticed. If they complained
that we had applied to the same schools and in the same order, we did not
hear about them.

1. Mary's College Namagunga 2. Nabisunsa Girls' School 3. City High
School. 4. Modern High School.

You got admitted to your first choice. I got my third choice. It was during
the holidays that we got a chance to see each other again. I told you about my
school. That I hated the orange skirts, white shirts, white socks, and black
boy's Bata shoes. They made us look like flowers on display. The boys wore
white trousers, white shorts, white socks, and black shoes. At break time, we
trooped like a bunch of moving orange and white flowers—to the school
canteens, to the drama room, and to the football field.

You said you loved your school. Sister Cephas, your Irish headmistress,
wanted to turn you all into black English girls. The girls there were the pret-
tiest ever and were allowed to keep their hair long and held back in puffs, not
one inch only like at my school.

We were seated under the jambula tree. It had grown so tall. The tree
had been there for ages with its unreachable fruit. They said it was there
even before the estate houses were constructed. In April, the tree carried
small purple jambula fruit, which tasted both sweet and tang and turned

our tongues purple. Every April morning when the fruit started to fall, the ground became a blanket of purple.

When you came back during that holiday, your cheeks were bulging like you had hidden oranges inside them. Your eyes had grown small and sat like two short slits on your face. And your breasts, the two things you had watched and persuaded to grow during all your years at Nakawa Katale Primary School, were like two large jambulas on your chest. And that feeling that I had, the one that you had, that we had—never said, never spoken—swelled up inside us like fresh *mandazies*. I listened to your voice rise and fall. I envied you. I hated you. I could not wait for the next holidays when I could see you again. When I could dare place my itchy hand onto your two jambulas.

That time would be a night, two holidays later. You were not shocked. Not repelled. It did not occur to either of us, to you or me, that these were boundaries we should not cross nor should think of crossing. Your jambulas and mine. Two plus two jambulas equals four jambulas—even numbers should stand for luck. Was this luck pulling us together? You pulled me to yourself and we rolled on the brown earth that stuck to our hair in all its redness and dustiness. There in front of Mama Atim's house. She shone a torch at us. She had been watching. Steadily like a dog waiting for a bone it knew it would get; it was just a matter of time.

Sanyu, I went for confession the next day, right after Mass. I made the sign of the cross and smelt the fresh burning incense in St Jude's church. I had this sense of floating on air, confused, weak, and exhausted. I told the priest, "Forgive me father for I have sinned. It has been two months since my last confession." And there in my head, two plus two jambulas equals four jambulas . . .

I was not sorry. But I was sorry when your father with all his money from the railways got you a passport and sent you on the wing of a bird; hello London, here comes Sanyu.

Mama Atim says your plane will land tomorrow. Sanyu, I don't know what you expect to find here, but you will find my mummy; you'll find that every word she types on her typewriter draws and digs deeper the wrinkles on her face. You will find Nakawa Housing Estates. Nothing has changed. The women sit in front of their houses and wait for their husbands to bring them offal. Mama Atim's sons eat her food and bring girls to sleep in her bed. Your mother walks with a stooped back. She has lost the zeal she had for her happiness-buying shopping trips. Your papa returns home every day as soon as he is done with work. My mummy says, "That is a good husband."

I come home every weekend to see Mummy. She has stopped looking inside her maroon case. But I do; I added the letter you wrote me from London. The only one I ever did get from you, five years after you left. You wrote:

> *A.*
> *I miss you.*
> *S.*

Sanyu, I am a nurse at Mengo hospital. I have a small room by the hospital, decorated with two chairs, a table from Katwe, a black and white television, and two paintings of two big jambula trees which I got a downtown artist to do for me. These trees have purple leaves. I tell you, they smile.

I do mostly night shifts. I like them, I often see clearer at night. In the night you lift yourself up in my eyes each time, again and again. Sanyu, you rise like the sun and stand tall like the jambula tree in front of Mama Atim's house.

## Pat Parker
# Metamorphosis

you take these fingers
bid them soft—
a velvet touch
      to your loins

you take these arms
      bid them pliant
a warm cocoon
      to shield you

you take this shell
      bid it full
a sensual cup
      to lay with you

you take this voice
      bid it sing
an uncaged bird
      to warble your praise

you take me, love
      a sea skeleton
fill me with you
      & i become
pregnant with love
      give birth
        to revolution

Pat Parker

# My Lover Is a Woman

1.

My lover is a woman
   & when i hold her—
      feel her warmth—
      i feel good—feel safe

then/i never think of
   my families' voices—
   never hear my sisters say—
   bulldaggers, queers, funny—
   come see us, but don't
   bring your friends—
   it's okay with us,
   but don't tell mama
      it'd break her heart
   never feel my father
   turn in his grave
   never hear my mother cry
   Lord, what kind of child is this?

2.

My lover's hair is blonde
   & when it rubs across my face
      it feels soft—
   feels like a thousand fingers touch my skin & hold me
   and i feel good.

then/i never think of the little boy

who spat & called me a nigger
never think of the policemen
who kicked my body and said crawl
never think of Black bodies
hanging in trees or filled
with bullet holes
never hear my sisters say
white folks' hair stinks
don't trust any of them
never feel my father
turn in his grave
never hear my mother talk
of her backache after scrubbing floors never hear her cry—
Lord, what kind of child is this?

3.

My lover's eyes are blue
& when she looks at me
i float in a warm lake
      feel my muscles go weak with want
          feel good—feel safe

Then/i never think of the blue
      eyes that have glared at me—
      moved three stools away from me
          in a bar
      never hear my sisters' rage
      of syphilitic Black men as
          guinea pigs
      rage of sterilized children—
      watch them just stop in an
      intersection to scare *the old*

*white bitch.*
never feel my father turn/in his grave
never remember my mother
teaching me the yes sirs & mams
    to keep me alive—
never hear my mother cry,
Lord, what kind of child is this?

4.
And when we go to a gay bar
    & my people shun me because i crossed
       the line
    & her people look to see what's
    wrong with her—what defect
    drove her to me—

And when we walk the streets
    of this city—forget and touch
    or hold hands and the people
    stare, glare, frown, & taunt
    at those queers—

I remember—
    Every word taught to me
    Every word said to me
    Every deed done to me
    & then i hate—
       i look at my lover
    & for an instant—doubt—

Then/ i hold her hand tighter
And i can hear my mother cry.
Lord, what kind of child is this.

# Pat Parker
# Sunshine

If it were possible
to place you in my brain,
to let you roam
around in and out
my thought waves—
you would never
have to ask—
why do you love me?

This morning as you slept,
I wanted to kiss you awake—
say "i love you" til your brain
smiled and nodded "yes"
this woman does love me.

Each day the list grows—
filled with the things that are you
things that make my heart jump—
Yet, words would sound strange;
become corny in utterance.

Now, each morning when i wake
I don't look out my window
to see if the sun is shining—
I turn to you—instead.

## Terri Jewell
# Celebrant

I have my rage.
I keep it inside,

                    tend to its startling core,
                    this ancient, sacred fire.
My rage comes with
                    lip spots pink as jazz,
                    full breasts and heavy thighs
              scarred in ripped plum satin.
My rage comes in books I keep face down
                                        at work—
                    Black books by June Jordan,
                    Lesbian books by Audre Lorde.
You know how people talk.
I have this rage.
I hold on to it like
                    nappy hair does lint.
                    Neither allows me
                        to forget who chooses
                        to remain ignorant of me.

If I lose this rage,
                    they got me.
                    I become like them,
                    assimilated ghost haunting
                    my own true treasures.
I do have my rage.
I will let it loose
                    and show it to you.
                    Only then will you hear me.

I have my pride

I twist its hair in

        gold-framed mirrors,
      make it fat umbilical linked
           directly to you.

I put my pride

      naked in the streets,
      fly this rainbow spangle
          to lift your downcast
          eyes to the wider sky.
    "A man in a dress,
    a woman in boxer shorts!
        A woman who builds fighter planes,
      a man who collects dolls!"

You know what people think.
But I have this pride

    just as I am.

I place cowrie shells, brass bells

    and African trade beads
    all through it.
        It allows me to remember
        the vortex of my dance.

If I hide this pride,

    they got me.
    I become like them,
    so lifeless and hard
        only a S.S. number
        distinguishes us.

I do have my pride.
I will snap it,

    let you stare in awe.
    Only then will you see me.

I have my love.
I feed it

     coconut and cassava root,

     pure spring water and lullabies.

My love of women

    and their saucy ways,

    their ruby-sharp minds

  and hands that knot thread

      into the Blues,

women arced in sex,

    carrying the world

      in the curve

      of their ribs

  "What DO women do with

  One another ANYWAY,

    those Radical Feminist

    Separatist Anarchists?"

You know how people are.

But I have this love,

     rub it down with the skin of lambs,

    press amber essence and myrrh

     into its lips

     behind its ears

If I deny my love,

    they got me.

    I become like them,

    liars and hypocrites

    who turn love into sin,

   then raffle it off

   at the next business convention.

I do have this love.

I hold it at the Mall,

    take it home to Momma,

    talk to my God about it.

I pin it up at Kwanzaa time,

and kiss it on the freeway.

                I will grieve it when it's gone

                and shout when it returns.

I do have my love.

And I will celebrate it

                today

                  and every day

                  among you

        Only then will you

                know who

                I really

                      am.

# PART II

# INTERLOCKING OPPRESSIONS AND IDENTITY POLITICS

## 1980-2020

I am Black, Woman, and Poet—all three facts are outside the realm of choice. My eyes have a part in my seeing; my breath in my breathing; and all that I am in who I am. All who I love are of my people: it is not simple.

Audre Lorde

. . . we were marginalized in the Black movement, in the Black liberation movement, certainly in the Black nationalist movement. And we were marginalized in the white feminist movement, for different reasons. One of the reasons we were marginalized in the Black movement, besides sexism and misogyny, was also homophobia. A lot of us were indeed lesbians. . . . We needed to have a place of our own. We needed to have a place where we could define our political priorities and act upon them. And that's where identity politics come from. . . . What we were saying is that we have a right as a people who are not just female, who are not solely Black, who are not just lesbians, who are not just working class, or workers—that we are people who embody all these identities, and we have a right to build and define political theory and practice based upon that reality.

Barbara Smith

## Anita Cornwell

# Three for the Price of One: Notes from a Gay, Black Feminist*

## I

For quite some time now, I have been wondering what kind of life I would have led if I had not become a Lesbian. Of course, at this late date, I am firmly convinced that all Lesbians are born, not made, but due to our rigid, heterosexual conditioning, most womyn† are seldom fortunate enough to discover the joys of being a womin-identified womin.

Which is not to say that Lesbians do not face problems in this society. We do. By and large, however, many of our difficulties would disappear if America would somehow overcome its archaic, homophobic tendencies. Obviously though, even if it did, the Gay womin would still be left with all the problems confronting womyn in a nation that—to quote one "expert"— worships the male.

Finally, if the seemingly well-nigh impossible should ever occur and we are freed from the bondage of sexism and homophobia, the non-white Lesbian would still be subjected to racism, that endemic virus that has plagued the nation since its inception. Dealing with any one of these demons takes quite a bit of doing; having to endure all three is worse than living in the crater of a volcano.

Fortunately, my Mother brought me up to be an independent womin. She had to if she wanted me to survive. This was because any Black female born

---

* Portions of this material first appeared in the *Los Angeles Free Press*, November 24, 1972, as "A Black Lesbian Is a Woman . . . . " *Wicee* (Spring 1974) as "Notes from a Third World Woman." Part of the material was written in 1972, part in 1974, and part in 1977; it was first published in its entirety in 1978.

† I am, of course, using the variant spelling. Many Sisters feel that *womyn* (plural) and *womin* (singular) are preferable to the old forms. See *Dyke*, A Quarterly, no. 3 (Fall 1976).

in America before the aftermath of the Civil Rights Movement could assure some measure of dignity and justice for the Black American, had to know how to shift for herself, otherwise she would surely have perished.

Consequently, inasmuch as I was brought up to be an independent womin, I could never quite get the hang of the game that so many straight womyn had to play if they wanted to land a man. And believe me, she who did not want a man back in those days of togetherness in the early fifties was in for a world of trouble. So trouble dogged my footsteps for many a year.

During those years, before I had even heard of the word *Gay*, I spent an inordinate amount of time fielding such questions as "When are you going to get married, Neet?" I never came up with a good answer, not even after I had had my first relationship with a womin. I was aware that it wasn't good politics to tell people I didn't want to get married. In fact, I knew it would have bordered on the disastrous.

Besides, although I was positive that I did not want a traditional type of marriage (which was the only kind one heard of in those years when the *Feminine Mystique* was ravaging the land), I was not at all certain what kind of alternative lifestyle I would be able to have. That one Lesbian relationship (with a married woman at that) did very little to help resolve my dilemma. I knew only her, and if she knew other Gay womyn, she kept them rather well-hidden from me.

As was the case with many incipient Lesbians of that period, I had read *The Well of Loneliness*, but that was even less promising than my elusive lover. Those characters seemed to exist in a kind of world that I had never seen and one that had vanished as completely as the dinosaur and the dodo bird.

Perhaps if I had not been so badly scarred from having been born Black, poor, and female in the Deep South at a time when all Blacks were invisible (and, of course, even today, being poor or female in affluent, male-oriented America is about on a par with having leprosy in India), I might have been more enterprising. Perhaps if I hadn't had to cope with all those battles, fears, phobias, and anxieties continually raging within me, I might have gone to live in Greenwich Village, or Paris, or Los Angeles, or any place except conservative Philadelphia, where we had settled while I was still in high school.

It wasn't until after I had had my fourth Lesbian relationship—sometime during the early sixties—that I decided that, for better or worse, I was irrevocably Gay. And from that time onward, I began to withdraw as much as possible from the heterosexual world. I found most straight men too sexist, and I was tired of listening to straight womyn complain about the problems they were eternally having with their men.

Not that I didn't sympathize with my straight Sisters and their oppression, but I was having a devil of a time trying to keep my own canoe from capsizing. Besides, even then I was baffled as to why so many heterosexual womyn continued to let men use and abuse them in the same manner that their mothers, grandmothers, and even their great-grandmothers—dating back to the rise of the patriarchy—had done.

## II

Not the least of the many problems that the Black Lesbian has to contend with is the extreme conservatism that prevails in the Black community. It is conservatism that most white people are totally unaware of. For some reason that has always amazed me, many white people seem to consider Black people "liberal" because of our insistence on racial equality. That is not liberalism but is simply a healthy instinct for self-preservation.

I suppose another factor contributing to this misconception is that living together "without benefit of clergy" was rather common in some Black circles at one time. But the truth is that most of this was done because of the extreme shortage of funds that has always been the lot of far too many Afro-Americans.

"No matter how radical most Black men may be, when it comes time to dealing with womyn they get their ideas straight out of *The Ladies Home Journal*," a disgusted Sister once complained. And Black men aren't the only ones afflicted with ancient ideas and precepts about womyn. Even unto this very day, all too many Black womyn are still so hung up on Jesus Christ and the Bible, they may as well be living in the time of Moses and the Burning Bush.

During the time of our greatest oppression in America, the Bible was about the only source of comfort for most Black womyn. They made it such a deep part of their lives it became rooted in their bones, so much so that in time it apparently became the only framework that sustained them. And if there is any document anywhere that is more anti-female and pro-male than the Bible, I simply do not want to hear about it.

In retrospect, I believe that's why many Black Lesbians feel so guilty about being Gay. I now think that factor was the most important one that made some of my Lesbian relationships with Black womyn such a harrowing experience. And probably the reason it did not occur to me at the time of the turmoil is that I simply was unaware of the terrible hold that religious beliefs often have on many people.

By some miracle or other, I escaped that curse. And since none of my lovers ever directly said anything such as, "This is a sin. The Bible says thus and so," I never made any connection between the two. This was in spite of the fact that one lover was a devout Catholic (or at least she seemed to spend half of her life going to Mass), while another lover would turn those Sunday morning, down-home church services up so loud they were most likely heard by Jesus Christ up yonder swinging on them Pearly Gates.

## III

If Black conservatism is one ogre that keeps the Black Lesbian forever wading in troubled waters, then white racism is the second demon waiting at the other end of the tunnel. For most of my life, I had always been reluctant to socialize with white people because I felt most of them really did not want to associate with Black people on a socially equal basis.

Yet, oddly enough, by the time I finally entered the Womyn's Movement, I had somehow convinced myself that the color of my skin would have little or no bearing on how Movement womyn would accept me. Although I am now hard-pressed to understand where I got that notion from, I felt the fact that I was Gay would count against me more than the fact that I was Black.

Perhaps my long distrust of the mass media prevented me from accepting the value judgment implied by the press when it repeatedly declared that most Movement womyn were white, middle-class, and under thirty. I also knew that the Lesbian issue had had unpleasant repercussions in other cities.

After I became an active part of the struggle, however, it was a pleasant surprise to find that Gay was considered good, by some womyn at least. Consequently, since I thought "Black was Beautiful," I felt I had at last found my place under the sun. And so anxious was I to hold to that illusion, many months passed before I finally faced the truth: racism did exist in the Movement.

The first major unsettling incident occurred at a weekend conference about two months after I entered the Movement. At this fairly large gathering, two white womyn began a formal discussion program by relating the actions of several Black womyn who had not in the least seemed displeased when foreign womyn had made several unflattering remarks about America.

"Of course, I can understand why they feel the way they do," one of the white womyn added when she evidently caught me staring intently at her. There seemed to be a frightened, or guilty, look on her face when she looked at me, and it suddenly struck me that she had absolutely no comprehension whatsoever why those Black Sisters were not ardent flag-wavers.

The second thing happened a week after the conference and disturbed me even more at the time. I was in the process of moving from one section of the city to another and needed someone with an automobile to help with this expensive undertaking. But none of the white Movement womyn with cars, and who I had been thinking of as Sisters, offered to transport one single item.

It is, of course, always more difficult to deal with subtle racisms than the more blatant variety. You're apt to think, "Oh, I'm just being too sensitive." And perhaps I was. But, in the meanwhile, I couldn't help but notice that So-and-So was given a going-away party, and invitations were issued all around me, *but not to me.*

Also, I often thought, "Well, I'm older than most of them, that's why they're a bit standoffish at times." But then I noticed that another Black womin, in her early twenties, who had wandered into the group wasn't exactly being overwhelmed with the welcome mat either.

Yet, I am not saying that I met racism every step of the way in the Womyn's Movement. I did not. It was there, however, and it is still there. I must also point out that during the time that I was having my most excruciating experience with racism in the Movement, a white Sister was of the greatest comfort to me. I shall always be grateful for that Sister's understanding because if I had withdrawn from the Movement then, I might have become embittered and never trusted another white womin again.

Not surprisingly, fear of encountering racism seems to be one of the main reasons that so many Black womyn refuse to join the Womyn's Movement. This is especially unfortunate for the Black Lesbians because, unless they have come across feminist ideas from somewhere, they are apt to remain in the old rut of sexual role playing that apparently affects all traditional Lesbian circles.

## IV

When I first became acquainted with more than one Lesbian at a time, these womyn immediately assumed that I was a femme, although I didn't know the word as it existed in that context. Then, as I grew older—and heavier—other Sisters automatically assumed that I was a "stud," a term that really made my hair stand on end when I first heard it directly applied to me.

One day when Dee and I were in her apartment rapping, I finally suggested that we go down to my place for a few cocktails. We were almost out the door when her telephone rang.

Impatiently, she yanked at the receiver, her face screwed in deep frowns. The frowns quickly evaporated, however, when she recognized the voice of a recent lover. "Hi, I was just getting ready to go down to Neet's place . . . ," she said.

Then, after a long pause, she declared, "Oh, no! Neet's a stud!"

I hadn't tried to overhear Dee's conversation, and after hearing it, I certainly wished I had not. And, to make matters worse, Dee, who also called herself a stud, thought she had done me a favor by "elevating" me to her level. There actually had been a note of pride in her voice when she said I was a stud.

It was such a frustrating business because if she had been trying to insult me, I could have felt justified in getting pissed off and acting accordingly. At any rate, I later tried to point out that I was a womin, and as far as I could recall, a *stud* was a male horse. But whether or not, *a stud was not me!*

I wasted my breath, of course, which I found out a few days later when I was up to her apartment along with several other friends. Sometime during the evening, while I was fixing myself a drink, she gave me a scornful look and declared, "You're the most feminine stud I have ever seen!"

Presumably, she said that because I was mixing my booze while she was drinking hers on the rocks. But she would seldom explain where she was coming from. And sometimes she seemed to come from far out, such as the time she told me, "You don't talk the way you look."

When I asked her how I should talk, she merely smiled and shook her head. Finally, really alarmed, I asked, "Then how should I look?"

Still she refused to comment. But as much as I could surmise, I think she believed that since I wore slacks most of the time, I should swagger around and boast about how great I was, the way she occasionally did.

One of Dee's problems seemed to be the same that affects so many men— she could not readily relate to womyn except on a sexual basis. Unless they were "studs." Consequently, most of her friends were Gay men. And she was forever urging me to "come up and meet the fellows, Neet."

I never did get around to doing that, however, and perhaps that's why she told me one evening, "You are not like the fellows."

"That's because I'm not a fellow," I replied logically, but it didn't seem to make much impression on her.

## V

Of course, most Black Lesbians that I have known do not fall into the kind of pattern that Dee was into. Still, I do believe that most white people simply do not realize what a devastating effect racism has on Black people in general and on Black womyn in particular. And, obviously, the Black Lesbian is usually the most victimized of all.

Perhaps one reason that white womyn do not realize just how crippling racism is, is that most Black womyn seem so strong to them.

Frankly, until I entered the Womyn's Movement and came into contact with far more white womyn than I had ever known before on a fairly close basis, I had assumed that white womyn were more self-sufficient and/or independent than Black womyn. I assumed that because, after all, white womyn have more affluence and influence than most Black womyn have ever heard of. Or so it appeared to me from afar.

Thus, at first whenever I heard a young white Movement womin saying such things as, "Mary Jones is such a strong Black womin," I would mentally conjure up a big, hefty weight lifter or some such creature. Only gradually did it occur to me that they were speaking of a different kind of strength. Then, as I got to know those young white Sisters better, I could well understand why Black womyn seemed so strong to them.

Yet it is simply a matter of the survival of the fittest, so to speak. Most Black Sisters still do not have influential fathers or husbands or white law enforcement institutions to lean on in some form or fashion. Most Black womyn learn very early in life that there is very little insulation between them and "the school of hard knocks," as my mother is so fond of calling life in the raw.

It is not my contention that womyn of any race should be exposed to the brutal experiences that Black womyn have endured in America so they may be "strong and self-sufficient." But why isn't there some middle ground? Why should womyn either be strong and independent because of societal brutalization or dependent and indecisive because of excessive sheltering or other restrictive influences?

As incredible as it may seem to most feminists, however, the often declared goal of many Black people is to achieve the life led by the typical white, middle-class, suburban family of the fifties wherein Mother is buried at home all day with two and a half kids, one dog, and perhaps a small swimming pool near the newly erected two-car garage, while Papa struts around with his attaché case, sporting his gray flannels and button-down, blue pin-stripe Van Heusen shirt. That or much worse.

"We want *our* womyn spoiled rotten," a well-known young Black actor once confessed to a news reporter. What he had in mind, of course, was his ideal female: the slender, beautiful, fluffily dressed young womin with nary a brain in her head who is mainly concerned with clothes, men, and beauty tips. Then, when *her man* gets tired of her or she loses her looks, out she goes, the same as any other disposable commodity.

## VI

The ideas that most Black men have regarding Black womyn are indeed fascinating to behold. A couple of years ago when I was a member of a colloquium held at a large, nearly all-white eastern university by the School of Social Work, I found myself, as a majority of one almost, having to point out in a firm (but not hostile) manner that Black men were just as sexist as other men. Then I eventually realized that most of the vocal members in the room were holding fast to the idea that Black womyn only had one of two choices: either we had to join the Womyn's Liberation Movement and be led by white womyn, or we had to become part of the Civil Rights Movement and let Black men run our show.

Finally, I put my question to this young Black dude who seemed even more insistent than the others—although they all seemed to have very definite ideas about the Black womyn's place, et cetera—"You seem to be saying that I have to be led either by white womyn or Black men. Why can't I lead myself?"

He hemmed and hawed, but never came out with any clear-cut reply. After all, what could he say? Certainly not what was on his mind. Or perhaps he wasn't entirely aware of what his deepest feelings on the subject were. But it was painfully obvious to me that he simply could not endure the thought that Black womyn are capable of running our own lives.

After the young man stopped sputtering, another caseworker student—a

Black womin—said to me, "Many Black womyn in my caseload tell me they would love to be able to stop working and stay home and just be a plain old housewife."

"That may be what they're thinking now," I began, "but once the marriage begins to go wrong and she gets knocked around once or twice for burning the toast or some other such business, she'll probably begin to see things in a different light."

The caseworker simply stared at me, as most of the others in the room seemed to be doing. Not that everyone seemed to think I was from outer space, but there were a great many perplexed expressions in that room. The group was about one-fourth to one-third Black (a rather large percentage for that university, but social work is one of our greatest domains), and for the most part, I appeared to be the only Black in the room in favor of the Womyn's Movement, which seemed to surprise about 95 percent of everybody present.

I don't know where all of this "Back-to-the-Doll-House Movement" is going to end for the middle-class straight Black womin, but it is certainly a disastrous voyage she is about to embark on. Because in a patriarchal society, the middle-aged womin is about as relevant as the square-earth theory, and even more ridiculed.

So, what would my life have been like if I had not become a Gay womin? I don't exactly know, but I am sure glad I will never have to find out.

# Ann Allen Shockley
# A Meeting of the Sapphic Daughters

## I

Lettie and Patrice arrived at their small apartment almost at the same time that evening as they rushed home from classes. They quickly ate an instant dinner of hot dogs and canned baked beans, bathed, and dressed. By 7 p.m., both were ready for the meeting of the Sapphic Daughters.

Patrice was more excited about the occasion than Lettie, mainly because initially, it had all been her idea. Lettie had entertained other thoughts for this Friday night, which did not include being with what she was certain would be a gathering of all-white Sapphic Sisters. But Patrice, whom Lettie sometimes affectionately dubbed her Oriole Cookie, had a habit of wanting to attend events for which she had no heart. Like the Gurdjieff lecture and Bartok concert last week at Jefferson University, where Patrice was working on her doctorate in American literature with the aid of a fellowship. Esoteric lectures and concerts were all a part of Patrice, who was a growth product of the fifties. She was one of the first to integrate the schools in Alabama, and later became a recipient of one of the rush of handout scholarships awarded to black students by one of the private predominantly white women's colleges in New England for the purpose of inviting federal monies. Patrice had been around more whites than blacks. Her whole life's itinerary had been a journey through a non-identifiable cultureless milieu. During this time, she was one of the lucky ones who had few problems, for her physical make-up of a light complexion, proportioned features, and curly sandy hair did not cause much of a panic among those white students who feared only the color of blackness.

With Lettie, it was different, for she halfway straddled another generation. Lettie had attended all-black public schools in Washington, DC, and completed her college work at Howard University, closing her circle of blackness. Even now, the chain had not been too severed, since she taught political science at a community college in a predominantly black neighborhood. The college had a smattering of white students and a top-heavy frosting of white administrators. She knew the whites disliked her, for she made them uncomfortable with her outspokenness.

Even her appearance seemed a threat to them. She wore her mixed gray Afro closely cut to the shape of her round head. The deep, rich ebony darkness of her skin reflected the mystery of her long-lost ancestors in the flowing ancestral heritage of her existence. Her dark flashing eyes could change from softness to a cutting penetration when adversely confronted. She was cynical; she knew the world, people—especially white people. About them, she would bitterly warn Patrice: *I don't care how friendly some of them are; when push comes to shove, they're white first!*

"You've tied that headpiece fifty times," Patrice snapped impatiently, watching her in front of the bureau mirror.

"Mind's someplace else—" Lettie replied shortly, now smoothing the folds of her long African dress.

"What's there to *think* about? We're just going to a meeting to hear Trollope Gaffney. The literature passed out at the college's Women's Center stated that *all* lesbians were welcome to attend."

"Uh-huh. But I'm just wondering how many *black* lesbians will be there besides us?"

Patrice garnered part of the mirror to apply lipstick. "It would be nice to find out, wouldn't it?"

"How can we when they're in the closet?" Lettie retorted.

"Well—so are we!" Patrice exclaimed in exasperation, turning to face her. "Have we come out to our colleagues, friends—students?"

"For what? To become ostracized? It's bad enough being looked upon as lepers by whites, let alone blacks. You know how blacks feel about—*bulldaggers.*" Lettie spat out the epithet deliberately.

Patrice shuddered, "I hate that word."

"So do I. But that's what our people call us," Lettie said, softly.

Suddenly a smile broke across her face, like sun chasing a cloud, as she took in Patrice's shapely form outlined in a sheer summer dress the color of violets. "You look beautiful—"

"And you look beautifully militant!" Patrice laughed, admiringly.

"I'm letting them know in front how I stand.'"

"Com'on, Angela Davis," Patrice teased, "let's go. The meeting starts at eight."

## II

The meeting of the Sapphic Daughters was on the second floor above a curio shop in a shabby brick building near a battery of dilapidated warehouses. A large, husky woman with a hostile face, dressed in faded denims, stood guard at the door, blocking their entrance.

Lettie purposely lingered behind Patrice, fighting off her natural inclination to simply ignore the woman and brush past her. She heard Patrice ask in her nicest Wellesley demeanor: "Is this where Trollope Gaffney is scheduled to speak?

The woman gave Patrice a long, hard, silent stare. Lettie smirked, thinking she was probably wondering if she were a nigger, and *if* so, where did she get that way of speaking.

"Yeah—" the guard finally grunted.

Deciding that there had been enough time spent on social graces, Lettie took Patrice's arm and forthrightly guided her past the door block. Immediately upon their entrance, they were washed by a shoal of white faces gazing at them from behind cold masks.

The meeting hall was an elongated, poorly lighted room bordering on bareness. A makeshift platform was at the front with three straight-backed chairs, a small table with copies of Trollope Gaffney's latest book, and a scratched-up podium. Decorating the wall behind was a large cardboard sign reading *Sapphic Daughters* with the interlocking Sapphic symbol beneath. Metal folding chairs had been placed in the center of the room. Along the right wall were two card tables pushed together, covered with white paper cloths, for serving refreshments. A large tin tub housed chunks of ice-sheltered beer.

Some of the women were seated, while others milled around in clover group clusters. "Br-r-r, I can feel the chill already," Lettie murmured, looking around.

"Don't be so negative. You just got here. Let's sit in the back row."

"No, indeedy! I've had enough back seat sitting in *my* lifetime!" Lettie retorted. "Front and center—"

The women seated in the fourth row they entered shifted their legs slightly to let them in. One attempted a weak smile. "I don't see one of us here—" Lettie observed.

"Sh-h-h—" Patrice hushed her. "I think they're getting ready to start."

Three pants-clad women strode stiffly down the aisle to the platform, feet grinding hard on the wooden floor. "That's Trollope Gaffney—"

Patrice whispered excitedly, "in the center."

"How could I miss her?" Lettie retorted sarcastically, watching the little group's important accession to the stand. "She wears the same kind of clothes all the time."

Trollope Gaffney was a tall, broomstick-formed woman with a hard, brittle face reflecting her forties. She was dressed in her usual attire as seen in the newspapers and on the covers of her books: tight sequined brown pants, braided shirt with a gold women's pendant embroidered on the breast pocket, and a beret. The two women flanking her were flushed with pleasure and excitement. One was young with a cupid face dotted with two splotches of rouge, and long brown hair. The other was older, tall as Trollope, and had a surly, self-important air about her.

Trollope Gaffney sat down first, cocking one leg halfway over the other, then the girl followed. The third woman stationed herself behind the podium, scowling darkly at the women who had not broken their cloistered groups to be seated.

"Please take your seats—" the woman commanded. "We want to start on time."

The groups obediently broke up as the women scattered to find empty chairs. Then the mistress of ceremony called the meeting of Sapphic Daughters to order. Before starting the program, she wanted to remind them about next Friday's potluck supper at someone named Cynthia's house; called for more volunteers to get the Sapphic Daughters' magazine out; and told them that dues had to be paid by the end of the month. Then, turning to the girl behind her, she said proudly: "To begin our program, Wendy is going to read us her latest poem, which is dedicated to Trollope Gaffney."

There was a smattering of light applause and a barely audible groan from the back. Wendy stood up nervously, taking a sheaf of papers from her bag. In a young, breathy intonation, she began a rapturous reading of her poem:

> *She is what I love*
> *She with her soft beauty*
> *    who can delight me to ecstasy*
> *Take me away on a cloud of*
> *Woman-an-ly lo-o-ve*

"Sounds like the shit I used to write in junior high school," Lettie murmured.

Patrice gave her a warning glance, thankful that the seats directly beside them weren't occupied. Lettie was pragmatic, a realist. She had found this out on their first meeting when they had served together on a Black feminist panel. They had talked after the discussion, talked into the following months, and talked until they discovered each other and how they felt.

When the girl sat down, there was another polite sound of applause. The mistress of ceremony told Wendy her poem was beautiful, so tender, full of love, such as only women can have for each other. Afterward, she began reading from a stack of publicity releases to introduce the guest speaker for the evening, Trollope Gaffney.

". . . one of our foremost lesbian/feminist writers. A leader, fighter—"

When she finally finished, the hall resounded with loud, appreciative handclaps for Trollope Gaffney. When Trollope got up, the room was stilled with attentive, respectful silence.

Trollope Gaffney had a high-pitched voice that derided her aggressive, bold, mannish appearance. She was self-assured and spoke without notes, having done this so many times before. Her talk was about the gay liberation movement, where it stood now and projections of how it would be in the future. She envisioned a world community of lesbians. "We have to assert ourselves—build. Identify ourselves to each other—this great army of lesbian women, because we are all sisters-s-s. We are all *one* in the beauty of Sapphic love-e-e!"

Later, when she finished, the hall's walls rocked with cheers as the women stood up. The Sapphic Sisters began crowding the platform to enclose Trollope Gaffney in a web of reverence. The young poet, Wendy, began selling Trollope's book, as the purchasers waited patiently for autographed copies. A record player was turned on, and the nasal voices of a lesbian group singing sad ballads of women in love with women saturated the hall in a plaintive, hollow sound.

"You want a beer?" Patrice asked, let down by the cynical look naked on Lettie's face.

"Now, what was all of *that* speech about?"

"About love and building a world community of lesbians," Patrice answered, as they approached the refreshment table.

"Who needs one? If I'm going to build a separate community of *any* kind, it'll be a *black* one!"

"How much is the beer?" Patrice asked the chubby girl with yellow bangs behind the table.

"Seventy-five cents for a beer, and fifty cents for a sandwich. We got baloney, cheese, tuna fish—"

"Wham!" Lettie breathed. "They must be already starting to finance that lesbian community."

"Two beers, please—" Patrice ordered, searching her purse.

The woman on the platform, who had taken charge of the program, came toward them in long, swaggering strides. "I'm J.L., president of the Sapphic Daughters." Her eyes were a sharp, glittering steel blue, like a frosty, clear winter's sky. She stood back on her legs, hands hooked over her belt, face closed.

"I'm Patrice and this is Lettie—" Patrice smiled, while Lettie eyed her cautiously.

"You live around here?" J.L. asked.

"Yes—" Lettie said quickly, taking the can of beer Patrice offered to her. She had played this scene years ago, many times before, going to places where colored, Negroes, niggers weren't wanted. J.L.'s question was a familiar conversation piece that dripped with subtle warning. Blacks who "lived around here" knew better than to go to places where they were not wanted.

"Hi!" The girl who had read her poetry came up to stand beside Lettie. "I'm Wendy—"

"Yes, we know—the poet," Patrice said. "This is Lettie and I'm Patrice."

Wendy stuck out an eager hand. "We've never had any black lesbians here before—"

"Oh?" Lettie said icily, raising the beer can to her mouth.

"We meet every other Friday. Sometimes we have rap sessions, consciousness-raising groups, and dances—"

"Do you people have any kind of an organization?" J.L. questioned, taking a cigarette from a crumpled pack in her shirt pocket.

"Frankly, we don't know any black lesbians," Patrice said, frowning.

"*Or*, if *we do*, they haven't *told* us," Lettie added, smiling venom.

"Do you know any?" Patrice said to J.L. She swallowed her beer hurriedly. This was a habit with her, to drink beer quickly before it got too warm and tasted like glue.

"Naw—" J.L. squinted over the cigarette smoke.

Suddenly, out of a murky past, Patrice was reminded of the rednecked hill crackers in Alabama. Revulsion shivered her spine. After all the transplanted years, she was surprised that she could still remember. Painful memories are never easy to forget, like being hurt in love. Women began drifting over to the table. A rock group record had replaced the melancholy singers, and a few couples had started to dance. Beer cans were opened and sizzling, popping sounds interspersed with laughter.

"What brought you here tonight?" J.L. went on persistently.

"A couple of things. Primarily, we wanted to hear Trollope Gaffney. I have assigned some of her writings to my students—" Lettie replied, feeling anger warm inside her. *Maybe what really brought her here was the devil to knock the hell out of the bitch.*

"And we wanted to meet others like ourselves—" Patrice added, gently.

Wendy edged closer to Lettie, gazing approvingly at her. "That's a lovely African dress—"

"Like *yourselves?*" The words were thrown like acid by J.L.

You goddam racist! Lettie thought, as the beer churned sourly in her stomach. Beer and anger don't mix. White racists and black militants don't mix, and white lesbians and black lesbians are white and black people first, instilled with personal backgrounds of distrust and hostilities.

Seeing the smoldering fire in Lettie's eyes, J.L. backed away, putting out the cigarette in an ash tray on the edge of the table. "Uh—well—you see, this is a kind of private organization." She conjured up a weak grin, which became a clown's grimace. "We meet at each other's houses sometimes and we are all—er—friends."

"Here comes Trollope—" Wendy interrupted.

Trollope joined them, still surrounded by her network of admirers. "I'm thirsty!" she giggled shrilly.

Someone quickly produced a can of beer for her. Over the can, her eyes glistened at Patrice and Lettie. "And who are you two?"

Patrice repeated the introductions, watching Wendy openly gazing at Lettie from beneath heavily lidded speculative eyes. For a flashing moment, jealousy singed her. *Yes, white girl, she's good in bed to me.* Angrily, she finished her beer, throwing the can in a wastebasket.

"We have your last book—" Lettie told Trollope.

"How nice. What did you think of it?"

Patrice held her breath, waiting for Lettie's reply. She knew from long ago how Lettie could raise her husky voice and let it all come out like thunder and lightning in a brass band. Only this time, Lettie was constrained.

"The section on political freedom for women was well-taken, but there doesn't seem to be anything in any of the lesbian literature on the lesbian movement addressing itself to helping the black lesbian to become free from racism—especially inside the lesbian community."

Trollope looked puzzled at first, then flustered.

"Will there be freedom from racism in your lesbian world community?" Lettie went on pointedly.

"Of course—" Trollope answered stiffly, looking over and beyond them.

"I had a black lover once—" Wendy blurted out.

J.L. shot her a mean look.

"It's easy to be liberal between the sheets—" Lettie said too sweetly.

Trollope let out a squeal. "There's Tommie! I haven't seen her in ages!" Moving away, she smiled broadly. "Nice meeting you—Patrice and Lettie."

J.L. grabbed Wendy's hand. "Com'on—let's dance."

Wendy waved back to them as she let J.L. lead her to the dancing circle. "Come again!"

"Got enough?" Lettie asked, deliberately putting her half-finished beer can on the table. She hated beer.

"Un-huh!"

"Then—let's go."

They left and no one said goodbye.

## III

In the bed, Lettie asked sleepily: "Now, has your curiosity been satisfied about the Sapphic Daughters, my little Oriole Cookie?"

"Umph!" Patrice grunted tiredly. "It was like crashing the DAR—"

"Maybe someday, we might find that silent legion of black lesbians. But until then—"

"We stay in the closet," Patrice mumbled, moving closer to her. "It *would* be nice to know—others."

"Perhaps we do. And, possibly one of these days, they'll let us know," Lettie said. "Let's go to sleep. You never know what tomorrow will bring."

# Dawn Lundy Martin
# To be an orphan inside of "blackness"

—is the condition of it (us). We can love it, sure, cradle its beautiful head, and eyes looking. It wants to be performed, leaping, but the *I* is not a good actor. The problem of the book is that it's never quite "black" enough. Language can perspire the thickest blackest blood but you are still the unheld nigger, the one inspiring the deadly shaking panicked rage. Your tennis shorts or salmon-colored pants will not help you. It's a good idea to have "black" in the title of the "black" book in case there are any questions as to its race. The "black" bits will be excisable, quotable in reviews. The book should be very interested in the thing you know as "blackness," all its clothes, its haberdashery. What the book actually wants, however, is to know the distance between the "I" and the "you," how it is drawn into space and action as when the white woman professor says you have written her a "vicious" letter and wants to know what's wrong with you. Claudia Rankine has reinvented this territory of the relation that is forever unrecognized in that relaxed [white] body. When one's actions have so clearly produced the interrogative text, the refusal to enter the text as subject. For you, the text lives in the floating unreal, a document that has nothing to do with you, but, my dear, it *is* you, the grotesque monument to the regime, so perfectly sculpted you cannot see yourself in the mirror.

## Kai Davis
# Ain't I a Woman?

I wake up with an apology already forming in my mouth
This is what it means to be a contradiction
Too Black to be a woman
and not man enough to be Black
This is what it means to occupy a vacant space
Have everyone slash each cross-stitched intersection of my identity with a
straight blade
Tell me to pick one label or none at all
But Ain't I a Woman?

When a Black man says I'm too thick for my own good
When he follows me down the street
When I say no in three different octaves
Ain't I a woman?

When a white girl in my class calls us "we"
Speaks of a universal need
Says woman is the new black
Talks picket signs like I've never marched before
Talks injustice like I've never met a cop before
When she hushes me then speaks on my behalf
Ain't I a woman?

Ain't I a woman when the moon is full?
When my mother rolls my naps in her palms
When my father shouts harambe seven times on New Year's Day
Ain't I been writing this poem for three years straight?
Ain't Sojourner Truth been doing the same?
Ain't bell hooks?
Ain't Ntozake Shange?

Ain't this the story that never makes the news?
The vacant space that fills the airwaves
The silence of unwritten eulogies
Ain't this Liberia?
Ain't this Haiti?
Ain't this North Philly?

Didn't a white woman close mouth smile at me today?
Tell me I'm beautiful then hack apart my body
Wear my lips ass and hair like a costume
Didn't she sell all thirteen of my children and lynch my husband?
Didn't she ask me to be quiet one too many times?

Didn't I bruise a Black man's ego swole today?
Ask him to stop calling my scars sacrifices
Calling my suffering an inconvenience
A blemish on the Black man's movement
As if MLK didn't suck milk from a Black woman's tit
But ain't I a bitch?
Ain't I bitter?
Ain't I divisive by accident?
Don't I complicate the revolution with all my grievances?
Ain't I still grieving?
Ain't this my middle finger?
Ain't I finally done apologizing?

I am not an obstacle to navigate through
I am the reason you are breathing
The feet that trod out the path even
The light that subverted all your darkness
Am I not the pulse of every one of your revolts?
Ain't I a woman?
Ain't I a woman?
Ain't this a rhetorical question?

## Kaila Story

# Not Feminine as in Straight, but Femme as in Queer #AF: The Queer & Black Roots of My Femme Expression/Experience

As a Black lesbian feminist femme, I have constantly had to navigate racialized and gendered projections upon my person. Many folks in the past refused to see and/or acknowledge that they were in the presence of a Black lesbian feminist femme. While my Blackness in many queer and non-queer spaces made me extremely visible, it was always the combination of my racialized difference coupled with my queer gender expression as a femme that seemed to deem who I truly was, invisible. Both queerness and Blackness, to me, have meant not letting society, institutions, friends, or loved ones define who you are, or who you hope to be. It has also meant defining yourself, for yourself. Further, it has meant living freely, unapologetically, and boldly. It has meant feeling so emboldened within your queer Black self that you freed others. That you challenged others. Lastly, it has meant working from your own center and letting others know and see that you are a force of freedom and light, who would rather live truthfully than live silenced, stifled, or afraid.

It took me many years to come into my unapologetic Black queer feminist stance, and even more years to come into how I defined my particular queer gender expression as a femme. My femme identity, as I see it now, is one that transcends and challenges white supremacist, homo-normative, and patriarchal ideas of femininity and queerness as white, and consequently challenges the hetero-patriarchal assertion that power, strength, and assertiveness are innate to manhood, maleness, and/or masculinity. My grounding within myself was made manifest by Black lesbian and queer feminisms as well as Black queer theory and queer theorists of color. It was through their writings and activism that I finally understood what it meant to be prideful of my

69

Black feminist lesbian femme identity.[1] Their works gave me the necessary experiential grounding, affirmation, and confidence in my identity as Black feminist lesbian femme. I knew after reading and studying their works and viewing their activism that I was a part of a wondrous and magical community. A community that has always been here, and a community that has had a fascinating and compelling history.

Shows like *Gentlemen Jack* introduce us to fragile and faintly white femmes like Miss Walker while shows like *Boomerang* introduce us to fierce and fiery Black femmes like Tia. Both illuminate that femmes have always been and continue to be here.[2] Femmes are both ancient and contemporary, and they have existed as long as queer folk have existed. Working-class lesbian and bisexual women popularized the term in the late 1940s and '50s "to describe the relationships they were forming: butch-femme."[3] Historically, femme identity was only discussed in relational terms to butch women and/or butch/femme relationships.[4] In Joan Nestle's essay "Butch-Fem Relationships and Sexual Courage in the Fifties," she contends that butch/femme relationships were never about mimicking straight relationships in any way, and that in fact, the butch/femme relationship model provided more visibility to queer folks, specifically lesbian couplings that would often go unnoticed. This street visibility to Nestle frightened folks and made them question the boundaries of gender and gender expression. "The butch-fem couple embarrassed other lesbians (and still does) because they made lesbians culturally visible—a terrifying act for the 1950s," she wrote.[5] In Nestle's later work, *The Femme Question*, she troubles the misconception that butch/femme relationships are nothing more than straight replicas. She writes: "Butch-femme relationships, as I experienced them, were complex erotic and social statements, not phony heterosexual replicas."[6] Nestle goes further and contends that "they were filled with deeply lesbian language of stance, dress, gesture, love, courage, and autonomy. In the 1950s particularly, butch-femme couples were the front-line warriors against sexual bigotry."[7]

With the emergence of queer theory and activism highlighting queer politics and bringing the queer movement during the late '90s and early 2000s to the forefront of mainstream media and scholarship, both butch and femme scholars amplified the subjectivity and individuality of the femme, removed from the butch-femme relational analysis.

I remember my first encounter with a femme like it was yesterday. Her name was Evie, and although this encounter wasn't in person per se, it still felt very real. Evie was the Black femme character in the film *The Incredibly True Adventures of Two Girls in Love* by Maria Maggenti. The filmmaker dedicated it to her first girlfriend. Something that I had only begun to dream about. A girlfriend. I had been struggling within myself about my own queerness. How to come out. When to come out, and who to come out as. It was 1995, and I was fifteen. Nicole Ari Parker played the Black femme character Evie, and the butch character, Randy Dean, was played by Laurel Holloman, before she was cast as Tina on the popular Showtime series *The L Word*. Evie and Randy Dean were from two different economic and racial backgrounds, but somehow found their first love within one another. Evie had box braids, a close relationship with her mother, got good grades, and was considered a popular girl in the film. Randy Dean by contrast was an outcast, already out of the closet in high school, and lived with her gay aunt and partner in the film. Evie was my first glimpse at the potential manifestations of Black femme possibilities.

Although I'd had glimpses of Black femmes before, Shug Avery's character in *The Color Purple* and Lorraine of "The Two," in *Women of Brewster Place*, neither one of those characters were as relatable as Evie was to me. The other two existed in worlds that I hadn't inhabited, nor would I ever come to know. My first encounter with a Black femme theorizing her Blackness in tandem with her femmeness was T.J. Bryan's work, *It Takes Ballz: Black Attitudinal Femme Vixen in tha Makin'.*" In the essay, Bryan explores how her femme gender expression has been tied to the same ways in which she has embodied and performed her Blackness. Similar to my experiences with not being seen as femme in both queer and non-queer spaces and in both Black queer and non-Black queer spaces, Bryan contends that it is her racialized difference that makes her Black femme identity not seen or felt by others. To Bryan, it was both her Blackness and her femme gender expression working together visually and ideologically that created the confusion about who she actually was. How she actually saw herself. It was the ways in which white supremacist conceptions of Blackness working in tandem with the misogynist ways femme identity was misunderstood that made the viewer of Bryan's racial identity and femme gender expression invisible. Bryan's work defines femme identity as part emotional strength and part spiritual perseverance. It also urges the reader to not link notions of traditional or conventional straight femininity with the femininity that is embodied and performed by queer femmes. Historically and presently, Black femmes have found themselves being read as conventionally feminine and/or not queer due to the white supremacist boundaries of Blackness and the homonormative boundaries of queerness.

Black femme theorist Kara Keeling explicates on the roots of racism and the misreading of Black femmes in her book *The Witch's Flight: The Cinematic, the Black Femme, and the Image of Common Sense.* She contends that Black femmes have always existed despite the many racist conceptions of Black identity, and like Bryan, Keeling argues that Black femmes are often read as masculinized despite their performances because of their queerness working in tandem visually with their blackness. She writes,

> The black femme is "black" . . . AND "woman" . . . AND "lesbian." She is each of these in such a way that each category's claim to be an expression of her identity is exploded by the effort required to maintain the validity of that claim. In each case, the black femme urges the project expressed by the category to recognize an alternative potential within it.

To Keeling and Bryan both, the Black femme has been historically and contemporaneously misread because of the multiple identities they embody and live simultaneously. Other femmes of color suffer from similar fates due to their racial and queer identities working in tandem visually, inevitably confusing any outsider as to how they should be read and seen. White femmes have never had to navigate their queer gender expressions/experiences in terms of their racial identities because of the ways in which white supremacist notions of humanity and identity have and continue to define whiteness as a standard and/or normative racial identity. Both Bryan and Keeling's work helped me to recognize that not only had the divine feminine been celebrated and exalted within ancient Black cultures, and contemporary Black communities, but it also solidified my own subjective feelings that my Black femme identity was an identity that came out of an ancient space of strength, power, and divinity. It was not an identity that was based upon heteronormative complacency and/or socialized expectations of gender. Their work allowed me to see my Black femme identity as one that was based and rooted within a Black feminist tradition of recovery and resistance that has always sought to undermine the racist and heteronormative assumptions that have chosen to see femininity as inherently white, and power as inherently male.

Trans and non-binary femmes have taken the expressions/experiences of femmeness even further, clarifying that femme identity is a queer gender expression and not a gender identity, clapping back at all the folks who continue to conflate the two. The popularized activist phrase "Women and Femmes" to many trans and non-binary folks does make this distinction clear. Although they recognize the phrase's potential for coalition building and solidarity, many still contend that these distinctions need to be made clear, so as to not, in an attempt to be trans and non-binary inclusive, that activists don't inevitably erase the fact that many trans and non-binary folks identify as femmes as well as women. In a *Slate* op-ed, femme theorist Kesiena Boom argues that the "modern day usage of femme is far more expansive: Now it's used throughout the queer community by people of any gender and sexuality as a label to name their intentional, feminine gender expression." Boom further contends that "when cisgender straight women have a feminine gender expression it's simply 'the norm,' not an intentional reclamation of femininity from the clutches of heteronormativity. Femme is an identity that queer people choose—it is not simply a description of a person's femininity."

Nuancing on Boom's piece, Black nonbinary femme B.B. Buchanan asserts that although the categories of woman and femme should be understood as two distinct identities, they also argue that this doesn't take into account recent Black queer and trans scholarship, which see the phrase as an attempt at coalition building and solidarity. Buchanan contends,

> Femininity, as a form of expression, is denigrated and devalued on all bodies; no matter an individual's self-identification. Fighting back against the neoliberal and modern understanding of a coherent and authentic self, I argue instead that identity is produced through structures and these structures exceed any one individual's claim on the gender order. Butches and trans men, because of the gender order, are seen as inherently or "really" feminine—in opposition to their self-identification—and the violence that emerges from that structural ascription is tied to disciplining them back into the proper gender order.

Buchanan, seeing the symbiosis of oppression that women and femmes have shared throughout time and space, makes the current activist phrase one that honors the distinction between the two, but also hints at the structural oppression that they share.

Although Buchanan challenges Boom to nuance their argument when it comes to the gender expression of femme, they also validate Boom's thesis, that femme identity needs to be understood as a queer gender expression/experience and not a gender identity. Both Buchanan and Boom also agree that you can't be femme and identify as straight either. Femme as a gender expression and experience has always come from a queer space and community, and for many, especially Black femmes like myself, femme has also always come from a Black space and community as well.

When one has the desire to call themselves a femme or call someone else a femme, they just better make sure that they are signifying a person's queer gender expression, and not a person's gender identity. This meditation on femmeness provides the reader with more clarity and nuance when it comes to thinking about and discussing femme identity. My ancient and current Blackness as well as my ancient and current femmeness have always worked together within myself to transcend and challenge white supremacist, homo-normative, and patriarchal ideas of femininity and queerness as white, while simultaneously challenging the hetero-patriarchal assertion that power, strength and assertiveness are innate to manhood, maleness, and/or mascu-linity. I have also learned over the years that if my Black femme identity con-tinues to remain unseen and/or invisible by others that I can take comfort in the fact that I'm not alone, nor have I ever been, and that this projection has nothing to do with me. Viva La Black Femme Power!

## Notes

1. These works include, but are not limited to, Audre Lorde, Cheryl Clarke, June Jordan, Pat Parker, E. Patrick Johnson, T.J. Bryan, Jose Esteban Munoz, Uri McMillian, Amber Jamilla Musser, Jasbir K. Puar, Omise'eke Natasha Tinsley, and Jessica Johnson. These are some of the Black lesbian/queer feminists and Black/queer theorists of color works that all help me discover my unapologetic Black feminist femme stance.

2. Lena Waithe, Ben Cory Jones, and Halle Berry, executive producers. *Boomerang*. BET. 2019. For more on *Boomerang*, see: https://www.imdb.com/title/tt9064792. Accessed June 4, 2019. Sally Wainwright, Sarah Harding, and Jennifer Perrott, directors. *Gentleman Jack*. BBC One & HBO. 2019. For more on *Gentleman Jack*, see: https://www.hbo.com/gentleman-jack. Accessed June 4, 2019.

3. Kasandra Brabaw, "A Brief History of the word *Femme*," *Refinery29*, June 20, 2018, https://www.refinery29.com/en-us/femme-lesbian-lgbtq-history. Accessed June 4, 2019.

4. The definition of *butch*, and/or *butch woman*, I am using has been defined by the University of Southern California's LGBT Resource Center and it reads as follows: "A person who identifies themselves as masculine, whether it be physically, mentally or emotion-ally. 'Butch' is sometimes used as a derogatory term for lesbians, but it can also be claimed as an affirmative identity label," https://lgbtrc.usc.edu/files/2015/05/LGBT-Terminology.pdf . Accessed June 4, 2019.

5. Joan Nestle, "Butch-Fem Relationships: Sexual Courage in the Fifties," *Heresies: Sex Issue #12*, vol. 3, no. 4 (1981): 21–24.

6. Joan Nestle, "The Femme Question" in *The Persistent Desire: A Femme-Butch Reader* (Boston, MA: Alyson Books, 1992).

7. Nestle, "The Femme Question."

# Mecca Jamilah Sullivan
# Wolfpack

For the New Jersey Four

*This story is for Patreese Johnson, Terrain Dandridge, Venice Brown, and Renata Hill, who, in 2007, received prison sentences ranging from three and a half to eleven years for the alleged felony gang assault of a man who threatened to rape them in New York City's West Village. The story is also for Chenese Loyal, Lania Daniels, and Khamysha Coates, who were offered plea bargains in the same case. The women have been known collectively as the New Jersey Seven.*

## Verniece

This is a story that matters, so listen. I'ma tell it. The summer my words were snatched away, the weatherman on Channel Nine kept promising a heat wave. Had me dreaming of days curled up under the dust and rattle of the AC with my son, Anthony Jesús, and nights out in the Village with my lady and our squad. It was the summer after high school graduation, and a heat wave woulda left my mother too drained to hassle me about my life, my weight, and my plans. None of her muttering: "What you fi do, Verniece, sit at home with that girl, getting big as this house while your baby starve? Yu na have plan?" My plan was I was gonna go to college to major in astronomy, back when I bothered with a future tense. When I told my mother this, she usually grunted. "No, yu nah gwan waste my money or yours, studying some devilment 'bout birthdays and signs." She would sigh her anger, sucking my dreams from me like the gristle from a chicken bone.

I looked forward to sweating it out that summer, gathering words for that fight. But the damn heat wave never came. Days, weekends, weeks, months passed, and nothing. I started to imagine myself leaping into the television with the weatherman and snatching the gray-speckled rug off his head, just to show him how it felt to have small hopes taken away. But that was not my spirit back then, before my words left me. I was patient, quiet. I waited.

I don't remember everything that happened that night, but the things that came before—I know those like my skin. Those stories—the ones that make what happened to us matter—are not about a man who tore into our summer and broke us. Those stories are about us—about me and my lady, our homegirls, and our son. Who we are and who we were, who we might never be again.

Before they took my words away, it was me and Luna and Anthony Jesús, plus my mother, when she wanted to act right. Even when she didn't, our family was the proudest thing I had. We were not like the teen pregnancy stories you see on television. I wanted Anthony Jesús as much as anyone ever wanted anything—a million times more than I ever wanted some man. Truth be told, my mother was happy to learn a baby was coming, too. Seeing Luna and me together and so strong for two years made her panic, started her in early on those things that middle-aged mothers go through—hassling me about when I'd find a husband, worrying endlessly about growing old on God's Green Earth with no grandbabies to care for. Sometimes, when the bookshelf buckled or a doorknob came loose, she would take an Olympic breath and sigh out: "Yu know we need a man in the family, with yuah papa gone now."

I would get up quickly from wherever I was and fix whatever was broken. Then I would remind her—silently, in my mind—that my father had died a decade ago, and had never been the handyman type in life. *Be careful what you wish for*, my fantasy self would say. I knew it wasn't a son-in-law, or even grandchildren, that she wanted. What she wanted was a different kind of daughter. If I had come to her at any point in high school to tell her I'd sworn off pussy and decided to go celibate, become a nun, she woulda flown to the church, tithed her whole pension, and sung the choir off the altar with the force of her gratitude. Her problem with me had nothing to do with motherhood. It was about womanhood, and which kind of woman I would be. In my mind, I told her all about herself. But in real life, I said nothing. Just counted the weeks till Luna and I had saved enough money to pay her cousin for his Y chromosomes.

Luna went to school and worked two jobs that summer, while Anthony Jesús and I kept each other company, held each other down in my mother's house. Luna would come home from her afternoon gig at the Pretty Look nail salon on Bloomfield Ave. with soul food dinners for all of us, my mother included. Every time, my mother refused. She would look at the bag in Luna's hand, all grease-heavy and smelling good. She'd breathe in the smell and you could see the want on her face. But she'd purse her lips, pat her stomach, and say "M-mm, no. Me nah feel settle," and turn back to her room. Then I'd hear her, late at night, muttering to herself as she crept to the kitchen, rifling through the leftovers, "Just fi likkle pick."

Luna didn't let my mother get to her. She just hid her hurt and kept trying. She sang to me and the baby whenever we needed it, brought home bootleg telenovela DVDs whenever I asked, and told me my body was her favorite place on earth. Her lips were like sponges just wrung free of cool water, perfect on Anthony Jesús's cheeks, perfect anywhere on me.

We weren't sweating what my mother—or anyone else—had to say back then. I still had the words I thought would protect me from everyone's opinions, keep me doing alright in the world. I found those words the same day I found our son's name, and I thought both would hold me down forever. That was a year before that night in the Village, four weeks after I pissed pink on the EPT strip. My mother dragged me to Saint Anthony's, eager to have me "put likkle face" in, let the old church ladies see me again before my belly started to show. Her face was a bright mix of shame and glee—happy about the baby, sad about me, and so I was sure the day would be miserable. I hated church usually—the slowness of it, the meanness of the women, the sour-breathed gossip and the eyes raking you down when you went for communion, looking to see if you'd put on weight. My father never went to church, and when I asked him why once, sometime in the third grade, he told me that being black and awake in America was enough of a double-bind for him; he had no interest in an afterlife that promised more of the same. I didn't know exactly what he meant, but it sounded right to me. I hustled my way out of going to church as often as I could, and when I did go I did my best to send my mind away.

But the day my words came to me, I couldn't get out of going. And so I sat in the pew with my mother, letting the music pass the time as always, thinking about eating fried wantons with Luna when I got home. But at the end of the service, something happened. The closing hymn that day did something—took me from the shaggy pew where I was sitting, made me forget the press of my too-tight pantyhose, my mother's hips against mine. I can't remember what the song was called, but I remember how the lyrics surprised me. They were not the usual tired mess about a man in the sky who said *Do This* and *Don't Do That* in a language nobody understood, or a ghost who played truth or dare games with your soul. There was no double-bind, no damned-if-you-do, no one saying what to do or be. The lyrics were just a name. And just like any word changes shape when you say it long enough, this word changed, too. Eventually I stopped hearing everything around it, and the name meant something simple: *You are a person. God loves you. That's it.* So I got up and I left the pew, but I took those words and the feeling with me. I put all that into our baby's name—Anthony Jesús—and let the past sag to the ground like a church lady's scowl.

For the next few months, I made those words a gate behind my ears: *We are people. God loves us. That's it.* I repeated the words in my mind wherever I went. Whatever was going to get to me had to fit through those words first. Those words kept me going with my head up when I walked around the city with my homegirl LaShanya—a slim, pretty, light-skinned-type girl with a long auburn weave. But after I found those words, I almost didn't care. I could walk with my homegirl and just be with her and laugh. When I went around Newark holding Luna's hand or pushing the baby, those words kept the frowns and pointing fingers at a distance, and made it so I almost didn't see the looks people gave us. By August, I thought I had gotten good at a new kind of hearing, a new kind of seeing—the kind that made no room for people's chuckles and the stares. I thought I had learned how to walk in the world just feeling like a person, no matter who else was around. But the night my words fell away, I learned I was wrong.

It was a Saturday night, and I remember the moon looking bright, like the white tip of a freshly manicured nail. It was hot, finally, and Luna had gotten off from the Pretty Look early, so we went with our girls to the Village to relax, do us, enjoy the summer. We were rolling deeper than usual that night—there were seven of us altogether: me, Luna, LaShanya (who we all call Sha), and our girl TaRonne and her woman, plus two of Sha's friends—a rich, Jersey City girl named Margina and a brown-skinned femme named Angelique, with dreadlocks and an eyebrow ring. Sha collected friends like jewelry, picking them up whenever they caught her eye, valuing them enough, but never crying too hard over the occasional loss. The people she brought around usually fell right in with most of us. They were Sha's people, and so they were cool with me.

TaRonne's teacher girlfriend, Arya, must have been upset about something, because she snorted like a sick dog every time TaRonne talked on the ride to the Village. TaRonne treated Arya's attitude like how a little kid treats a video game, pushing random buttons and giggling at the response. "Arya's in a bad mood," she announced to all of us from the back seat. "She don't understand why we always walk around in the Vil when we could be sipping sherry with other *young professionals* like her." Arya huffed and looked out the window. "Nah, I know what it is," TaRonne said after a few seconds. "She's just worn out from being so intelligent, and accomplished, and fine. It ain't easy being a dream come true." She squeezed Arya's waist and let her head fall onto her chest. Arya sighed and ran her hand over TaRonne's fade, pushing her own cheeks toward the window to hide her smile.

We parked on West Street and walked up to the pier on Christopher to drink Coronas and watch the rich people's lights flicker on the other side of the Hudson. When we got to our regular bench, Sha turned to Margina and asked if she knew anyone who lived in one of those apartments. "I just want to know who my neighbors will be when I blow up," Sha explained, crossing her legs and fanning her dress out behind her on the bench. Margina leaned her back against the railing and said, "Um, I don't think I know anyone there," her voice all nervous and small. I decided then that I liked Margina— she was quiet like me. But TaRonne liked to make waves.

"Right, right," she said. "I guess you not in the habit of mingling with Daddy's tenants. I know how it is." Margina turned the color of Pepto-Bismol and tried to sound hood. "Nah, it's not even like that, yo," she said. Then she gave an awkward smile, crossed her legs, and looked down at her shirt.

We could all tell the little girl was feeling TaRonne, but Arya wasn't bothered at all—she was out for fun. She uncapped a bottle of beer for Margina and raised her own. "To new experiences!" she said. Then she tongued TaRonne down right there, hands palming TaRonne's skull like a basketball, her eyes wide open and staring dead at Margina. The couple's love tiff must have dissolved by then, because they didn't stop kissing till Luna busted out in her jingle-bell chuckle. Then the rich girl went from pink to purple, and turned her face back toward Jersey. Luna put her arms around my waist and we threw our heads back, drinking our laughter like raindrops.

That was the last thing I remember before the man showed up—all of us laughing, kissing, feeling at home in the night. I keep that moment high up on a shelf in my mind now, in a row of important times I do not want to forget: the first time I saw my baby smile, the day my father gave me a toy telescope for no reason other than it made him think of me. The day I found my words—the words that left me, in a second, for a lifetime, that night on the pavement.

Now that my words are gone and I have nothing but time to think back, I remember another moment that belongs on that list, too. It's another story that matters, even if it only matters to me. It was months before that night in August, but I see it clear as yesterday. Anthony Jesús hadn't been born yet, but he was one of our plans, along with my astronomy and Luna's zoology and a tall house in the suburbs with mango smoothies always in the freezer. Luna was reading on the sofa while I sat at my father's old desk, making flashcards for a Spanish test. The day was so still it almost seemed fake. For hours, it seemed like the only things moving were the little bits of dust that floated in the strip of light between my mother's curtains, tumbling slowly over themselves like cells under a microscope. Suddenly, Luna slammed her book shut, the smack of the pages cutting into the silence.

"People talk," she said. She was looking at me but past me, like how my father used to do. Then she paused and focused. "The only real difference between people and animals is that people talk. That's it."

It was the kind of moment that flags itself for you, announces its importance right away but waits till later to be explained. I thought of plenty of reasons to remember the moment right then—how beautiful Luna looked with her face pinched up in thought, how nice it was to know that no matter what anyone said about me and my girlfriend, they couldn't say we weren't smart. But as time passed, what Luna said stayed with me, and soon the question came up: if that's true—if talking makes a person—then what's wrong with me? Why don't I speak?

That's when I started looking for words, I realize now, now that I am still and boxed in quiet, with no one to listen and everything to say. Those words meant the chance to be a person, in my own language, for real.

That moment is as big as a planet for me now. Every day I think about it and find new stars, new rings. I remember it together with our laughter at the pier, just before my world fell from its socket. Now, in the quiet, I remember the seven of us, Luna, LaShanya, TaRonne, Arya, Angelique, Margina, and me—chilling, glowing, taking gulps of the night and sprinkling it out in laughter. I remember our loudness, how huge we felt, in the best way, and how free. I can't say exactly what happened after that, how it started, what the man said, what he did, how we responded. But I remember opening my mouth, saying, *"We are people,"* and feeling, believing, that words could help us.

## TaRonne

We left the pier with our faces tied tight into smiles, me and my lady in the front. Arya was laughing, her hand all warm and wet in mine. Verniece and Luna were behind us, quiet as usual, cuddled up in each other like West Fourth was their living room. Sha's little friends were holding down the rear, and Sha was on the near side of the curb, brows sharp as switchblades, face in full glow like she was a drag queen walking for femme realness. Before shit went down, the night was nice, cool, everything peace. Then I saw it happen in sepia tone, time winding down to slow motion. I knew shit was wrong before the dude threw his cigarette at us, before he touched Arya's neck, before he slung his threats at Sha. As soon as he called Verniece what he did, I knew there would be a fight.

Me and Arya had had some problems in the car, but she had brought it down to a simmer by the time we got to Sixth Ave. She was finishing up the summer session at Morton Street Middle School, and someone had asked her to make a list of the students that should be kept apart in the future, just so that a gun or a baby didn't show up in class one day. I told her I didn't think that was her place, that by the time they're twelve, kids should be allowed to conduct their little romances and tragedies as they please. She shot me an icicle stare and told me I was naïve. "You can't pretend the teacher's role is strictly intellectual in 2006. Things are not that simple for us, TaRonne." Full first name. I knew she was tight. I told her I knew she wasn't simple, that I liked how complicated she was. She told me "Complex!" and started popping some shit about transitive verbs. I put my arm around her, said I didn't know the difference but was ready to learn. She liked that. By the time we walked past the movie theater on West Third, we were back to our black-dyke-hood-love like in *Set It Off*, all Cleo and Ursula again.

We walked past the newsstand, where some skaters and rich kids and a handful of gay boys were scattered around, all talking kiki and enjoying the night. Merengue horns and hip-hop beats hovered over the pavement, and the smells of beer, smoke, and McDonald's French fries mixed thick on the street. In front of the sex shop on West Third, a homeless woman was sitting on the ground, talking to her scarf, and when we passed the woman, Sha's little richgirl friend stared like she saw an alien, then stepped over the woman like if she wasn't there at all. I whispered in my lady's ear: "Arya, what you think would happen if we brought her back to Newark with us, or took her up to Harlem?"

Arya laughed. "She'd probably front like she wasn't scared, just like she's been fronting all night, trying to be smooth."

I laughed. "I don't know. Maybe it's not a front. Maybe there is some smoothness to her, after all, deep, deep down."

Arya slapped my finger and shot me a look that made me wish we'd stayed in bed that night.

Then I saw him, half a second before he saw us. He looked about thirty-five, although I found out later that he was in his twenties. And from the table he had set up on the pavement, covered with DVDs, I would have sworn he was a bootlegger, although the papers, the prosecutor, and everyone else who mattered called him a "filmmaker" from the next day on. When he opened his mouth at Sha, I didn't care what he called himself.

"Hey, princess!" he said. Sha didn't respond. He didn't give up.

"Sweetheart, I'm talking to you."

"She's not interested," I told him from the far side of the pavement.

"Why don't you let her speak for herself?" He moved from behind the table and took a pull from his cigarette, stretching his neck to see where my voice came from.

"She doesn't have anything to say to you," I said, loud now, getting hot. "She's gay."

Then he looked dead at Verniece, thinking she was the one talking, instead of me.

"Who asked what you think, you goddamn elephant!"

Verniece was shocked frozen, like if someone had snuck up on her and flashed a camera in her face.

"Fuck you, nigga!" I shouted.

"Oh, that was you?" he said, taking another pull and finally turning my way. "You look like a fucking man. What, you sticking up for your woman? Don't go that way, sweetheart." He looked at Sha and grabbed his fly. "I'll fuck you straight!"

I shouted something—I can't remember what, the words and the spit and my teeth all mixed up in my mouth. He flicked his cigarette at us, the cherry arching across space toward Angelique and Margina, who looked like they would piss on theyselves soon, if they hadn't already. We were in motion before the fire landed. I can't really recall what happened after that. Wild how time and space make perfect sense up to a point, but then unravel like shoelace threads in the tick of a second. I saw his hand on Sha's neck, in her hair. I felt my fists pushing hard into his shoulder, the blows never landing heavy enough. I saw Angelique and Margina get some hits in too, felt my surprise. I heard some words come from behind me, from Verniece maybe, but I have no idea what they were. I never saw a knife, and I never heard the muthafucka cry. I wish I had.

Arya is the only one who hears me when I say I saw it coming from that one word—elephant—before the spit and the fire and the bodies flew. Everything after that was like dominoes falling into place on a track. Tell my femme friend you want her pussy. Fine. Call me a man. Whatever. None of that is new. But what he had for Verniece was something different, like she wasn't even human. He tore the person out of her, like he tore out that clump of Sha's hair, like the judge tore up our lives and everything we know, chunks of us missing like the truth missing from news stories.

The cops, reporters, lawyer, jury, everyone but my woman skips over that part, that word—elephant—like they want to press fast forward and get to the part of the story that really matters. When the first report came out without mentioning what he called Verniece, Arya said it was because the white reporter didn't see why that kind of "dehumanization" would mean a fight to us. I realized then that Arya is the naïve one. I tried to let that word sit in my ears for a long time after she said it: *dehumanization*. By then I knew I wouldn't get to hear her talk like how she does for a long time. That was our good-bye.

I can't speak for the rest of us, but I was glad when he took that step and put his hands on Sha. Hands you can see, touch, prove. Hands you can bite and burn and tear away. But words, I'm learning, ain't shit.

Sha doesn't know if she stabbed the man. They screamed the question into her face for hours and each time she said "I'm not sure." But I know this—I wish I'da had a knife in my hand, wish I'da heard him shriek like a dying cat under my fingers. I can see that night however I want to see it now, and I see it this way all the time: I'm the one with the knife, and I am sure. This woman sticks it in that nigga real fucking good.

# LaShanya

The knife was a gift from my mother. She gave it to me to keep in my purse, because she loves me, because she didn't want me to be the first of the two of us to leave this world. They were killing black dykes in Newark—like they always are, here and everywhere. But now there was Sakia Gunn, my cousin's sister-in-law's friend. Sakia with the deep eyes and the sweet, shy smile, Sakia who was fifteen and could've been me, stabbed to death on the same corner where I used to catch the bus to work, right by the twenty-four-hour police booth, and still nobody saw. Walmart doesn't give time off for hate crime danger, and I had to work late nights all the same. My mother called that knife my bodyguard. She gave it to me to keep me safe. To keep me whole and coming home.

When I think of that night, I think in lists of things. The courtroom is a big wooden box, and as I sit here, my heart tries to fly away from me, but the lists bring comfort, something solid, like place. I think of the smell of my hair grease melting under the streetlights. I think of my newest sisters, Angelique and Margina, wailing behind me as the fire flies at my eyes. I think of the man, the stripes on his shirt getting bigger and bigger until they are on me, right on top. I do not see my knife. I try hard, plunge my fingers into memory. I try to see myself pulling the blade from my bag, try to feel what I have never felt before, my knife slipping past skin, sinking quickslow into flesh. But all I can remember is the weight of his hands on my scalp, those stripes falling on top of me, like how this judge sits on top of the room, hovering like Jesus hovers in holographic paintings on project walls.

Judge McBain, sitting on top of me, his face breaking like a cloud, his cackle crashing over me like lightning. "Sticks and stones may break my bones," he says. He tells us that's what we should have thought. That was the command that should have traveled like blood from our brains to our bodies. Not DUCK, not BLOCK, not PROTECT YOURSELF, YOUR GIRL. As though "I'll fuck you straight" was just a pack of words.

The man has a name, but I'd rather not say it. He's sitting up in the wooden box, just like he sat up in some reporter's face, saying he didn't think it was a crime to "say hello to a human being." I've never felt more alone, more confused than in this moment. I feel like this man and Judge Dickbrain—that is what I want to call him, where they've got me to now—I feel like the two of them come from the same place, someplace where a bootlegger without a pot to piss in and a white man with power dusting his shoulders like dandruff can be two sides of the same damn coin. This is not a place I ever thought I'd be. I did not know I lived there.

But Dickbrain is the bootlegger's parrot in his sentencing speech. "Sticks and stones," he says first. And then: "Words don't justify hurting a human being."

I sit and remember stripes and sounds and hands flying into me like arrows, wonder if either of them knows how good "human being" sounds right now, as a thing to be. Sounds like a safe place in the flow of words and things, something as sure as the ticking of the clock at the back of an old, hollow room. I wonder if either of them will ever know how hard it is to think human, to *be* human, when someone is threatening to knock, force, fuck the *you* out of you.

I hear our names hit like tennis balls across the courtroom and I think: we are women whose names mean things. Luna is bright and distant like the moon she is named for. Verniece is named for her mother, who's more like her than either of them can admit. Arya is named for a beautiful kind of song. Angelique is named for an angel that welcomed her mother to heaven in a dream. Margina is named for her father's choice to forget the center of things and live well on the sidelines. TaRonne is named for a grandmother who spat in a white man's face for calling her "girl," and an aunt who raised all her sisters' children on the salary of a maid. My name comes from Hopi and Spanish and Newark Ghetto, my mother's imagination and a mix of things. I wonder if Judge Dickbrain would have anything to say about that.

But when the thunder quiets and the cloud seals up, what he has to say becomes clear. He forgets about names and drops numbers on us all. Angelique Ramos, Margina Thompson, Arya Lewis: *Six months probation.* Luna Martinez: *Three years in prison.* TaRonne Daniels: *Five years.* Verniece Smith: *Eight years.* LaShanya Parish: *Ee-leh-ven.*

I will be nineteen tomorrow. The next time I am able to run through a sprinkler on my mother's street, kiss my girlfriend in a quiet room, make myself a turkey sandwich, dance or sing with no one watching, I will be thirty. I will never remember a bloody knife in my hand. No one will ever have to prove it was there.

When we left Verniece's house that night, her mother was on her way to church. While they got the baby dressed, Mrs. Smith asked Verniece over and over to come with her to the service. Verniece said, "No," sweetly, then strapped on a baby sandal, pulled up a tiny sock. Her mother asked one more time on her way out the door, and Verniece said "No, thank you" again, like she was turning down butter for her toast.

Mrs. Smith held the baby and said to all of us:

"Alright, then. You girls be safe."

We were seven girls to her. Seven women to us. Either way, we were people, sure as time.

## Verniece

All I do now is remember: I am wrapped up in Luna, my girls, and the warm, licorice sky. The man tears like a bullet through our night.

"Who asked what you think, you goddamn elephant?"

I am afraid for my girls, for Luna, and for myself. I see him reach for Sha, his palms spread wide and ready to grab, and I think of her mother, of my mother, of Anthony Jesús. I don't know what will happen. Then, the thing Luna said wails in my ears: *The only difference between people and animals.* And my own words swirl up into orbit: *You are a person.*

So many things are going on in this moment, I feel like my mind is breaking down to mesh, to screen. I cannot tell what is happening inside, what out. I see a man in pink come, I see a woman run away. I see fingers and DVD cases and a nugget of fire fly. I see Luna and my mother holding the baby, smelling good like ackee and saltfish. I see blood curled around stripes, and Sha holding a silver-soaked blade. From one side of my ears or the other I hear him say again: "Goddamn," "God-damned," "God-dammned elephant." I feel my words popping like firecrackers inside my mouth, and I let them blaze the air:

*You are not a man—Your sneakers are cheap your clothes are corny you have no job—You are not a man, hands on your sleepy little dick trying to prove it's there—You are not a man, what you know about God some white man in the sky—If your God doesn't know me blackdykemanwoman god fuck him he doesn't exist—You are not a man—You are a joke.*

All those words, all that time, beat into nothing like bubbles on the wind.

Columns of newspaper ink are burned into my eyes now. I try to make faces out of the lines and curves. I do not want to read what they say about us. I would rather see anything else. In one paper, I see my mother's head turning toward our apartment door, an almost-eclipse of black hair and a crescent of powdered cheek. In another, I see Luna's proud neck, Anthony Jesús's sourdough chin. I say nothing, think less than nothing—just try to pull their faces through the ink.

My first night here, I make a decision: pretend. I play games with myself, pretend to fool myself like my mother used to do when she didn't want to really see me. I tell myself things are not what they are. I pretend that things are me and Luna and the baby, slow-swirling mornings dappled with laughter, endless hours of warmth and clean air. If I want to share my dinner with Anthony Jesús, I decide he's on my lap, his polka-dot bib brushing my wrist. When I miss TaRonne and Sha so much it hurts my chest, I decide they're here on the cot with me, and we laugh.

I wade through the sea of orange suits, eat my food, and do what I'm told. I try not to think in days, how they close me up in darkness, stuff all my holes with funk and pain. I try not to think of how time is crusting over, baking me deeper into stillness each time the moon brings a day to its end. But there is always the ink, running like blood up and down the newsprint paper. Even when I say nothing, the headlines are always there: KILLER LESBIANS' TRIAL BEGINS . . . SEETHING SAPPHIC SWARM DESCENDS . . . BLOODTHIRSTY PRIDE ATTACKS.

On the morning after my first night here, someone puts a newspaper in my hands. It's folded open, and before I read the headlines, I find my name in the middle column, a gnarl of ink at the center of the page. "Verniece Smith, 19, was hauled out of the courtroom after an emotional outburst. 'I'm a mother,' Smith wailed." I read up from there, wading back through the spread of letters, grabbing onto the lines and curves I can find sense in. I float up through my girls' names and ages, the number of years each of us will lose starting now. Then I see the headline: LESBIAN WOLFPACK HOWLS ITS END.

This is when I decide to make things whatever I want them to be. If I cannot be a person I decide, then anything can be anything at all. I find Luna's hand in the paper, our baby's eyes in the black of the ink. From the space around me, I carve my mother's smile and a deep, wetwarm sky.

I get up, tighten my grip, and breathe. Then I part my lips, clear my throat, and say—out loud—*"Let's go."*

# Pamela Sneed
# We Are Here

It was before I'd seen it, but I started reading reviews about
the new Wonder Woman movie and my heart started aching.
It's all about a tough white woman who kicks ass from Amazonia
but it made me miss the real life Wonder Woman
warrior poet Audre Lorde with cancer and the one breasted
Amazons of the Dahomey
she spoke of so valiantly
brown women soldiers
an army
I love fictitious woman super heroes like Wonder Woman,
Xena and Buffy
but I'm tired of all the whitewashing.
I want to ask,
*Where are all the brown/black lesbian women?*

At the time I thought it was silly but
I dreamt of it again,
I wanted to start a sticker campaign to say
Black lesbians were here and place them
in unsuspecting places
Like sewn into a garment or work of art it might say made by
Black lesbians.
Like what about instead of emoticons and lemon yellow smiley
faced stickers
the face of a fierce happy black dyke popped up with
a shaved head, a buzz cut or an Angela Davis type Afro?
What if X-men star Storm with the silver mohawk or Isis had
their own movie?

I can't remember specific details but there was a Latinx
performance artist who once performed
an action in a supermarket and replaced all
the Chiquita banana stickers in a supermarket with
something like harvested by slave labor to show the labor
of where real bananas come from.
As I go to more and more vigils and protests about violence
against black men and marches for white women
I want to say Black lesbian lives matter too
And there's been so much violence enacted against us
amongst each other too.

I feel stilted at times with the language of identity politics.
I feel as if I'm in the Stone Age using crude and rudimentary tools
to discuss something so complicated.
I once wrote about lgbtq identity and said "the real freedom is
going to come when being lgbtq won't make or break us."
Sometimes when I go around speaking I meet young Black
lesbians who even in urban populated landscapes are isolated.
They are hungry to have someone say they exist.
They want need to hear me say proudly as Audre Lorde once did,
"I am a black lesbian warrior poet doing my work coming to ask
Are you doing yours?"
It saves their lives and mine too.

For all the world's seeming progress
I feel like black brown lesbian women have disappeared in all
the dialogues.
What about our bodies?
I want to start a sticker campaign that people will read in unlikely places
to say
My people

Black lesbians
We were
Are here.

# PART III

# COMING OUT AND STEPPING INTO

## 1978–2020

And surely Black lesbians have been central in American cultural production and political debate. Whether or not they and their work can be quickly identified or marked simply as "Black" and "lesbian," their experiences and position bear deeply on their work, and it is out there!

Catherine E. McKinley and L. Joyce Delaney

Black women have a rich oral history of lesbianism: Everybody knows of the bulldagger up the block that their mamas used to talk about. Of the auntie the family used to dog. Of the rumors about the basketball player at college. And when Black women talk at get-togethers, the coming out stories fly! "What was your first girlfriend like? When did you know you were in the life? Did you think you were the only one? Do you remember the first girl you kissed? The first girl who kissed you?"

But I realized that these stories weren't written; there was nothing that a young black lesbian—riding the train, passing for boy with a good-looking woman on her arm—could go to for reference, to know that she's not the only one. That she has stories of bulldaggers and he-shes and femmes and butches and old maid aunties. Old ones and young ones. And that we are here, we've always been here, and look how glorious it all is!

Lisa C. Moore

## Beverly Smith
# The Wedding

*The following is based on writing I did during the weekend of my friend J.'s wedding in 1975. J. and I met each other in September 1974 when we were beginning graduate school in public health. The fact that we were the only two Afro-American women in our class helped bring us together, and we were "best friends" for much of our first year. J. was engaged to H. when we met. I had been married about 3½ years in March 1974 when I left my husband.*

*Part of the significance of this writing to me is that I did it a few months after I began to consciously realize myself as a lesbian. This writing was also done before I had been involved in a lesbian sexual relationship. I am fascinated by what it reveals about my development as a lesbian. It's also important to me because it tells something about the juxtapositions of living as a Black woman who is both lesbian and feminist.*

*The type of writing that is here, journal writing, is something I have done since my first or second year of college. A major impetus for this writing for me has been my need to make sense of my life and to manifest my life in writing. It is a survival tool. As I wrote in this journal, "The only way I've kept my sanity is by writing every chance I get."*

*I burned all the journals I'd kept up to that time during the second year of my marriage, partly because I felt I had no safe place for them away from my husband and partly because one of my duties in that marriage was to forget who I had been before it. I did not keep a journal again until about a month before I left him. Much of that journal has to do with the process of leaving, and I feel that I literally wrote my way out of the marriage. I am grateful that our movement has provided me with a safe place for these words.*

August 22, 1975 7:10 P.M.

At the Rehearsal

I'm in the bathroom trying to get down some notes on this mess. . . . I feel so cynical, so frustrated, almost hysterical and bored.

The "cast" is from the Black bourgeoisie, Frazier would have loved it. No one has real faces. I was looking at the women and thinking of our friends' faces, the spirits that reveal themselves there, Demita particularly. God, I wish I had one friend here. Someone who knew me and would understand how I feel.

I am masquerading as a nice, straight, middle-class Black "girl." I changed into my costume in a dressing room at Penn Station. A beige "big dress," earrings, a scarf.

August 23, 1975 2:00 A.M.

At Mrs. Brown's

[Mrs. Brown was a neighbor of J.'s family with whom I stayed.] I'm now in a place that unlike the one above is totally familiar. The room I'm staying in reminds me of the first places of my childhood . . . the ambience created by an old Black lady. Dark old furniture and photographs. A picture of FDR above one of Martin Luther King. Two pictures of Jesus and several of trains—from when trains were important.

This whole scene is unbearable. The rehearsal dinner was awful. I abhor these tight, proper, nasty-nice people. There were Black servants. A maid, a cook, a waiter, and a bartender.

I can't go on. All of a sudden I feel nauseated.

August 23, 1975 8:00 A.M.

. . . Back to the wedding. I loathe the heterosexual assumption of it all. I can imagine how these people would act if they knew that I was a dyke. It's funny, I've been questioning my right to classify myself as such. ("Right." Most people would see that concept as absurd.) But in a context like this I realize that it's correct.

Why am I so upset? Because I realize now . . . that in some sense I want J. for myself. I am shocked as I write this, but it is true. My dream helped me see this, and as I sat at that deadly party last night waiting for J. to arrive (she's been late to everything so far, the rehearsal, the dinner—a clue?) I thought about this, about the dream I had this week. In the dream I was in the front seat of a car and J. was in the back. I kept asking her whether she was all right and she assured me that she was. She put her arms around me over the back of the seat and kissed my face. She got into the front seat and just as we were starting to talk and were getting ready to drive off Terry (a boy Barbara went out with in high school) came up to the car. Of course I was furious. This morning when I woke up I thought of that dream and particularly of what Terry meant in it. Of course he represented men in general and more specifically H. (The names are similar, perhaps coincidental in the dream context, but everything about the two is symbolically identical.) I realized that Terry was the first male to come between Barbara and me. . . . I remember how hurt I was by all those goings-on.

She is irretrievably lost to me and I to her. She's getting married and since I'm a dyke I am anathema to her. She's made her feelings on homosexuality clear on several occasions. [I no longer use the terms *homosexual* or *homosexuality* to refer to lesbians.]

Two last things and then I'll stop. Last night I was on the second floor after going to the bathroom (I must have gone four times, I was hiding and trying to maintain my sanity). I went into a bedroom where J. and three of her bridesmaids and Susan (the wife of a friend of H.'s) were talking. J. was talking about what still needed to be done and about her feelings concerning the wedding. Mostly anxieties over whether everything would go well. But at one point she said something to the effect that "It seems strange. We've been together all our lives (her three friends) and after tomorrow we won't be." Her friends assured her that they'd still be a part of her life. Ha! I know better. She'll be H.'s chattel from now on. It occurred to me that celebrating a marriage is like celebrating being sold into slavery. Yes, I'm overgeneralizing (I'm only 90–95 percent right); but in this case I feel sure.

One piece of evidence for the above. At the rehearsal yesterday J. was on the fourth floor shouting to someone. H. yelled up to her, "J., don't shout!" J. replied, defending herself, and H. interrupted her by saying sharply, "J.!" as if he were reprimanding a child or a dog. I was sick. This is the essence. He will try to make her into his slave, his child, in short, his wife.

I must stop now. Mrs. Brown just brought in a clock, not wanting me to be late. Did I mention that this is frightfully badly organized? Everything is chaos. But I have no doubt it will come off. Unfortunately.

At the Reception 6:35 P.M.

I'm sitting on the floor of the first floor bathroom. I'm so tired of this. I wish I had somewhere to go, a movie, or a friend. Of course I don't have the latter and I don't have enough money to pay for the former. I wonder how long before I'm discovered, i.e., before someone wants to use the bathroom. Fortunately there're not many people on this floor.

I feel so out of place. Twinges of self-pity. I haven't felt like this in a long time—since before I began to create my life.

I am so overwhelmed by the fact that heterosexuality is so omnipotent and omnipresent (though certainly not omniscient!). Not only is it casually taken for granted but it is celebrated as in this bacchanal, announced in the *New York Times*. And homosexuality is so hidden and despised. Homosexuals go through torturous soul-searching, deciding whether they should come out. Heterosexuals get announcements printed . . .

Of course this is not the only source of my dislocation. All of this represents a lifestyle I abhor. This is nothing more than a Black emulation of the super-rich. A catered affair with a vengeance.

How could anyone with a social conscience or just simple common sense perpetrate something like this?

I've gravitated toward the "servants" both today and last night. They are about the only people with whom I feel comfortable. Precisely because they are clearly not a part of this. I hardly know anyone here, and the only person I care about is J. This is the kind of jive socializing that we've always hated—the kind that made Aunt LaRue call us "anti-social."

I keep thinking of the Meg Christian song, "The Hive." . . . I keep thinking of Mrs. Brown. I wonder is she as lonely as she seems. If I'm not mistaken, she's the woman who used to take care of J. when she was a child. J. came over this morning to get me and she hugged Mrs. Brown and said goodbye to her. J. cried and I began to cry too. I went into the bedroom so they wouldn't see. I'm not allowed to cry. No one would understand. People would wonder. After all, as a woman this type of event should make me happy. After all, J. has achieved the supreme goal of any "real woman." Not only is she married but her husband is a Harvard Law School graduate. A fine young man.

I find myself hoping that this might be the rare, good marriage for J.'s sake, but I'm skeptical.

At the Reception 10:25 P.M.

The crowd has thinned considerably. I don't have much more to say. I'm played out. Maybe I can escape soon. I want to prepare for the meeting and I don't want to be as exhausted as I was at the last one. [I was meeting with a group in Manhattan the next day to work on the creation of the Gay Caucus in the American Public Health Association.]

I just had a long conversation with Art, one of the bridesmaids' husbands. . . . H. reintroduced me because I committed the horrible sin of sitting by myself, not talking with anyone . . .

. . . one thing he [Art ] said that I totally disagree with is that interest group politics (defined by ethnic group or gender) are not ultimately productive. The larger women's movement and Black feminism come out of broader, supposedly comprehensive movements whose net result was to fuck women over.

It's fine to coalesce on common issues but the plain fact is we don't want what they want. At least half of the people (men) in this country don't want women to live. Approximately 80 percent could care less about Black people. Ninety percent (who really knows?) are adamantly opposed to homosexuality. So who is going to fight for our lives but us? . . .

*The next day I managed "to escape from Queens." I had decided before I went to sleep that "damn it, the good dyke thing to do was to get to the city by myself" and not depend on J.'s father to drive me. I had told him that I wanted to leave early to get on the train. The actual reason was that I needed to get to my meeting. After the meeting I took the train back to Boston.*

*I have kept the writing I did that weekend, some of it on the backs of the printed wedding program in a worn white envelope labeled "The Wedding," for* the last four years. Soon after the wedding I read parts of what I'd written to Lorraine Bethel, one of the editors of the Black women's issue of Conditions. She said it sounded like perhaps I could make it into an article. That seemed like an extremely remote possibility then since I had never published anything before. But her comment always made me think of this writing as a potential article—maybe. In March 1978, our third Black feminist retreat was held in Boston. I had not read "The Wedding" in some time. I was afraid to look at it. Afraid that it couldn't be made into an article because it wasn't good enough. As a result of the support and inspiration of being with the women the first evening of the retreat I got up the courage to read what I had written the next morning as I rode the subway to our meeting place. I told some of the women about this experience that day.

I know these were crucial steps in the creation of this article. There have been many other contributors to this process. My sister Barbara Smith's encouragement and nudging has been essential. I include this description because I would like other women to know something of how I managed to get this into print and how important other women's help was to me. One hope I have is that after reading this other women, especially Black women, will be enspirited to tell their own essential stories.

## Dionne Brand
# poem from *No Language Is Neutral*

Someone said this is your first lover, you will never
want to leave her. There are saints of this ancestry
too who laugh themselves like jamettes in the
pleasure of their legs and caress their sex in mirrors.
I have become myself. A woman who looks
at a woman and says, here, I have found you,
in this, I am blackening in my way. You ripped the
world raw. It was as if another life exploded in my
face, brightening, so easily the brow of a wing
touching the surf, so easily I saw my own body, that
is, my eyes followed me to myself, touched myself
as a place, another life, terra. They say this place
does not exist, then, my tongue is mythic. I was here
before.

# Angelina Weld Grimké (1880–1958)

## Part III

*Editorial Note: This section is a condensed and edited version of the larger essay on Grimké's life by Akasha Gloria Hull. Below, Hull succinctly describes Grimké's love lyrics, which evidences Grimké's lesbian-themed poetry, like "A Mona Lisa," which can be found in Part I of* Mouths of Rain.

Angelina Weld Grimké's poetry can be roughly grouped into five general categories: (1) elegies, (2) love lyrics, (3) nature lyrics, (4) racial poems, (5) philosophical poems about the human condition. Love lyrics constitute one of the largest groups of her poetry. These poems are, as a rule, very delicate, musical, romantic, and pensive. "A Mona Lisa" and "When the Green Lies Over the Earth," two of her best-known works, probably belong in this category. Practically all of these lyrics are addressed to women. One that she never published is called either "Rosabel" or "Rosalie":

> *Leaves that whisper whisper ever*
> *Listen, listen, pray!*
> *Birds that twitter twitter softly*
> *Do not say me nay.*
> *Winds that breathe about, upon her*
> *(Lines I do not dare)*
> *Whisper, turtle, breathe upon her*
> *That I find her fair.*

> *II*
> *Rose whose soul unfolds white petaled*
> *Touch her soul, use white*

*Rose whose thoughts unfold gold petaled*
  *Blossom in her sight*
*Rose whose heart unfolds, red petaled*
  *Prick her slow heart's stir*
*Tell her white, gold, red my love is—*
  *And for her,—for her.*

In these poems, Grimké was probably not simply assuming the mask of a traditional male persona, but writing from her own true feelings and experiences. In February 1896, one of her school friends, Mamie (Mary) Burrill, sent her a youthful letter, where, mixed in with apologies, school gossip, and church news, she recalled their secret good times together and reaffirmed her love: "Could I just come to meet thee once more, in the old sweet way, just coming at your calling, and like an angel bending o'er you breathe into your ear, 'I love you.'"[1] For her part, Angelina was even more ardent. In a letter written later that year while she was in Northfield, Minnesota, at the Carleton Academy, she overflows: "Oh Mamie if you only knew how my heart beats when I think of you and it yearns and pants to gaze, if only for one second, upon your lovely face." With naïve sweetness, she asks Mamie to be her "wife" and ends the letter: "Now may the Almighty father bless thee little one and keep thee safe from all harm, Your passionate lover."[2]

Mamie went on to become a teacher in the Washington, DC, public school system, an actress, and a playwright. Her 1919 one-act drama *They That Sit in Darkness* concerns a poor black woman with too many children who is mired in childbearing and poverty because the system denies women access to birth-control information.[3] It appeared in the same special issue of the *Birth Control Review* as Grimké's story "The Closing Door." Exactly what happened between Grimké and Burrill is not clear. She may or may not have been the partner in the disastrous love affair mentioned earlier that Grimké set down in her diary, July 18–September 10, 1903 (although it is a bit hard to imagine Grimké speaking forthrightly about a female lover to her father). Later in their lives, Mamie alluded to their girlhood relationship in a brief note that she wrote to Grimké in July 1911 after Grimké had been injured in a train wreck: "If I can serve you at all, for the sake of the days that are a long way behind us both, I trust you will let me do so."

The manuscript poems that Grimké wrote during the early 1900s parallel the diary's story of heartbreak and unhappiness and indicate, further, that the lover was female—either Mamie or some other woman. "If"—one copy of which is dated July 31, 1903—is divided into halves. The first speculates that if every thought, hope, and dream the speaker has of her love became a pansy, rose, or maidenhair, then the world would be overrun with "rosy blooms, and pansy glooms and curling leaves of green." The second part, though, posits that if every look, word, and deed of the lover became ice, sleet, and snow, then "this old world would fast be curled beneath a wintry moon/With wastes of snow that livid glow—as it now in June." Another poem, entitled "To Her of the Cruel Lips" and ending "I laugh, yet—my brain is sad," was written November 5, 1903. And, on January 16, 1904, Grimké is asking "Where Is the Dream?" and "Why Do I Love You So?"

Nothing else exists to tell if and whom and how she loved after this. She followed the external resolutions that she made in her diary to forego marriage and children and occupy her life with writing and her father—and probably continued to desire women, in silence and frustration. Unlike Dunbar-Nelson, Grimké does not appear to have acted on her lesbian feelings with continuous and mature assurance. But—perhaps because she did not—they provided greater impetus for her verse.

Her first developed piece, "El Beso" (quoted earlier), reveals one way that Grimké handled in her public art what seem to be woman-to-woman romantic situations. Here, she writes of "your provocative laughter, / The gloom of your hair; / Lure of you, eye and lip"; and then "Pain, regret—your sobbing." Because of the "feel" of the poem and its diction ("sobbing," for example), the "you" visualizes as a woman—despite the absence of the third-person pronouns and the usual tendency most readers have (knowledge of persona, notwithstanding) to image the other in a love poem as being opposite in sex from the poem's known author. "A Mona Lisa" is similar in tone and approach. It begins:

> *I should like to creep*
> *Through the long brown grasses*
> *That are your lashes.*[4]

As one might predict, Grimké's unpublished poetry contains an even heavier concentration of love lyrics. In these can be found the raw feeling, feminine pronouns, and womanly imagery that have been excised or muted in the published poems:

> *Thou are to me a lone white star*
> *That I may gaze on from afar;*
> *But I may never never press*
> *My lips on thine in mute caress.*
> *E'en touch the hem of thy pure dress*
> *Thou art so far, so far . . .*

Or:

> *My sweetheart walks down laughing ways*
> *Mid dancing glancing sunkissed ways*
> *And she is all in white . . .*

Most of these lyrics either chronicle a romance that is now dead or record a cruel and unrequited love. The longest poem in this first group is "Autumn." Its initial stanza describes a bleak autumn with spring love gone; stanza two recalls that bygone spring, with its "slim slips of maiden moons, the shimmering stars; / And our love, our first love, glorious, yielding"; the final stanza paints the present contrasting scene where "Your hand does not seek mine . . . the smile is not for me . . . [but] for the new life and dreams wherein I have no part." The anguish of the second type is captured in poems like "Give Me Your Eyes" and "Caprichosa," distilled in lines such as:

> *If I might taste but once, just once*
> *The dew*
> *Upon her lips*

Another work in this group, "My Shrine," is interesting for its underlying psychological and artistic revelations. The speaker builds a shrine to/for her "maiden small, . . . divinely pure" inside her heart—away from those who might widen their eyes and guffaw. There she kneels, only then daring to speak her soulful words. This poem was carried to the typescript stage and, having reached this point, Grimké substituted "he" for "she" where it was unavoidable. In many of these lyrics, the loved one is wreathed in whiteness (even to the mentioning of "her sweet white hands").

Needless to say, most of this poetry is fragmentary and unpolished. One reads it sensing the poet's tremendous need to voice, to vent, to share—if only on paper—what was pulsing within her, since it seems that sometimes she could not even talk to the woman she wanted, let alone anyone else. "Close your eyes," she says in one poem, "I hear nothing but the beating of my heart."

These romantic poems, as well as all the other types of Grimké's poetry, draw heavily on the natural world for allusions, figures of speech, and imagery. However, some of her work can be strictly classified as pure nature lyrics. Perhaps the best of these are "A Winter Twilight" and "Dusk." The latter reads:

> *Twin stars through my purpling pane*
> *The shriveling husk*
> *Of a yellowing moon on the wane—*
> *And the dusk.*[5]

She also writes about the dawn ("Dawn," "At the Spring Dawn"), "Grass Fingers," and the "green of little leaves" ("Greenness").

Grimké produced relatively few racial poems. Of her works with racial overtones, the one most often reprinted is "Tenebris," which is about a shadow hand "huge and black" that plucks at the bricks of "the white man's house": "The bricks are the color of blood and very small. / Is it a black hand./ Or is it a shadow?"[6] These poems are indirect and merely suggest the sensitivity to injustice and the political zeal that characterize her prose.

Finally, there are her philosophical poems about life. A varied lot, these treat regret, religious themes, the need for peace, "The Ways O' Men," a "puppet player" who "sits just beyond the border of our seeing, / Twitching the strings with slow sardonic grin,"[7] the "Paradox" of two people who are spiritually closer when physically apart than when "face to face,"[8] and many other subjects of universal human experience. Generally, her first-person observations resonate more broadly, as in these lines from "The Eyes of My Regret":

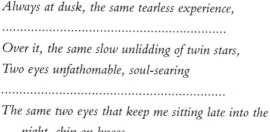

> *Always at dusk, the same tearless experience,*
> ..................................................
> *Over it, the same slow unlidding of twin stars,*
> *Two eyes unfathomable, soul-searing*
> ..................................................
> *The same two eyes that keep me sitting late into the*
>     *night, chin on knees,*
> *Keep me there lonely, rigid, tearless, numbly miserable,*
>     *—The eyes of my Regret.*[9]

Grimké was not a literary theoretician, but on one occasion, she impressively explained her own creative process. A young man named Adolph Hult, Jr., a senior at Augustana College, Rock Island, Illinois, was studying her poetry as part of a class project in black literature. He wrote her on November 28, 1925, requesting information about her work. Almost immediately, she responded; what she wrote is one of the few self-critical statements that exists from a black writer of the period. It is introspective, sophisticated, even philosophical:

I think most [poems] that I do are the reflections of moods. These
appear to me in clearly defined forms and colors—remembered
from what I have seen, felt. The mood is the spiritual atmosphere.
Symbolic also. I love colors and contrasts. Suggestion.

Whatever I have done it seems to me is a reflection of some
mood which gives the spiritual atmosphere and significance. The
mood has a physical counterpart in Nature in colors concrete
images brought out by contrasts. Often to me the whole thing
is not only a mood but symbolic as well. The more vivid the
physical picture the more vivid the vibrations in the mind of the
reader or listener. Each word has its different wavelength, vibration. Colors, trees flowers skies meadows. The more concrete,
definite vivid the picture the more vivid the vibration of word in
the reader or listener.

And what is word? May it not be a sort of singing in the harp
strings of the mind? Then on the principle of sympathetic vibration is there not in nature a harp singing also to be found. . . .[10]

Her theory of composition here is essentially romantic (even more theoreti-
cally so than Dunbar-Nelson's). First of all, the poetry arises from within
herself; it is, as she puts it, the reflection of a mood. Her "appear to me" suggests the kind of spontaneous coming of a poem that Coleridge, for "Kubla
Khan," called a "rising up." As for the romantic poets, nature is also a primary force that, in her case, furnishes the physical analogues for her moods. And
nature, as well as the experience of it and the images in which it is clothed,
is symbolic. Finally, she states, in the favorite romantic harp image, the sympathetic correspondence that was supposed to exist between the poet's mind
and external nature.

Grimké's poetry accords very closely with her theoretical description of
how she writes. Being expressions of the moment, her poems are usually
brief. They present the scene or thought as swiftly as possible in sharp, concrete images, and then abandon it. This trait causes critics (like Robert Ker-

lin, for example) to compare her with the imagists. However, Grimké cannot usually refrain from comment, and thus violates the suggestive objectivity that is a part of their creed. Her poem "The Black Finger" is an excellent case in point. Here is its middle section:

> *Slim and still,*
> *Against a gold, gold sky,*
>   *A straight cypress,*
>   *Sensitive*
> *A black finger*
> *Pointing upwards.*[11]

Those seven lines have the haiku-like, symbolic compression that the imagists prized. However, the poem consists of three additional lines—a beginning statement, "I have just seen a beautiful thing," and two closing questions, "Why, beautiful, still finger are you black? / And why are you pointing upwards?"—which alter considerably its tone and effect by making attitude and meaning too explicit.

Ironically, this predilection for brevity is also the source of one of Grimké's weaknesses as a poet—her occasional over-reliance on fragmentation and understatement. Sometimes, more often in early poems, her lines are too cropped and ejaculatory, resulting in a series of disjunct, giddy phrases. Something of this can be seen in the second half of "El Beso," quoted above.

Without a doubt, Grimké's greatest strength is her affinity for nature, her ability to really see it and then describe what she has seen with precision and subtlety. Take, for example, this stanza from her elegy "To Clarissa Scott Delany":

> *Does the beryl in tarns, the soft orchid in haze,*
> *The primrose through treetops, the unclouded jade*
> *Of the north sky, all the earth's flamings and russets and grays*
> *Simply smudge out and fade?*[12]

Describing nature gives Grimké her freshest, most original and graphic expressions and helps her avoid the trite or threadbare diction that now and then entraps her. As she says in her poetic statement, she loves color and contrast. She handles them well and builds many of her finest effects upon them.

The mood of Grimké's poetry is predominantly sad and hushed (one of her favorite words). Colors—even when vivid—are not the primary ones, but saffron, green-gold, lilac. Sounds are muted; effects are delicate. Emotion—even when intense—is quiet and refined.

> *A hint of gold where the moon will be:*
> *Through the flocking clouds just a star or two:*
> *leaf sounds, soft and wet and hushed.*
> *And oh! the crying want of you.*[13]

Grimké's poems are written in both rhyme and meter, and in what Sterling Brown calls "a carefully worded and cadenced free verse."[14] In some poems, she wavers between the two. Related to this metrical uncertainty is her major fault of repeating words, phrases, and lines in a manner that suggests padding. It seems that when inspiration waned, she sometimes resorted to the stock poetic technique of repetition to try to achieve some easy lyricism. Very few of her poems are written in the jazzy, syncopated style that was in vogue with black writers of the 1920s, like Langston Hughes and Helene Johnson. One of them, which is "At April," has this rhythmic beginning:

> *Toss your day heads,*
> *Brown girl trees:*
> *Toss your gay lovely heads . . .* [15]

Generally speaking, Grimké's excellencies as a poet outweigh her weaknesses—especially in the handful of well-wrought lyrics that secure her literary fame. However, assessing her accurately requires thoughtful consideration of the personal and social conditions under which she wrote. Clearly, her poetic themes of sadness and void, longing and frustration (which commentators have been at a loss to explain) relate directly to Grimké's convoluted life and thwarted sexuality. One also notes the self-abnegation and diminution that mark her work. It comes out in her persistent vision of herself as small and hidden, for instance, and in the death-wishing verses of "A Mona Lisa" and other poems.

Equally obvious is the connection between her lesbianism and the slimness of her creative output. Because of psychic and artistic constraints, the "lines she did not dare" went almost as unwritten as they were unspoken. Being a black lesbian poet in America at the beginning of the twentieth century meant that one wrote (or half wrote )—in isolation—a lot that she did not show and could not publish. It meant that when one did write to be printed, she did so in shackles—chained between the real experience and the conventions that would not give her voice. It meant that one fashioned a few race and nature poems, transliterated lyrics, and double-tongued verses that sometimes got published. It meant, finally, that one stopped writing altogether, dying "with her real gifts stifled within,"[16] and leaving behind the little that managed to survive of one's true self in fugitive pieces. Ironically, the fact that Grimké did not write and publish enough is given as a major reason for the seamy recognition accorded her (and also other women poets of the Harlem Renaissance).

# Notes

1. Letter of Mamie Burrill to Angelina Weld Grimké, February 25, 1896.

2. This letter exists in a draft written on the back of some physics notes dated October 27, 1896.

3. This play is included in *Black Theater, U.S.A.: Forty-five Plays by Black Americans, 1847–1974*, ed. James V. Hatch with Ted Shine (New York: The Free Press, 1974).

4. Quoted from *Caroling Dusk: An Anthology of Verse by Negro Poets*, ed. Countee Cullen (New York: Harper and Row, 1927), 42.

5. Quoted from *Caroling Dusk*, 46.

6. Quoted from *Caroling Dusk*, 41.

7. "The Puppet Player," *Caroling Dusk*, 46

8. "Paradox," *Caroling Dusk*, 43–44.

9. Quoted from *Caroling Dusk*, 37.

10. These remarks exist in an incomplete holograph draft.

11. Quoted from *American Negro Poetry*, ed. Arna Bontemps (New York: Hill and Wang, 1963), 17. This version of the poem has been slightly revised from its form in Locke's *The New Negro* (1925).

12. Quoted from *American Negro Poetry*, 16.

13. "The Want of You," *Negro Poets and Their Poems*, 154.

14. Brown, *Negro Poetry and Drama*, 62.

15. This poem is reprinted in *The New World Split Open*, 262.

16. Alice Walker, "In Search of Our Mothers' Gardens," *MS.* (May 1974): 67.

# JP Howard

# aubade, in pieces, for my ex-lovers

I am letting go of ex-lovers
ancient I.M.'s on my blackberry, deleted
"I will love you forever Boo! 😊 "
an ex-lover cheated with my neighbor's girlfriend
I screamed and meant it
crumpled in her pocket, damp from a rainstorm
rain-soaked, on our first night together
a woman has always felt like coming home
I want to hold onto young me
I've saved a space in my heart for
crushes explored in bathrooms
on a conference room meeting table
I'm holding onto lessons learned
I wonder what happened to that lover
And the next woman after her
Goodbye to the lover I followed 3,000 miles
Thank you to that same woman
so long to the Ph.D. who left her lover for me
I'm still thankful for the 1st lover I lived with
and called it my writer's den

I am saying goodbye in between stanzas
that tear-filled message after our 5th breakup
a favorite photo of us, torn in half
**"If you see me on the street, cross over!"**
I saved my 1st love poem from my first lover
we were eighteen, she was my first poet
I cried when she handed me that love poem
every goodbye feels like leaving home
my only cue, love and deep kisses
women's bars that held secret lovers
even an angry lover who dumped my panties
during a staff meeting at my first real job
Mama said *"Don't shit where you eat chile"*
she only wanted to sex me all summer long
held onto my every word
only to learn she saw us as "just friends"
who gifted me her home that sweet summer
yet insisted on *"No PDA in public J!"*
she painted a tiny room Navajo white
Anita Baker's "Sweet Love" was our jam.

# Janae Johnson
## Black Butch Woman

Black Butch Woman be strong

Black Butch Woman be silent

Black Butch Woman be thick as thieves

Creatures of the night

Be emulating Black Man's genius

& his broken

All in one stride

Black Butch Woman learn from Black Man

Black Man scared of Black Butch Woman

Be disgusted

Be conspicuous

Be wide-eyed & closed fist

Be at war

But Black butch woman be ready for war

Be strong

Be protector of identity

Because Black butch woman be knowin

Black butch woman be knowin their history

Black butch woman have no history

Be born & forgotten

Be four layers of oppression

Be in no white man history book

Be unwritten

Be Grammy's nightly prayer

Be a high functioning closet

Be up for interpretation

Be artistic expression

Be bow ties & boat shoes

Be WNBA with a perm

Be secret partner

Be lifelong lover

Be Auntie

Not mama

Be failed crushes

Be college experiment

Be dagger in flesh

Be scarred

Be wounded

Be *you could've been so beautiful*

Be born beautiful

Be complimenting their way out of suicide

Be affirmation

Be certain

Be not a phase

Be in love all the time

Be carry heart in shadows

Be *careful they don't see us*

Be touch here . . . here . . . here . . .

Be no mascara

Be no proof of crying

Be heartbreak over gospel

But be no trace of a tear drops

Be strong

Be locked jaw

Swallowed insult

Be like Black Man

But stronger

Black butch woman stole woman from black man

Be baggy jeans & fitted caps

Be fades & loc'd hair

Be tattooed & blemished

Be on the wrong side of the store

Be on the wrong side of the dressing room

Be *Sir! Sir Sir!*

Be left

Be sideways

Be queer

Be tomboy

Be sports & only sports

Be good

Now Black Man feel endangered

Black Butch Woman is endangered

Be misrepresented

Be unrepresented

Be trying to exit without living

Be learnin everything she know from Black Man

Who hate him a Black butch woman

He be wide-eyed & closed fist

Ready to swing

But Black Butch Woman

always be ready

For war

# Jewelle Gomez
# Curtain 1983

Sandy stood behind the curtain, stage right; waiting. Although she was doing more than simply waiting for it to open. Her body was rigid with longing. Attention coursed through her as if it were what held her upright. If that attention were drained from her, she'd be a glittering heap of clothes on the backstage floor.

The sound of the band rang like an alien noise in her ears. Even though she'd rehearsed at least four hours each day with these guys she didn't recognize a thing they played in the overture. And they were her songs. Panic started to meet the longing and ride a tide of nausea. She wanted to run back.

Her shoes were stuck to the floorboards, which creaked as she tested them.

She expected the floor to crack open in jagged pieces and she'd be sucked below. Looking down at the sparkling blue of her heels, the panic dissipated; she almost laughed at the image of a crime boss out of a movie . . . instead of a "cement raincoat" he'd glued her feet in place.

She could hear them on the other side of the curtain; despite its toxic fire-proofing, she could feel their heat. The fans anticipating; the newbies skeptical, shifting and shuffling as if she were a holy visitation not just a colored girl from Queens. The curtain muffled their sounds with its thick velvet and asbestos fabric but they were there—voracious.

Sandy glanced behind her, offstage where Denise stood, her silk shirt and tailored slacks the exact same shade of blue as Sandy's shoes and gown. How did she always do that? Sandy wanted to run back and ask her DeeDee, but her feet would not come unstuck.

Denise did not smile as she recognized the paralysis in Sandy. It was a moment they'd been working toward for the past decade. They'd started the journey almost before they'd returned their high school caps and gowns. Sandy wielded her big voice and Denise found those who help her shape it and cut the path they would take. Denise expected Sandy's terror in this moment. In fact, she'd embraced her own with the soothing toke from the stuff the spotlight guy sold her. But none of that for Sandy, she needed to be sharp. She would be out on stage when the curtain opened in place by the microphone with laser focus.

Denise nodded—actually the opposite of a nod. More like she raised her chin twice slightly as if she were shooing chickens away from her back door. The gesture was subtle, seen not even by the puller who stood at her side. He was poised to catch the curtain as it slid on its rails and then steady the leaded velvet into stillness.

Sandy felt Denise's nudge in her body like a wave carrying her into shore. She smiled, not so much at Denise but at the sensation of connection. She looked toward her mark, a tiny snip of glow tape that called to her as if it were a docking station in deep space. Her feet became light and she glided for it in long strides. The motion toward the mark was electric on her skin just like the moment that she slid between the sheets next to Denise. The feel of the slit in her dress as it brushed her dark legs sparked her further as if it were Denise's hand on her.

On the other side of the curtain the electricity was even brighter than the lights footing the stage. Sandy sensed their power and was both warmed and chilled. Once she stepped through to the other side all would be changed. She didn't need applause or a reviewer to tell her that. The lights were shining bright now, and she knew they'd flame even higher once she stepped out and sang. This was what she'd been longing for most of her life. She and Denise. All the rehearsals and the gritty night clubs; outdoor concerts and the women's festivals.

The women. Many would be here tonight to see what heights "their Sandy" could attain. But they would be outnumbered by the new devotees who'd heard her only on radio, or heard tell of her from others. Others who were waiting too—for the newest voice.

Their applause would take her far and high, past the lights above her head now. Far and wide, away from the women who'd first lifted her up. Far and away from Denise. They would not want her to have Denise there on her arm or in her bed.

Sandy could feel Denise—her DeeDee—as if it were her energy that fueled the lights and would bring the audience to its feet. This is the moment they'd worked toward, and they both knew it would be more than a single moment in their life. It was a catalyst for change.

Tomorrow would not be simply the next day; it would be the new day. Some of the old would come along, of course, but there was no way of telling what of the old would make it through. That unknown whispered the chill into the air beneath the heat of the lights but Sandy refused to let it cool her. Now she was not immobile but sensed each molecule crashing around inside of her. Just at the back of her spine, though, she felt a stillness, the preparation for emptiness. The place where she and Denise had been would soon be gone.

Sandy stepped closer to the curtain and exhaled as deeply as she could, the air leaving her lungs, as if squeezed from below by a bellows. Her darkened lashes lowered, blanking out the hazel of her eyes, then swept upward again toward the lights suspended above her head. The sound of the motor hummed behind her and Sandy succumbed to the intoxication of the scent of the old and elegant curtain as it swung back, revealing her to the 1,239 individuals seated ready to stand and become thousands.

She glanced quickly toward her DeeDee, aware it might be the final time they could live in this intimacy. There she saw Denise recognise the same sea change this moment would make in their relationship. The sadness of it was dulled somewhat for Denise by the small toke she'd taken. She often tried to reassure Sandy that times were changing but she had no real picture in her mind what that meant for them. Sandy told herself that no matter the outcome she and Denise would always be friends. Their passion might be forced into some other form but the work was what was important to them both now, Sandy used to say.

As the curtain spread like wings Sandy pulled her gaze from Denise and turned to the audience. She couldn't actually see anyone but she focused outward, piercing the darkness with her intention to deliver exactly what they wanted and more. Sandy didn't look back as she rose like the smoky mist captured by the lights.

# Michelle Cliff
# Notes on Speechlessness

The condition of affliction—as described by Simone Weil—is the primary condition of the powerless. This condition is characterized above all by speechlessness. It is important to realize the alliance of speechlessness and powerlessness; that the former maintains the latter; that the powerful are dedicated to the investiture of speechlessness on the powerless.

Speechlessness—as I have known/know it—is implosive, not explosive. That is, it is most effective—most devastating—against the speechless person. It may seem explosive: it may seem to affect those around and those in opposition to the speechless person, but its real effect is against she who will not! cannot speak.

Speechlessness begins with the inability to speak; this soon develops into the inability to act. The inability to act is part of the implosion.

Speechlessness is always directed against the self, never directed outward, except indirectly.

Speechlessness involves self-denial:

> the denial of rights
> the right to express, to choose
> to choose to express
> to choose to express anger
> to choose to assert a separate self
> > in the expression of ideas.

If the choice for expression—the separation which will come from real, rather than speechless expression—is not made, the person is speechless.

The non-expression implodes into depression.
This denial of the self is the origin/outcome of speechlessness.

It is self-annihilation.

The phenomenon: From my journal 2/7/77

> Myself: the old feeling of not being intellectually up to it—when asked to perform. The idea of being revealed as a phony in every sense . . . my heart palpitating because my turn to speak was next.
>
> Devising sentences in my mind.
>
> Then, later, realizing that these women were women, this place a place I could be with/in, where to talk would not be the experience it has been . . . but something different. I don't know . . . I have so much to realize.

★★★

On one level I have experienced my own speechlessness as:
fear of being judged along the lines of male modes of thinking and argument.
fear of being thought "stupid" as defined by those modes.
feeling of powerlessness when dealing in those modes.
fear of revealing I have never understood properly all along;
that I am a liar and a fraud.
belief that everyone speaks from clarity where I do not.

These attitudes lead to a genuine difficulty in understanding, since in any situation—a seminar, a meeting—these fears take precedence. The fears settle like a mist; then turn to concrete—encasing. Disallowing communication.

In those situations where absolute silence is impossible, the option for the speechless person can be a trivializing mode of speech—e.g., humor: this can be a mechanism for deflection.

Speechlessness as self-punishment: as something self-induced to preoccupy in order to preclude growth.

★★★

The importance for women to realize and understand the causes of our speechlessness. How it is our collaboration with our oppression. How it has been applied by us to protect ourselves from our oppression—but the cost has been ourselves.

*Persona:*

a film about a woman who has stopped talking and a woman who is a chatter-er; about the non-communication of women—within/between themselves. During the film the faces of the two women split and merge; they become one person: which they are. They share the identity of speechlessness.

We have been quiet. Or we have chattered.
Speechlessness is not simply being quiet—more about this later.

I am reminded that a great compliment of my childhood was: "She's such a quiet girl . . .
"i.e., speechlessness as a quality—a behavior—held to be positive and encouraged in young girls. Therefore speechlessness is connected with being "good."

"Let the women keep silence in the churches: for it is not permitted unto them to speak; but let them be in subjection, as also saith the law." (Virginia Woolf quotes this from Paul, the First Letter to the Corinthians, in a footnote to the second part of *Three Guineas*. In the note she connects not-speaking with chastity: the transgression of both of these with "shame." She observes that these two admonitions enforce the patriarchal notion that a "woman's mind and body shall be reserved for the use of one man and one only." Thus does speechlessness enforce powerlessness.)

★★★

The necessity to relinquish male parlor games:

My choice of dissertation could be a trivialization of male history and also the trivialization of myself as a scholar. But "The Intellectual Game in

Italian Renaissance Culture: 1400–1600" is also an investigation of those modes which seem to terrify me. In the dissertation I reduce the modes to game-playing, which in a sense they are. By choosing male intellectualism but treating it as it was played—usually for the benefit of women—I reduced the principles to a size I did not find intimidating.

★★★

I see my own speechlessness as an outcome of various factors:

1. Being female forced into male modes of thinking and argument. Excelling but never belonging.

> She is defined and differentiated with reference to man and not he with reference to her; she is the incidental, the inessential as opposed to the essential. He is the Subject, the Absolute—she is the Other.
>
> *The Second Sex*

Being the Other conversing in the language of the Subject is a condition of my speechlessness.

2. Being a lesbian in the same circumstance. Concealing lesbianism and thereby entering a dual masquerade—passing straight! passing lesbian. The effort of retaining the masks enervates and contributes to speechlessness— to speak might be to reveal.

A dream:

> I am in a small town in Europe. I enter an old-fashioned butcher shop. The men wear straw hats; there is sawdust on the floor; marble counters. The place is brightly lit, filled with townspeople doing their marketing. I am an outsider, I am having trouble speaking their language. There is a paper container of sausage meat on the marble counter. The butcher tells me it is for tasting. I taste—it is sweet. I realize suddenly that the meat in the shop is the dead flesh of lesbians. I escape.

I feel when I wake up that I have engaged in an act of auto-cannibalism. The sausage meat is unrecognizable, mixed up. I couldn't have said what it was originally. I can speak the language in the shop but haltingly. Whatever else this dream stands for, it is a clear illustration of what I am doing to myself when I take part in a double masquerade. I can't pass myself off as straight, because I can't speak their language. But by remaining silent and denying myself any real knowledge, I am forced (forced meat) to devour myself. I am as identifiable as the sausage meat when I engage in this double masquerade. Unknown even to myself. Speechless about myself.

3. Being my parents' child—which perhaps should be #1. For me, the symbolic origin of my speechlessness lies in an event of my childhood: the diary-reading. When I was thirteen, the place where I wrote things was broken into. In one afternoon my words and thoughts—my attempt to recount my own reality; to assert my separateness—were trivialized, shamed, ridiculed, ultimately denied. I was called a liar.

For me, part of my speechlessness originates in my fear of the lies in my childhood/life. It was a childhood in which lies were punished/encouraged, encouraged/punished. In which lies concerned the definition of my identity. Lies (or silences) about my ethnicity/race/name/sex. (I was my father's son . . . for a time.)

★★★

The analogy of Victor, the wild boy of Aveyron, with whom I have identified.

Victor never learned to speak—
a scar on his throat.
He was "rescued from the forest (parents, mother, family)" and taken to a "civilized" place (learning, separation, growth). But the damage has already been done—his throat has already been cut—he has been rendered speechless.
Victor returns to the forest.
Then chooses to return to the civilized place.

The fear is that the throat has already been cut; that speechlessness will be lifelong.

★★★

In my journal I find that I have written about Virginia Woolf: As a survivor, but also as someone who used withdrawal and humor to deal/not to deal. As I have done.

Both withdrawal and humor are types of speechlessness.
The obscuring and trivialization of what is real is also speechlessness. Speechlessness is not simple muteness—it is the inability to speak but also the inability to reveal.

Speechlessness—whether muteness, withdrawal, humor—seeks to "avoid" lies; to avoid real expression or revelation. Muteness and withdrawal avoid the possibility of being caught in a lie by their outright silence; humor allows the use of a lie—essentially—and if the lie proves too much, then with a laugh or a disclaimer the lie is defused/negated. Escape is possible. Truth has once again been deflected.

★★★

Survival:

To not be speechless: to seek those modes of thought and articulation which will assure the unity rather than the division of myself.
To separate out and eliminate those elements which split me.
Those elements which have divided me into mind/body, straight/lesbian, child/adult.

This means nothing more or less than seeking my own language.
This may be what women will do.

# Moya Bailey
# Living ~~Single~~

I hate the term *single*. Despite the fact that most of us come into this world by ourselves and leave that way there's an expectation of partnering in the interim. And while you are granted a bit more of a reprieve from single shade* in queerdom, there's still a palpable partner privilege that operates. Couples-only hangouts, automatic invites to your partner's friends' functions, less unwanted amorous attention because you're read as off-limits, more respect for your time as it's obviously being impacted by another person, etc. I've had the unfortunate but not uncommon experience of losing friends to relationships, only to be heard from again in the equally unfortunate but not uncommon instance of the breakup. As a non-partnered person I also feel some pressure when hanging out with half of a coupled couple. I sometimes sense suspicion of my intentions. It seems non-partnered people are read as a roving threat to relationships. There's always some pop culture plot point where a generally good person, usually man or masculine, is tempted by an evil single seductress who doesn't give a damn about the existing relationship. Y'all saw *Obsessed* right?

As I age, I am curious about that moment when singlehood switches in peoples' minds from the willfulness of youthful independence to tragic pathological existence. I think that timeline is too short, maybe even non-existent, for straight women, and while there's a bit more leeway in the queer community, there comes a point when casual dating isn't cute anymore or perhaps even possible because folks are booed up. It has me wondering if there's room to maintain a single life as an older person, like still dating in your 50s and 60s? And how do you find folks to date if all your peers at that age are married or partnered? I mean the Golden Girls had it rough but they'd all been married before. I really struggle with this as someone who is ambivalent about romantic relationships, particularly as constructed in this society.

Co-dependent love is constantly represented as the ideal. "I can't sleep/think/live/function without you, romantic partner" leads to the inevitable crash of despair when things don't work out because you've set up someone else to meet the impossible expectation of completing you. "Forsaking all others" doesn't just imply sexual partners but in a nuclear model of family, seems to also speak to friendships and extended family. Why do mothers-in-law stay getting a bad rap?

And yet, there's something really real about co-dependence in a culture that doesn't value interdependence. A romantic partner is expected to be there, in "sickness and in health" in ways that we don't demand of friendship. Subsequently, a spouse or partner has legal and social rights that a friend does not. For queer folks this is particularly important when unsupportive biological family can legally trump chosen family. Our legal system actively limits who we can call on, which reflects and exacerbates social beliefs about relationships.

I have a more playful, flirtatious way of thinking about intimate relationships which usually rubs up against (and not in a good way) a social expectation for monogamy. I have romantic friendships that are not quite platonic, sexy time friends that aren't quite lovers, close kindred spirits that should really be on my insurance before a romantic partner. And while pop culture flirts with poly possibilities, it never quite goes all the way. There are an endless number of songs that reference men cheating or women cheating on their boyfriends because of the supposed sexual prowess of whomever is singing/rapping the hit. So while there's a tacit tolerance of cheating, intentional polyamory remains off the table. And even with an occasional "my girl's got a girlfriend" and "ain't no fun if the homies can't have none," women are tools for male fantasies, heterofying homosocial sexual behavior. Folks are more into the illicitness of affairs and the freakiness of multiple sex partners than building articulated intimacy with more than one person. I digress . . .

I want to live in a world where there isn't a hierarchy of relationships, where romantic love isn't assumed to be more important than other kinds, where folks can center any relationships they want whether it be their relationship to their spiritual practice, kids, lovers, friends, etc. and not have some notion that it's more or less important because of who or what's in focus. I want to feel like I can develop intimacy with people whether we are sleeping together or not, that I will be cared for whether I am romantically involved with someone or not. I want a community that takes interdependency seriously, that doesn't assume that it's only a familial or romantic relationship responsibility to be there for each other.

I didn't just dream this way of relating to each other up. Other cultures and communities throughout time have had more options in terms of how they construct connection. And we are doing it now. Folks are creating interdependent relationships and community that disrupt popular perceptions of appropriate partnering. I just wonder what it will take to get more of us to honestly evaluate the realities of our love and determine whether we are actually getting what we want. Love is abundant, not scarce. Why would we ever want to limit or narrow its flow?

# Pat Parker
# funny

Once upon a time there was a young woman. Her name was Doris, or Sarah, or Sue; I never knew. She walked the streets of Sunnyside, the beaten seashells dusted her feet and she always walked alone. She wore men's clothing, long before profiteers had developed unisex wear: flannel shirts in fall, covered by an army field jacket in the winter; white T-shirts in summer, and khaki pants. Not blue jeans, which were acceptable for young women after school and on Saturdays, but beige khaki pants. Men's pants.

Every evening around dusk she walked the three blocks from her house to Mr. Isom's store. She passed my house with long strides, her arms swinging; a steady rhythm, not too slow, not too fast. Her eyes were always forward. She never turned to the people sitting on their porches, never nodded her head, never said, "How you do?" She always walked straight and purposefully, and she always walked alone.

One day I asked my parents who she was, and they closed around me. My mother, who had taught me to always be nice ("if you can't say something good about a person, then say nothing at all") looked embarrassed and told, "You stay away from her—she's funny." I didn't understand. Had never heard anyone called funny except on radio and television as we crowded around the small screen, or box, and watched Amos and Andy, or George Burns and Gracie Allen, or listened to Fibber McGee and Molly.

"What do you mean, *funny*?"

I should have known better. I had lived with my parents long enough to recognize "the look." The look that said a subject was closed—no discussion here. You're too young, or innocent, or female, or Black to learn about this.

"Never you mind, girl. You jist do like your mama say and stay away from her. She's a disgrace. If I had a daughter like that, I'd kill her."

My father was not embarrassed. He was angry. The look that he wore when he came home at night. The look he wore when he had to change his plans cause Mr. Jenkins from the Oldsmobile place called and wanted to come retread his tires the very next day, not two days later. The look he wore when he had to wait for an hour to get paid while Mr. Jenkins waited on his customers, even though Daddy was done and needed to get to Mr. James's Buick place to retread tires that he also had to have done that same day.

I had seen that look, but I had never seen it directed toward a Black person who had said nothing, done nothing to my father and what was his.

So, I didn't find out what funny meant that day, and I never asked that woman her name or why she always walked alone.

The Fuqua family moved next door to us the year I was seven. There were four children: Joyce, Barbara, Howard, and Anthony, in that order. Joyce was four months younger than me.

We became inseparable. We rode bikes, played jacks, football, and paper dolls. Paper dolls were our lives. During the summer we would cut out models from ads in the *Houston Chronicle*. We had to use summer models because they wore shorts or bathing suits. We pasted cardboard on their backs to make them sturdy. Then we'd draw clothes—hundreds of outfits, many copied from JCPenny catalogs, or just what we thought the well-dressed doll should have.

Each of us had complete families. A mother, a father, a boy, and a girl. All-American nuclear family, and white.

We played paper dolls for hours. If Joyce's siblings had been good, or her mother insisted, then they were allowed to play with us. More often, we played alone.

The game changed the summer I was fourteen. In the past, we would press the dolls' faces together for their goodbye-I'm-going-to-work kiss and continue to play. This time it was different. Joyce reached out as the dolls touched and pulled me to her and kissed me. To this day I'm not sure why. Perhaps it was the sexual playing we had begun with the boys in the neighborhood, allowing them to sneak kisses and fast feels during hide-and-seek. Perhaps it was simply the time, as puberty took control of our loins and senses. Perhaps it was Joyce acting out what she had been secretly learning at Mr. Isom's store from Mrs. Isom. I don't know why but we kissed.

From that moment, the games changed. We played paper dolls as often as we could, and we played alone. We never admitted that what we were doing had nothing to do with the paper dolls. We always took them out and dressed them; then we laid them down and took each other.

We kissed long, slow, passionate kisses, mounted each other rubbing our genitalia against one another, feeling our budding breasts.

Our parents marveled at how wonderfully we got along. We never fought; we cried when we couldn't spend the night at the other's house. Yes, we played paper dolls at night, too.

The summer I turned sixteen was the most exciting summer of my life. All my sisters had gone off to college and both my parents worked. That meant our house was mine and Joyce's. We spent hours each day exploring each other's bodies—until the day my father came home early.

I don't know how long my father had been standing there. As Joyce and I pulled apart to say goodbye, I saw him and I died. My heart stopped, my breathing stopped. I was numb. I knew in that instant that my life was over. I wasn't going to California that next year. I wasn't going to college. I was never going to see my mother or sisters again. I was never going to ride my bike or wrestle with my dog. I was going to die by my father's hand.

He didn't hit me. He told Joyce to go home, and then he turned and walked away. Joyce left immediately. She left her dolls, and left me to face the wrath of my father.

My father, who was known throughout my entire life as crazy, the man who insisted that all boyfriends came to our house and meet him, come pass his test of approval—and no boy ever passed—the man said not one word to me.

My mother came home and the two of them went into their bedroom and talked. Not for long, not more than two minutes. Then they came out. My mother cooked dinner, and I went into my room and prayed. I prayed that it was all a bad dream and I would wake up quickly. I prayed that my father would have a heart attack and die. I prayed that time would suspend itself and I would never have to deal with the next moment.

We ate dinner in complete silence that night. Not one word was said by anyone. I ate trying to pace my meal. I did not want to finish ahead of my folks—no way did I want to ask permission to leave the table. I wanted visibility. I don't know what I ate, I only know it was heavy. Tons of rocks being passed down my throat. After dinner I went to bed and lay there, still praying: my father had that look, and my mother was worried.

My mother came into my room the next morning and told me to get dressed. To put on one of my school dresses. I asked no questions. School dress on a Saturday? You got it, Mom. We climbed into my father's car and drove to Third Ward. My curiosity was being squashed by fear. And my parents said nothing.

They took me to a doctor's office. I waited outside as they went into an exam room. A few minutes later I was called inside. My father left and my mother watched as this physician had me disrobe and looked at my breasts—not touching, just looking.

Then he had me lie down and looked at my genitals. Again not touching, just looking. I was told to get dressed and wait outside. My father re-entered the exam room. Less than ten minutes later we were out of the doctor's office and back in the car and headed home.

Still no one had said anything to me.

When we got home, my parents told me to go into the living room and sit down. They walked in together, and finally someone spoke to me. My father.

"The doctor says you are alright. You're not funny, so I don't ever expect you to do what I saw you and Joyce doing again."

They left the room. That was it. I was still alive, and now I knew what funny was.

The following day, after morning church service, my father took me to all of our neighbors' houses. I had to sit while he told each neighbor what he had caught Joyce and me doing. I didn't understand then that he was employing their aid in watching the two of us while he was at work. I thought the man had lost his mind and simply wanted to see me die from humiliation. Yet it didn't make sense because he had already told me I was alright—not funny.

Joyce and I still saw each other, still explored each other. We continued to do so until I left for college.

We didn't know the name for what we were and what we were doing, but we did know it had to be a secret. We had received our first closet keys. But faith, or time, or the goddess placed us in an era where closet doors would at first creak, then slide, then blast open. And unlike Doris, or Sarah, or Sue, or whatever her name was, we would not have to walk alone.

# PART IV

# THE SACRED

## 1970–2020

The Divine call to the Divine, inside of a meeting of self with self, a practice of alignment with the Divine. Yemayá, that broad expanse of Ocean, who lives both on sea and on land, has pushed past modernity's mode of reason and taken up temporary sojourn on the insides of this artificial enclosure, come to accept, to cleanse, to bless, to remind us that in the same way the breaking of waves does not compromise the integrity of the Ocean, so too anything broken in our lives cannot compromise that cosmic flow to wholeness. The body cannot but surrender in order to make way for this tidal flow. And this, too, necessitates practice.

What would taking the Sacred seriously mean for transnational feminism and related radical projects, beyond an institutionalized use of value theorizing marginalization? It would mean wrestling with the praxis of the Sacred. The central understanding within an epistemology of the Sacred is that of a core/Spirit that is immortal, at once linked to the pulse and energy of creation. It is that living matter that links us to each other, making that which is individual simultaneously collective.

M. Jacqui Alexander

# Alexis De Veaux
# Inter**species**

They did not speak the same way.

They did however talk.

With looks, stares, they gave each other.

They'd lived as such, each learning the other, for the better part of several years.

They were companions.

Any other word for what they shared would unleash the stench

of the proprietary

Fhill was thinking that as she side stepped Nommo outside her bedroom door. There was a splash of water on the floor coming from the bathroom. Nommo saw her see it. Then he casually looked away, seeing something she did not.

Good morning, Fhill said. Hungry? Nommo's look told her, as it always did, the rhetorical had no meaning. And she let out a soft chuckle. As they made their way downstairs. Quietly tiptoeing. As one. For they'd lived so closely so long it was hard, sometimes, to tell when the canine was not human and the human not canine

On the first floor of their home spears of light hummed through the shutters. Cascaded over the dark, well polished wood floors. The light shadowed the window seat in the foyer. Fhill could see that the hibiscus and fica and arugula cohabitating in pots in the living and sitting rooms were erect, awakening to the morning. Nommo mosied over to them. She carefully sniffed each one ferreting out the scent of growth night deposited. Fhill collected the wine glasses and juice bottles from the coffee table. And then, as did Nommo, followed a scent into the kitchen

Emma sat at the table. Her black notebook open. The poem she was writing, in her eyes. Her hands cupped a mason jar of fresh brewed black coffee. She managed a thin smile when Nommo came and sat beside her. The dog was nice enough but. It wasn't clear what Nommo was. Why his tail and left hind leg was black. Why he was missing a toe on that black paw. Why the rest of him was bleach white. The dog had a penis and full breasts.

★★★ ★★★

In the city's Harbor Park, Fhill walked down by the river. It was her day off. The look of the day was maudlin. The weather upstate was just turning cold. The usually boisterous seagulls nested at the pier. Fhill spotted the lump beneath a bench. As she approached it she could see the dog. Closer, she could see the litter of dead pups. The dog stared at her a while. Then it looked at the huddled dead one last time. The dog followed Fhill the whole walk home

The *Art of the Dogon* was the title of a book she'd found in a closet the first week in the house. She'd discovered, flipping through it, the Nommo were believed to be water spirits

★★★ ★★★

How'd you sleep? Fhill took the carton of Half n Half out of the refrigerator. Nommo watched intently.

Emma yawned. Not too well. She massaged her protruding belly. She said, this one is a night owl.

Like father like daughter, Fhill said. She poured some coffee and some Half n Half into a tin bowl. Before she could put the bowl down on the floor Nommo was in his spot. In three quick slurps the bowl was empty. And Nommo swiped his whiskers with a long, pink tongue.

Emma yawned again. I'm happy for Fawnie, she said. Having a sister means a lot-

You taught me that, Fhill said.

What we've taught each other, Fhill said. Grinned. Poured herself some coffee and sat at the table. She sipped from the mermaid shaped mug while Emma jotted something in her notebook

Nommo marched out of the kitchen. As if someone, or something, had called. Went upstairs. Went into the bathroom. Jumped over the lip of the tub. In the just enough water Nommo happily splashed, doing his ritual. He was on his back, panting into a furious kick when his ears lifted. Emma stood in the bathroom doorway. She watched him baffled. With a scowl meant to punish. Why was this dog in the tub again. What possessed the dog to bathe, if that was what he was doing, where she and her six year old washed naked. How did this dog get water in the tub. Fhill knew. Fhill knew what the dog did in her bathroom. But why did she allow it still. Why didn't this fucking dog stay in its own lane. He just looked at her. Like she had lost her mind, she felt. He waited. His legs suspended in the air

Momma? Fawn came up behind Emma. The freckles swam across her nose. Her doe-y red curls tossed by dream. She rubbed sleep from her eyes. I gotta wee, she said.

Emma glanced over at Nommo. So still the dog was, for all intents and purposes, invisible. O sure baby, Emma said to Fawn. Then glanced at the statue dog

Fawn pulled on her pajama bottoms and wiggled them to her ankles. She scooted over to the toilet. Stopped and blinked at the sight of Nommo. Momma, why she froze like that?

Nommo likes to play hide and seek, Emma said. Pretend like you don't see him. She gonna be in the tub with me? Fawn sat on the toilet.

Let's skip the bath today, Emma said. Just wash your face and hands. And brush your teeth baby. Hurry up.

A bowl of granola and blueberries and tall glass of milk waited for Fawn in the kitchen. Fhill emptied the dishwasher. As Emma came in holding Fawn's pawish hand.

Good morning Fawnie, Fhill said. We got you your favorite breakfast. She nodded at the blue cereal bowl.

Good morning Goddess Mother, Fawn said. Sat down wide-eyed.

Your dog is in the bathtub, Emma droned.

Uh huh, Fhill said. Thought, canine. She put away the silverware.

Don't you wonder about him, even a little? Emma said.

Nope, Fhill said.

Didn't you tell me you've seen him-Emma glanced at Fawn then spelled out, f-u-c-k-i-n-g the neighbor's dog? Ringo?

Yep, Fhill said. She put away some pots and pans.

And wasn't it their other dog, Lily Pad, who was doing it to

Fhill shot Emma a look. So?

So he goes both ways, Emma said.

She is both ways, Fhill said.

Well there's different, and then there's different, Emma said.

Don't you love Lune? Fhill said. Ain't Lune some different?

And what could Emma say but that look. You'd have to be blind not to see. Lune had whiskers where another had a mustache. He was feline. He made his living hunting and killing rats for the city's overwrought restaurant owners. Much to Emma's amazement, he perched atop the refrigerator to eat tuna out the can. When he was satisfied he purred. He insisted she call him Big Pussy when he made love to her. It made him hard. His loving, wild. Emma'd known for some time. She was living with a hybrid

Nommo padded down the back stairs. She stopped at the bottom and shook water from her fur. Then she gave Fhill side eye as she went out his door and into the patchy green yard

In humans, it is said, the spirit lived in the body, unseen and unseeable. Dependent, and wedded, throughout the life of the body, to the body. But Nommo's spirit ÷ from Nommo's body when it wanted to, because it lived on its own. Because every species has a talent. And every living thing hungers to be seen. Which made it possible for Nommo to be in a here and in an otherwhere at the same time. In the backyard, Nommo's spirit took off

Fhill wiped up Nommo's wet tracks and finished tidying the kitchen. She reminded herself what day it was. For Nommo and the others. Beast Valley-as the humans called it- was for canine wilding out. Once a year, the city's officials encouraged "dog own-ers" to bring their "pets." To mingle with the canines who live there without leashes, sit commands, or human rule. As Fhill watched Nommo from the kitchen window. Just standing in the yard, looking at something she could not see. Fhill was sure Nom-mo knew today was the day

Nommo was sitting upright in the back seat of the Cadillac convertible, waiting. When Fhill and Emma and Fawn finally emerged from the house. Emma looked at the dog. Shook her head in resignation. This just didn't match. It did not match Fhill's tales of having grown up in a neglected neighborhood in the South Bronx. Where mangy dogs terrorized the residents night and day. They mauled garbage cans, she'd said, in search of food. If humans got too close, they'd bare their teeth. They'd foam at the mouth, she'd said, she was petrified at the sight of a dog. She'd run into the nearest store front, the nearest building. Sweating fear. How many times had she'd said, baby I hate dogs

Emma hoisted Fawn into the spacious seat, beside Nommo. She watched Fhill round the wide front of the car. Her breasts full under her clothes. The way her pelvis rolled as she walked. Her keys in her hand. The easy way of charisma.

★★★ ★★★

She was later than she'd planned to be, though she loved making an entrance. Emma slinked through the apartment full of women perfuming the air. The black silk sheath she wore highlighted her curvy frame in fact. A woman approached her. Staring down at her feet.

I like your shoes, the woman said.

Thank you, Emma said.

Are they Tookie Smith's?

Emma's eyes locked the nattily dressed woman. I'm impressed, she said.

So am I, the woman said. You pamper your feet. I'm Fhill.

Emma, Emma said.

You know anybody here? Fhill said.

Aurora and Hamp, Emma said. They always throw a good party.

Fhill took a swig of her beer. I like your feet, she said into her bottle.

Now, of course, there is no such love as heaven. In brief time, they each felt the sweet go. So they went from being lovers to fondly friends

★★★ ★★★

Emma got in the front seat. Fhill guided the tank of a car out of the driveway. Emma noted that it was still spotless. Still smelled of new car leather. Fhill's

Cadillac still had those white wall tires. Out of the city the two-door silver blue convertible truly looked much happier

You know what Goddess Mother? Fawn said from the back seat.
What baby? Fhill said.
Nommo is licking my leg. And before, she was licking my face.
Fhill glanced at her goddaughter in the rear view mirror. That's how he kisses people he likes, she said.
Isn't this fun-Emma said. No matter what, it was good to see Fhill. It'd been too long. They'd always have what they'd always had. She could feel it. Emma threaded her fingers through Fhill's free hand. And when Fhill gave them a gentle squeeze, Emma settled into the ride out to Beast Valley

The breeze washed Nommo's face and he greeted its insistent touch sticking his nose into it. He looked about. To everyone else in the car he was enjoying the ride. But part of him, the ÷ part, was already where they had yet to come. That part went into the bushes of Beast Valley. And stopped in a corridor of trees. A humanoid in a dark hoodie peeled off the ground. It was luminescent. It shimmered, like a hologram. And though it was three dimensional, the Ever All violated logic as it hovered slightly above the ground. It was an astral rapture, the Ecstatic Word, originating in the answer to a question:
what more
and more precisely
what else
what else was there
of life
of its forms
its hybridities

The figure walked toward Nommo. When they were only a few feet apart Nommo bent his head in deference. The figure came close.

Nommo collapsed onto her back. She let the shimmering figure rub her belly with vigor. The humanoid got down on all fours. Then the two muzzled and pawed each other.

Admired one another. And sat, side by side, looking at what only they could see. Their thoughts and feelings bleeding through epidermis for what did not feel like, but was, a long time

★★★ ★★★

The area where the humans parked their cars was on a hill. From there the full vista of Beast Valley was visible: It was a tract of land outside the city proper. The prehistoric, densely spaced trees were matted together in families. Their towering necks bent at the top, competing for shits of sunlight. They communicated, through electrical impulse and their own senses of smell and taste. The ground beneath was choked with bulbous crawling roots. An umbrella of smaller trees weaved beneath the taller ones. They nurtured the stump of a felled tree, feeding it sugars and other nutrients. Even without a breeze, everything was in motion, preening, adrenalized.

The canines were not visible at first. But then the prehistoric green began to mutate. And there they were: tails wagging. Roaming about in tribes. Standing still. Staring up at the humans on the hill. Though Beast Valley had been designated by the city's humans as "a dog park," humans were neither in control nor welcome within it. In fact, it was the canines who'd chosen this place to be

Nommo bolted from the back seat. He tore down the embankment, along with several others. The newcomers let their butts be sniffed. Until what was to be known about their diets, genders, their emotional states-written in the biographies of sharp odor and pheromones-was known to the waiting pack

Emma let Fawn out of the car. She squinted at the scene below. I see what you mean, she said to Fhill.
Yeah, it's pretty wild, Fhill admitted.
Inhospitable, Emma said. I wouldn't call this place an enchanted forest.
People say, Fhill said, there's something in there. That can change humans into

dogs.

Emma sucked her teeth in loud disbelief. Gurl, please.

Fhill chuckled. Come on Fawnie, she said, let's get a balloon. And with that, Fhill took Fawn's hand and started for the concession area

At a nearby table, a city employee, with the name tag Huber, announced the city's animal rescue hotline with a pile of brochures and free buttons. Huber hovered between long ears, dog paws and an elongated, hound dog nose. Huber wore baggy jeans and an oversized tee shirt. And scratched, from time to time, with one paw, furiously. The city employee was accompanied by a teen aged human who handed out balloons. He handed Fawn a blue and green balloon on a long string. It resembled planet Earth. Emma came up behind them

Well that's stupid. Fhill frowned.

What? Emma said.

Hot dogs, Fhill pointed at the lone food truck. Why would they have hot dogs, of all things to eat, here?

Emma regarded the truck. Animal behavior. Animal behavior and other human activities.

Yeah, Fhill grunted, let's sit down.

A few feet away Emma and Fhill settled onto an unoccupied bench under a tree. Fawn hovered off to the side. She gazed, transfixed, as a tiny girl consumed an enormous hot dog. A blob of yellow mustard dirtied the girl's otherwise pristine white dress. As the girl swiped at the stain she looked to see if anyone was watching. She stuck out her tongue at Fawn. It was littered with half chewed bun and meat. The sight made Fawn blink. Irritated, the little girl stomped off. And Fawn stuck out her tongue at the girl's back. A flirty breeze whipped the balloon about

Emma surveyed the thin crowd at the food truck. She watched a woman in line ignore the insistent chihuahua who humped the woman's leg. Animals did what they wanted. Clearly. Upstate, people were just as wild as their creatures. Anything was possible, Emma thought. She gave Fhill a quick once-over. There

was something different. She sensed it. Sure as someone without sight, sensed
light

I never thought you'd be out of the city this long, she said to Fhill. You must like
it–
Too much drama in the city, Fhill said. Turned to look at Fawn wandering around
behind them. Fawn talked to her balloon.
What happened to you? Emma said.
All the feet started to look the same. Fhill studied the thin black leather straps of
the sandals across Emma's thick toes. The manicured toes lay atop one another
polished black. The bunions on the sides of her feet swelled outward. A stunted
sixth toe on her left foot had changed its mind about coming out mature.
That married woman still seeing you? Emma said.
Fhill's laugh was from surprised. Why? You jealous?
Emma brushed a lick of red curls from her face. Then massaged her belly.
Laughed too. Maybe, she said.
A squat, sweating woman deposited herself at the other end of their bench. She
held tight to the leash of the large black and grey German Shepherd attached to
a choke collar. The dog's tail dripped between his hind legs. He waited until the
woman looked at him before he sat down. Fhill eyed the German Shepherd and
the woman he was with. There was no mistaking. He lived by her rule. He had a
place in her home because he was obedient. He ate good, at her expense. She
expected him to protect her. Here, and everywhere. She was the alpha dog

Nommo appeared on the periphery of the embankment. He sat on his haunches.
Glanced back over his left shoulder. He looked at the Ever All shimmering inside
its hoodie. When Fhill spotted Nommo she wondered what Nommo was looking
at

The early spring wind belched around them. Fawn squealed as her balloon
became kite. The woman felt pinched by the child's sound.
Get that thing out of my face, she barked. And slapped Fawn's kite away from
her. Fawn ran into her mother's arms.

Hey! What's your problem? Fhill said to the woman.

For Christ's sake, Emma said, it's a fucking balloon-

The woman sprung up, wound tight. The world was scary without Jimmy. Jimmy had loved and protected her forty two years. He'd understood she was nervous by nature. Change was hard for her. When no one else did, he'd understood she needed a rock. Jimmy had been her Lollipop and she, his Plum Pie. Now, all she had was his walking buddy, Pal. Was company enough but no dog, nothing, could replace her Jimmy. Gone to glory, bless him. What was she to do

She snarled even louder. I said keep it away from me!

Nommo crouched forward, stalking the woman. With the humanoid beside him. He let out a low, rattled growl. Fhill stood up just then. She towered over the squat woman shaking visibly.

Look lady, Fhill said, you need to calm the hell down-

The woman jerked tighter the choke collar around Pal's neck. The pinch of it momentarily strangled. She shook violently now. You don't tell me what to do you you you, you nigger!

And right then the hooded figure hovering beside Nommo, the figure only Nommo could see, brightened in frequency. And Fhill sprung forward with vicious speed. As canine and incisor, as premolar, teeth flashed. Fhill's bite slit the woman's mouth.

What the! - Emma said, baffled. She and Fawn stood at Fhill's back. Emma kept one eye on the few people watching. The woman backed away from Fhill. Though she tried, she could not speak. But she tasted the fact: Fhill had spit in her mouth

You okay? Emma said to Fhill. Still baffled by what she'd seen.

Goddess Mother? Fawn said.

I'm fine baby, Fhill said. Glaring at the woman as she pulled her dog toward the parking area. It wasn't clear now which one of them was on the leash.

Nothing's changed, Emma said.

She has, Fhill said. She'll watch her mouth from now on.

Nommo walked up to them. She gave Fhill a tender look. Then she sat down, lifted that left hind leg and licked herself. And the space of the missing toe of that black paw. When she was finished she looked over her left shoulder. To see t he humanoid headed into the dense bush, its light less intense. Nommo headed for the car

That night, after Fawn was asleep, Emma headed for Fhill's bedroom. And later, when all the humans were snoring at last, Nommo went out her door and into the backyard and collected her spirit. And then went through the gate, pass the convertible sleeping in the driveway, and down the street's deserted black. As if someone or something had called him

# Alexis Pauline Gumbs

## her relationship to Africa lives in the part of her that is eight years

old. that is seven years old. when did it start? her relationship to
Africa lives in the part of her that doesn't know how long a year is
or that it will one day be divided into seasons. at least three-fifths of
which will make her sick. Africa is not her mother, but her relationship to Africa lives in the time machine of her body on the same re-
boot date as her relationship with her mother. i mean they ended at
the same time.

restart. her relationship with her mother lives in the place behind
her eyes where she saves headaches for later and pretends to be surprised by them. the place where she doesn't eat. the place where she
has braces, where she braces. her relationship to Africa lives in the
place in her mouth where she bleeds and grows soft callouses. the
place in her mouth where she forgets how to speak the words her
mother used to sing. she will learn every western language and not
fill that soft red place.

her mother is not Africa. Africa is the place where she swam in the
dark. no. Africa is the place before she screamed chained there in
the dark. her memory of her mother is the truth that taught her
shallower breaths would save her in that cold place that wet place
where ever after it hurt to breathe. her mother is the warning that
said use your brain to protect your heart. her mother is not that
dark place she doesn't remember. her mother is not a ship. her name
is not phillis. her name is her mother's name. her mother's name is a vessel
she screams in alone and surrounded and chained. this is not
helping.

her relationship to her mother is different. her relationship with her mistress is different from her relationship to her mother. her relationship with her mistress is bigger than her relationship to Africa. she would travel the ocean to see her. she would send her across the ocean (not) to free her. she would understand her words. her relationship with her partner is different from her relationship with her mother. she would never approve. she would never prove her love by finally getting it together. mother is the name of the one who can save you. mother is the name of the one who comes when you scream. mother is the name of the one who keeps you warm. where were you when the sun died?

okay stop. her mother is not god. her relationship to her mother is not Africa. her relationship to her mother is a ship in the angry ocean. her mother is not god. Jesus is not her mother. but she doesn't know yet. she doesn't know yet. she is eight years old. her relationship to Africa is three-hundred years old. her relationship to breathing only thirty-four years old. brilliance is a respirator. all those smarts. how can she run her heart. how can she heal her lungs. when she dies the floor is wood again. and someone is screaming. mama.

Restart.

## Arisa White
# Black Pearl:
# A poetic drama for four voices

**Voices:**

Narrator

You

Driver

Deejay

**Time:**

Your darkest hour

**Setting:**

A crossroads where a street meets an avenue

*Here you have fallen to a ground unfamiliar with your stomp, your corners and your beefs, no body is calling your name—a mispronounced anomaly. Too blur to be understood, you are where the ground done shake, done burn, done sink into itself to show you Her insides—a cave for all our birthings, a pitch black wonder, a solemn O.*

*Oh*

*oh the silence it volumes tunnels into the O of your canals, into an Oh off your drum, out of an O of your breath, out of the Oh of your mouth, washed from the O of your teardrop*

*Drops*

*drops you here in this place. A water rough goes through you. Here in this place, on your knees, knocking on this earth to call your people's music into your bones, their laughter with no syntax, loose and fresh their tongues, all them rhythms to heal. Your heart thirsty for love is but a cup compared to your body. Here, east*

150

*of your spine, the ocean, a conjunction in your story; the ocean, filled with vows
and hunger, and here you are—*

Waiting

> *for a Black Pearl Taxicab
> to take you to the Lake,
> jeweled with lights
> the City keeps running.*

forgotten in your circuitry
remembered after the fact
the fact that is
twenty-four and seven years
I am hours
I am fumes
these pieces you rather not puzzle
10,000 portraits of dust
small confessions r.i.p. my palm—

> *Black Pearl pulls up before you. On the radio, the
> deejay says,* Dedicated to the children, women
> and men, to them all who died at the hands of
> loveless hearts, apathetic laws, became bricks
> in blue walls, and called back too soon—our
> plots cannot contain the sour.
>
> *A litany of dead names is said and remains in the
> atmosphere as a veil of sound.*

I am not a star
I am missed and ancient
I am not heard

I am not blue eyes
I live these pages turning wild
I am not recognized

*The backseat door opens before you can apply your*
*pull. Driver greets you with obsidian eyes. Her*
*dreadlocks, silver as a full moon, fall to her elbows.*
*She speaks like a chorus of ancestors drives her*
*lungs,* I got you.

I am saying, where is the love?
I am saying, I'm the promise to hold
I am saying, how many rounds of names
must pass through my throat?

*You clear the tears from your eyes.*
*Driver asks,* Where you want to go?
*You say,* Take me home.
*Driver keeps her eyes on the road, her hands at 3*
*and 9, and all of her sees you as a true spark. She*
*holds you in a body gaze—you've forgotten such a*
*communicating touch and remember again the lan-*
*guage of your own presence. Speech happens with*
*lips parted or in silence. She meets your eyes in the*
*rearview, and the ancestors declare,*

The dirt is
where the bloom
comes from the buried

All these sheeps want to sleep me, *you say*

Before and unborn

our mothers carry
blood that brought us alive

      push shush on my lips—shush me, *you say*

Her tears echo in US
like a canyon speak back to us
You've forgotten your voice made grand

      silent to myself, silence builds me, *you say*

These crooked rooms,
not meant for standing,
let them tumble and fall

On the earth's door, you raised
your fist full of want, knocking
for an answer, knocking

      master-tools be the house that house me, *you say*

And the ancestors want to know:
Why you knocking for?

      I want these bricks out the walls of we, *you say*

Your fist full of thunder, knocking
for a beat to lay a rhyme, knocking

      out from beneath His missionary hide, *you say*

And the ancestors want to know:
What you knocking for?

set free my tender-headed kitchen, *you say*

Your fist full of vex, knocking
for an angel to flex, knocking

cross my wounds with love, *you say*

The ancestors want to know,

What's all this killing for?

*The deejay says the litany of dead names like the veil of sound lifted and the ocean took over his tongue and names come to the shore salted and ready for land.*

My body I fear to swim,
    fear disconnects my line:
white noise has become the ghost of me,
    I hear myself haunt the dead silence
deaf and dead in this rift, a spook, a little am I.
    no continuity to dream of. No peep to my back,
no peep to eye. Alone and alienated in a construct
    they call me black

loud
wild
intimidating
too fresh
Bland
and my red is spilled all over

dirty
soucouyant
monkey

bitch
too Proud
by news so splitting it herds

> *You and Driver sync into a rhythm, your words
> share the same root, be of the same mother, act
> contrapuntally.*

I've been called
three-fifths        regarded
angry               inhumanely
disadvantaged       by people
nigger              fashioned
Brown               by colonizer's colors
capitalizing off our beads

> *You keep your fingers butterfly on your chest like
> your heart is the vinyl you're not allowed to touch.*

This violence
on the heart
skips on "Nobody"
"Bumbaclot" "Ugly"
and their kin
cuts through
my veins.

*Who you knocking for?* is the bridge that Driver lays into your grooves.

> *You look at the passing lights, the night, the still-
> ness as prayer atop these roofs, the sky in shades of
> navy and ash, and you can taste the silence before it
> breaks,*

Mothers, Mae I, Rae I, Pearl,
Esther, Gail. Mothers, May I, Margaret,
Carol, Elsie, Carol, Mariana, and Madeline,
and Mable. Mothers, Mae I, Rae I, Anna B, Jean,
Josephine, Ethel, Karla, and Lucinda, Jo. Mothers, May I,
Eleanor, Pat, Barbara, Ruby, Judy, Karen. Mothers, Mae I,
Rae I, Florette, GrandMother Rose is who I knock for.

> *Driver stops Black Pearl near a curbside garden and
> your door opens,*

Take from your mother's garden
A pistil to put in your braids—

> *And you take a blossom that looks like a trumpet of
> wind and Indian gold and you wear it like a Holiday.*

Sweet reminder to keep Her blessings
when beneath the spell of sorrow

> *You return to Black Pearl and Driver resumes the
> engine's purr, and her words,*

Pick and eat Her yams and yucca,
Swiss chard and snap peas—

Your mother's garden isn't all peach.
What you take, you can't mistake

There's not a strange fruit
and forbidden is for pussies—

the reason they try to shut this mother down

*You bring them to the up, to the air to breathe,*

Mothers, Mae I, Rae I, Pearl,
Esther, Gail. Mothers, May I, Margaret,
Carol, Elsie, Carol, Mariana, and Madeline,
and Mable. Mothers, Mae I, Rae I, Anna B, Jean,
Josephine, Ethel, Karla, and Lucinda, Jo. Mothers, May I,
Eleanor, Pat, Barbara, Ruby, Judy, Karen. Mothers, Mae I,
Rae I, Florette, GrandMother Rose, who I knock for.

*Driver drives Black Pearl to an oak that fell when a*
*storm rolled through and now its roots starburst from*
*the dirt. Overlooking the Lake, Black Pearl is put*
*in park and Driver turns her obsidian eyes on you,*

There is no peace in running the truth of you,
no justice in naming your inheritance shatter,

all have trembled in your mask, but you are found
In your lagoons and liminal paradises, a tree grown

from the menses the baobab drank—
its diameter the weeks in a year, its bark generous,

around its circumference women on their haunches,
evenly spaced in preparation for flight

Your knocking resounds, spreads before your heart's pride,
roaring, roaring right from all these mouths of mater

GrandMother Rose is who I knock for.

*The door opens again, and you hold your grand-mother's name in your mouth like hard candy.*

Rise yourself to enter roots,
framed as a doorway, as a window,

the height for you to passage through

You rise through her name,       Rose
you grow yourself to standing,

from the ground no longer fallen,

        Rose

*The deejay plays some keys of life and tells you about your Rose Carter, your Geechee parts, from when your people were down South,*

      Petals and thorns
      grit and perseverance
      ego soothed by your knees'
      arthritic crunch—you getting up,
      to the deep side, where
      roots reach, where
      Rose rose from
      Her red clay sleep,
      Boo creeping in just
      when the moon
      makes Her descent,
      when Rose smelled
      that same toilette
      water from another
      toilet piece of ass,
      and when Boo pulled

them sheets to see
a shotgun, Rose said,
This's who *I'm* fuckin wit.

*You say,* Never knew GrandMother Rose had that kind of bitch and spice.

> *You reach your hand to the roots of this oak, more*
> *old than old, and you feel its memory. The roots*
> *reach back to you and Driver remarks on where you*
> *stand,*

Here, your shadow retires. Put to rest your restless, enter into the touch of
things, what the body senses. You must look by listening to free you from
the power of what them say. Feel our names inside. That core of you is the
core of you is the core we're rooting for. Here, is the will to endure.

> *Driver meets you at your side, brings you into an*
> *embrace that makes you feel the goodness inside. She*
> *points her finger to the crescent above, the grass, the*
> *skin of the Lake, then here, and then there, until*
> *her finger has made a constellation of life and things*
> *and all things being. Her palm rests at the back of*
> *your heart, and when her hand returns to her hip,*
> *the heat it leaves, melts your ice. The water is filled*
> *with Driver's voice,*

Without Her, you
have no body to feel
to feel the feel
to know the feel
to swear on the feel—
it's mighty real

In Her body, your
body, the sweet preverb
quiet, the sea untranslated
body is Her
body is a body
of unimaginable real
where what we call
magic is dark depths
where no Sankofa reach
in the woe
in the wonder
in the wick
that stands to burn
for your body

give Her praise
up high, your palms
contralto, you bear
Her note, surviving
in our words
Ma
Ma
Ma
Ma
arrives from all our fragments
and steps foot here

Where you from?
          *You stand more strong, more sure,*
          From here.

                    *Driver sits down on the grass, with its blades long*
                    *and glowing. With a pound on the ground, she*

*invites you to sit next to her. Driver gives you a*
*moment to abide, and you do, and she lets her 'locks*
*flow down one shoulder. She holds your hand, while*
*she drops this knowledge,*

When it does not suffice that you are USAmerican,
that you must be somewhere not BedfordStuyvesant,
it is that rebel pearl-diver blood that makes this skin other
than what is expected. Is it Negra Azalea, Venezuelan born,
beneath shade of trees that scream their hurt when roots are torn,
the Isle of Las Tetas de Dolores. Her, the woman who planted it all,
our freedom seeded. She's the tierra that features most.

    Who am I?

That depth of sea survived. . . .
When I say ship, I mean the one from Dutch—
Prima Madre in its belly, learning ways she is peri-
carp around a seed. Azalea in her belly, put there
by a dull and fiery face, on an afternoon, rape
joined our helixes. Her tongue held on to No.
When I say ship, I mean Prima was. Shipped
then shipped, she didn't know where she was.

She wanted for her daughter swimming ways.
Cape Verde, her island, taught her so.
Prima slaved for pearls. Carried down
into feet by boulders, Prima's body greased,
a slick allegiance to finding Negra Paca's black pearl—
in a league she couldn't quite descend, in the mouth
of a ladena named Paca was Prima's freedom. The pearl
the size of your eye, and many lost sight to getting it.

What emerged from Prima's darkest deep
wasn't the jewel of another's suffering, but home
she tasted too frequently in these waters. She blacked out,
gave up her air for the drink of it, and rested on oyster beds.


    Where am I bound?


Azalea motherless, and the magic of never
been born a child, she was a sure profit.
She had a talent for holding breath, fainted
never, not a shark touch her, like a dolphin,
her body with no death in it, ode and spring to sea.

She was able to find the pearl on a full-moon night.
In a dream, Prima came to her, and Azalea followed
her mother to the sea. There, glowing in the low tide,
a trinity of albino stingrays that led her to where Paca
drowned. The black pearl steady in her mouth.


    Where do I come from?


Azalea's lips,
that kiss,
to Paca's mouth.


> *Driver opens her hand, and there, balanced on her
> lifeline is the black pearl. You wonder, Is this for
> me, and Driver answers back with, Yes and a Yes,
> some more. You smile, feeling happiness like a friend
> you haven't seen since elementary, and gratitude
> reveals its source.*

*On the radio, the deejay stirs the litany of dead names into a house-beat, into an*
*indigo pulse, into the joy we summons to gift our dead.*

You are awoken,
we see you through

Love you strong,
these blues make violets
with your redbone

We walk the path,
the paths you walk,
our feet the meters          *You respond to the melody with all the*
your talk come through       *choreography carried in your bones. You*
                             *abandon your shame and let your limbs*
Through us, you are alive,    *celebrate: Wops and Running Mans, Pepper*
no lie can tell about you     *Seeds and Whines and the madras your*
                             *hands sign.*
You are awoken,
your shells, you shed
to know truth

For you, our tears, our kinks,
our how-we-do, our milk,
yams, our breaths, little
deaths, these mending needles,
roots and rivers, what we do with rue

Your blood a hive, oh honey,
sweet your pulse brings you close to being
Your heart is unblinking
Your spirit wolf

You are awoken,
a cosmological we,
infinite pearl—you are precious.
So it be, your back, we at,
we got you.

*The litany of dead names becomes a murmuration of swallows. The veil of sound is more like crisp, the first bite into, like honey on a spoon to gild your song, like the bling of a ray served to break your fast.*

> *Driver and you sit watching east and you notice how the Lake rises and fall, and you notice, too, the swell in you. When the embankments go invisible, you feel its stillness convincing you to walk across it. The morning is yellow in you and Driver's eyes, and you have something to say,*

I am here in it, in love
with the for-sense to whole
myself whole again.
Love is its own enough
as its own presence—
I've been labored here.
The people I love are in it,
and we breathe to attest
our love is for certain.

> *Driver ponytails her 'locks, and they fountain from her crown,*

You are sharp for the real,
your breaks give you an edge
Loud out comes your laughter, it raises the roof
Your anger is an organizing sound

*Driver walks back to Black Pearl, and begins to
warm the engine. You return to the backseat and
Driver continues with sense,*

Riot against the guards—civil is a judgment
Your beauty is a truth that doesn't crack—take the flags down!
Your inhale removes the robes off this eroding empire—
see behind the trees to where your hands made a beat:
You're a river, that sweet fresh, a breath of first take.

*Driver goes in the direction of home, down First
Avenue. She turns the volume up, and the deejay
says the litany of dead names like they are dressed to
the nines in red silk, fashioned from rainbows whose
arrows call us into a familiar and safe high, and your
skin shines. When the names turn into aerosols, you
put the black pearl in your mouth, and savor these
three words,*

I
L-O-V-E
You

I
L-O-V-E
You

I
L-O-V-E
You

I
L-O-V-E
You

I
L-O-V-E
You

I
L-O-V-E
You

I
L-O-V-E
You

I
L-O-V-E
You

I
L-O-V-E
You.

# Cheryl Boyce-Taylor
# How to Make Art

her sharp mouth a bright silver revolver
fingers a scorched iron train
stop
that hurts
sweeter than I found you
next day
      open each section girl
you make me weep
      is sun leaving
I always want to praise sky & Ceni
my night rider
22 years and I can still drown in her wildness
all the while praying calling Jesus Jesus
who gets to be called daddy first
      to paint your toes bright orchid
teeth disguised as new bones to
      tame a wild woman worship her like a poem.

doris diosa davenport

# Erzulie-Oshun (Georgia Style)*

1

the arch in her back
increases five inches when
she lays on it or
kneels


2

before she grew 2
big toe double nails
ingrown to her feet,
her feet was the
spot. "Oh, touch
my feet please
do it (she said) to
my feet . . ."


3

she had it cast in silver
because her clit
is a major work of art
not one of the seven wonders
of the world but

---

\* Erzulie is a Haitian Voodoo Loa—Goddess—of passionate love, as described by Z.N. Hurston. Oshun is a Yoruba Goddess of love, sensuality and water, and other life forms (described in many sources). The poem pays homage to and "claims" these Deities and acknowledges the powerful spirituality of sexual love between black wimmin-loving wimmin. Further, it describes specific attributes of two of my ex-lovers, from my time in Los Angeles, in the 1980s. First published in *voodoo chile slight return: poems* (1991).

a wonder all the same

    4

not to mention her
major African inheritance, that
ass that conjures
that conjures
lampposts & cars
seduces in sweatpants
sways with a natural breeze
sometimes force of a hurricane
wind even when it's
still, it says
uh huh. uh huh. Uh HUH and
some people have been
blown away

    5

her body in
orgasm
ripples like a
wave
it ripples like a
wave sometimes of
hot
lava not scalding but heating the
room all the same some folk got
drowned. some got burnt
up but they always
resurrect for
more.

## Pauli Murray
# Without Name

Call it neither love nor spring madness,
Nor chance encounter nor quest ended.
Observe it casually as pussy willows
Or pushcart pansies on a city street.
Let this seed growing in us
Granite-strong with persistent root
Be without name, or call it the first
Warm wind that caressed your cheek
And traded unshared kisses between us.
Call it the elemental earth
Bursting the clasp of too-long winter
And trembling for the plough-blade.

Let our blood chant it
And our flesh sing anthems to its arrival,
But our lips shall be silent, uncommitted.

# SDiane Bogus

# Fighting Racism: An Approach Through Ritual

In a query in *Lesbian Contradiction* (Summer 1984), Rebecca Gordon asked for some feedback on her idea that "we . . . start attacking the outward manifestations of racism, its political and economic effects in women's lives" rather than acting only according to the belief that "the best way to fight racism is through self-examination and self-improvement." Most of what she said was directed at white womyn whose racism tortuously reveals itself in the "anti-racism workshops" that are convened to "examine and remove" racist attitudes. For one, I have always believed such sit-down-and-talk sessions to be a step in the right direction. It seems to me that any attempt to work on racism has always been worth the effort because, when we meet, we move in the same direction as do those larger organizations, say, for example, the NAACP. What we do in small groups is as viable as what larger groups do, because we are all busy working together or separately to establish order, harmony, justice on this planet. The large and small of it is that we're trying to do what we can to eradicate the beast of skin distinction.

I've found interracial groups even more strenuous in their efforts to accomplish the same kinds of goals no matter how hurtful the revelations, no matter how painful the sharings. It all looks very needed to me. But in our small groups, of one kind or of interracial mix, what has always been lacking is the profound sense that we *are* sisters and lovers. It appears that, when we come together, we do so as strangers or acquaintances. Somewhere in the back of our minds there is some literary or rhetorical *fantasy* of sisterhood, which we want to believe is true but don't accept as a valid truth. So we deal with each other like estranged lovers, trying to talk through a haze of issues that have clouded our once familiar love for each other. But I tell you now, we *are* sisters and lovers. We are our mother's and father's daughters, dust of the same earth. We may never have shared the same upbringing, but we have shared the same planet on which to be brought up. It is this great sphere revolving in the heavens that gives us life, the very ground on which we take our stand; and each day that we rise clothed in the flesh of life, we rejoin humanity in a vital and moving way.

When we meet each other, in the flesh of our flesh, we validate that vital connection to the other. We find acknowledgment in our shared lesbianism; we find strength in our shared ideology; we find joy in the company of womyn; we find power in working out our feminist politics. But that kind of knowing, loving, has become so commonplace that we take each other for granted. When we meet to talk, we let the assumptions about our shared lives carry us into discussions that take our love for granted. But I tell you, we must remember we are lovers, that our lives are interrelated because we stand on this planet together and have the kinship of the earth. That context—that we are lovers and sisters, given to one another by virtue of our shared humanity, preferences, and ideologies—must be made the over-riding consideration for every attempt we make at gestalt.*

Note, for example, that even when we sit in groups governed by an appointed facilitator—respectfully following her rules of order, trying to play fair and sane without denying ourselves the utterance of what is in our guts—we are not entirely given to each other. The formality, the civil arrangement of the process, creates distance, makes what we are trying to share more unnatural to get at. Such interactions are confined by a kind of "reasonableness," and *it is* because of that reasonableness that tensions arise. A meeting meant to be reasonable will break down, because everyone does not reason the same way nor perceive another's reasoning as more valid than her own. When the structure for sharing is to be reasonable (i.e., listen rationally and respond in kind), then that structure lends itself to ultimate unreasonableness and disruption. Loving-sharing is "unreasonable" mostly because we've never believed it is possible.

---

* *Gestalt*: "a unified whole; a configuration, pattern, or organized field having specific properties that cannot be derived from the summation of its component parts."

# Focusing on the Spiritual Core

I would like to suggest a symbolic approach to our interactions, a ritual approach. By so suggesting. I am saying I don't think we should abandon our intergroup work on racism, but continue it by exploring new ways to communicate. In this way, we may break through to each other so as to really make a difference "out in the world." To begin, I believe we need to start focusing on the spiritual core of ourselves in our group interactions. To do so, we will need to draw upon all that is good and loving inside us. Then, when we work together, our work will reflect an intimate harmony based on self-knowledge and personal sharing. For when it comes to attacking the welter of racial antagonisms out in the world and within our own hearts, nothing less than our sharing the hope and trust of our soul will do.

When we sit together, it must be in pow-wow, in council. We each are to act as elders and protectors of that which is sacred to our love. We each must know that such gatherings of spirits are courageous, morally responsible acts, so it can be taken for granted that we are spiritually ready to confront what has the Appearance of Disharmony among us. Those who become disgruntled or offended, those who recoil and withdraw, will only be reflecting the phases in the process (as you know, and as Bernice Reagon discusses in her "Coalition Politics: Turning the Century" essay in *Home Girls*), and those seeming squabbles should be accepted as "seeming," never as the truth of what we are about. Built into every session, to offset such impasses, should be the uttered willingness of each sister/lover present to remain committed to the transformation of racial relations in the world, and to the best possible outcome for the day's work. Our willingness to say we are glad to be engaged in the struggle, doing what we are doing, fighting as we fight, will allow us to grow bigger, broader, more receptive to others. In time, we will become big enough to genuinely live and let live. And that leads me to the edge of a discussion on moral truths.

## Acknowledging Moral Truth

Tolerance, Forbearance, Harmony, Understanding, Receptivity, Loving are not just catch words from philosophy or religion; they are actual moral principles already alive in each one of us. If we care enough to sit and fight out our differences, then, by virtue of that caring, we are capable of and fully prepared to put those principles into practice.

Our interactions, especially our consciousness-raising efforts, can be grounded in neoancient ritual (which we can create), and through a ritual approach, we can make way for a new ambience of communal and spiritual touching. Before starting any meeting, the peaceful burning of calming incense might do much to evoke spirits of peace; candles could be burned to signify the search for light in our hearts, light to guide ourselves. A bit of silent meditation would please the spirits of harmony that, no doubt, will attend such devoted and sincere attempts to touch hearts. A womon could spend a few minutes looking at what is in her own heart, trying to think which would be the best way to speak of what she feels. She could look about the room, at the faces of her sisters, seeking in them signs of grace and honesty. She could look for it in the curve of their brow, in the shape of their eyes, in the line of their lips. Perhaps a cup of herb tea, individual introductions, and a few yoga exercises might add to the context of intimate sharing and exchange. But mostly during this period of readying of the spirit, the thought of blessing the interaction to come should be uppermost in every woman's mind.

You may gather that such preliminaries as I am suggesting will take time, and they will. But isn't the act of coming together to work out the antagonisms between us (and to look for solutions to those in the world) an act of taking time? Giving up whatever other enterprise we might be engaged in to come and talk politics and strategies is taking the time to set right our lives. Rushed interactions conjure up tension. Slow evolution into discussion would ensure that what comes out of our mouths would not be indictments against any womon present nor of any racial group, but the testimony of experience, meditated on, centered in love and delivered with loving intention. Yes, tempers flair; yes, we do not always agree; yes, there will be uncomfortable moments where no one will know what to say or do, but the love between us should be recalled to the fore of the meeting, to enfold us once again, to renew us in common bond.

Should a woman in such ritual council ever allow her anguish over past or present racial injury to govern her talk with another, should she become so upset as to be also unkind, this special ritual, ideally, would dictate that she become silent until she is clear of the upset and ready to speak again without unproductive anger or harshness. And out of tolerance and forbearance, those womyn hearing her must receive her shattered emotions as witnesses, but not as the offended. Each of those present must be willing to be slow to anger, slow to be offended, slow to criticize, and slow to perceive negative behavior in those present. At such moments, a chant could be begun: "'Know that we are not responsible for the persistence of racial antagonisms in our culture." "Know that we are not willing to have them separate us." "Know that we are lovers and sisters." "Know that we perpetuate love and harmony here. None else. None else." These or similar words could be chanted before, during, and at the end of such meetings. I believe the power in the words they affirm will begin to undo some of the conscious and unconscious ways that racism insinuates itself among us. By chanting these or like affirmations, we can dispel that which we most wish to dispel: the appearance of disharmony.

Oh yes, we are different from each other; but aren't sisters in the same family different in character, temperament, personality? These are the differences that we must begin to deal with, not the implied distinctions, of color and the attendant inferior or superior positions of class privilege. Our councils, in their deeply telling way, will meld our common experience into a montage of relatedness. As ritual events they will provide a way for each of us to perceive our humanness, and they will provide a way for us to disregard that which others allow to divide them.

## Acknowledging Confusions of Spirit Within

I opened by saying we must be in to draw upon all that is good and loving inside of us in order to work together; now I must acknowledge that the other half, "the dark side," if that is an acceptable term, has some play in how we interact as well. I must ask, from where do pettiness, intemperance, conceit, and envy spring? From where do lack of self-control, laziness, uncooperation, avarice, and cruelty spring? From where any negative behavior, attitude, thought, or expression? I think you know. Yes, they spring from inside of us. Inside of us rages, always, a battle to be our better selves. That better self would be good to our lovers, kind to our parents, generous to the poor; honest and fair in our dealing with humanity at large. That same self wants to be more fulfilled, smarter, richer, more gainfully employed, more artistic, more settled, less shy, more assertive, or less limited—a host of "more" and "better," and an equal host of "less" and "no worse." Knowing that we are always at war with ourselves to improve, to grow, change, how can we think that we can come to any consciousness-raising meetings, any council on race or other political issue, free of the deeper stuff that troubles our (human) spirits? How can we presume to think that we can produce harmony in the world, or among ourselves, when we have such confusions of spirit at war within us?

Well, there's a bad and a good to the answer. The same inner forces that tug us to grow also lend themselves to the outward struggle. Vanity makes us think we can solve the problem of race between us, the very vain notion that we can do whatever we set our minds and hearts to. No matter how impossible the struggle, we are vain enough to take it on, even when the odds say that we are just flawed human beings struggling against our own flawed natures and against the flawed nature of the world. Either way you go, in your struggle, out to the world or back to the private interface, it is all the outworking of the arrogance in human nature which is known as vanity. Vanity, indeed, won't let us accept a concept of ourselves as permanently flawed beings. Do you see how the bad side works to support our inner struggle? Well, the obverse of vanity is inner vision, and inner vision gives us sight. What we think we can do, we see(k) a way to do. What is good within us is sighted by vision, and struggled for through the mocking of vanity. It is this unconscious interaction within us that lends itself to our efforts to coalesce, to sit down and talk. We know quite consciously that we have natures that are in eternal contention, but through the unconscious alchemy of the struggle between vanity and vision, of the faith we need to overcome the internal chaos, that faith gives those of us who grapple with the question of racism the confidence to write and talk about it, to take it on. And so, for all our confusions of spirit, we do take on that which seems even more confused and outside of ourselves.

What this means is that, in those moments of contemplation before attempting dialogue, we must consider that we all have our private wars within us. We must know before we speak a word to one another that we are being driven by needs of spirit and flesh, hardly within our conscious grasp. Knowing that we have secret needs, desires, problems, we must have everything out and above board—through sharing introductions, through the natural exchange of interactions, or through chants—but out, so that those agents of the silent war within us won't dictate to us how we are being and acting with our lovers/sisters. Only by knowing who and how we are individually will we be able to speak to the soul of another.

The question of *how* to change, *how* to grow, *how* to transform our lives is ever at the essence of confusion. Having always lived with "what can I do?" "how can I do this?" when we arrive at plateaus of self-revelation, at breakthrough points in our interpersonal relationships, we cannot always recall the path we took. Hence the route to harmony, within ourselves, within our communities, even out in the world, is neither straight nor charitable. We are called upon to live day to day with our dissatisfactions and inadequacies they clear up, however they do it. Meanwhile, we engage in self-help therapy, we read, we subscribe to our religious beliefs, we meditate, jog, walk, talk with our friends, lovers, parents, sisters, brothers, our groups. Meanwhile, we take whatever small steps we can toward transformation, satisfaction, self-revelation, change. Sometimes those changes, revelations, etc., will come in a beautiful flash of insight; sometimes, after long reflections and worry; sometimes, in retrospect. That is all.

So again, when we come to our consciousness-raising, problem-solving groups, especially those designed to work on racism, we must remember that the private self dictates to the public self. And, just to bring it out of the moth balls of what is often taken for granted, I will add this: another's race has nothing to do with the desire to meet heart to heart in the arenas of controversy. Each of our selves has in common with every other self/soul/spirit/human in the room the desire to show her best self to the world.

That is why I recommend that we change the context from which we have been dealing with each other. A bit of incense, a few lighted candles, some tea, moments of self-reflection, even some sharing of what we perceive as our personal struggles: these elements of ritual before any encounter session will help the womyn there perceive their shared humanity, because shared humanity is the key. I do not mean to turn our meetings into transactional analysis sessions, nor into confessionals; only the womyn who are ready for a transformation of the way in which they have been interacting will know how to implement what I am saying here. But though what I say may seem far-fetched and untried, I am sure that should we strive to contact the great sleeping rituals within us, when we come to talk over race or any other problematic matter, what we will hear from our sisters/lovers will be heard by the heart.

# Sangodare Akinwale
# Anew

*An invocation written and activated by Sangodare. Anew was commissioned by
Daniel Alexander Jones, who embodies and enlivens the energy of Jomama Jones
on the occasion of her album release concert and party at Joe's Pub at the Public
Theater, New York City, on February 14, 2019.*

Who's ready to have a good time? How 'bout an extraordinary time?
My name is Sangodare! Sango-dare.

Well, I'm here to invite you to prime the pump with me. To prepare the
way. . . . To put some energy in . . . offer up our intention tonight. Is that
alright? Can we get it hot . . . get it right out here for this Jomama Jones
experience?

This is an Invocation . . .
*(Humming "Purple Rain"—hmmm mmm mmm mmm; hm mm mm mm)*

> We invite
> We call out to the highest vibration of our own being-ness
> to Great spirit,
> to the divine indwelling intelligence,
> to lov
> to the uplifted and enlightened energies that support this evening's
> love intention,
> we invite you to be present with us with grace and ease.
>
> we offer as libation our presence,
> our applause,
> our uplifted voices,
> our joy and laughter.

and we release the pain of the past
lest anything stand in the way of tonight's revelation

we release the stories from friends, family, and society
we step into a new possibility right now
we activate the infinite in a space called Joe's Pub
in an institution called the Public Theater
in a city called New York
on a night some call
Valentine's.

we open the portal
we activate the vacuum that removes all the old
and flood the space with universal love energy
right now!

Those of us who have felt despised and rejected
will be embraced, tonight.
Those of us who've known sorrow
and been acquainted with grief
will be lifted up, on tonight.

[Lorde have mercy]

Those of us on the shoreline . . .
Those of us who love in doorways coming and going . . .
Those of us who love in the hours between dawns . . .
For those of us imprinted with fear . . .

Those of us . . . !
[Can't help but wonder is anybody here a *those of us*?
Anybody prayed those of us prayers
or ain't nobody here cried *those of us* tears.]

*in the bedroom as a kundalini lover*
*or in the boardroom as purpose or partnership.*

*Anew:*
*Like the kiss of the morning sun on the horizon.*
*Like the golden hour of sunset.*
*Like the Lorde, Audre,*
*acting on us "like a drug or a chisel*
*to remind you of your me-ness,*
*as I discover you in myself."*[4]

[Oh, I wish somebody, anybody, would pray with me, right now!]

*Anew:*
*leaving the sunrise,*
*leaving the heat of the day,*

*Anew:*
*leaving even the voluptuous rivers in the desert,*
*and embracing the peace, the abundance*
*of a sun setting in love.*

*Anew:*
*embracing the cycles—*
*embracing the sunset*
*embracing the night*
*for we know the night time is the right time*
*but not only that,*
*we embrace the night shift (y'all),*
*the work we are here to do*
*in love and in each loveship.*

*Anew:*
*embracing each new dawn.*
*"Opening UP our eyes"*[5]
*every day*
*"to a dawn that we have long imagined"*[6]

*Anew:*
*Knowing*
*"Love is the revelation*
*Love is the true salvation"*[7]

And . . . as long as love is what we are making
there will always be enough (Yeah, Alexis)

For we know
Love is Life Force (Yeah, June Jordan)
And as long as we have love
the sun will rise again.

for all is
created anew
by love
created anew with love.
created anew AS love!

I can hear the Purple One say Jomama
I know, I know,
It's time we all reach out for something new.
That means y'all too.

As we sing
these words of love
these melodies sent from above

we lift up this higher vibration
we can
we are
and we will
create the world ANEW!

and so it is.
Ase.

*[Humming "Purple Rain":*
*Ooo hoo hoo hoo*
*Oo hoo hoo hoo*
*Oo hoo-oo oo oo]*

# Notes

1. Jomama Jones, "Wild," *Anew* (Daniel Alexander Jones, 2019).
2. Jomama Jones, "Revelation," *Anew* (Daniel Alexander Jones, 2019).
3. Jomama Jones, "Dead & Gone," *Anew* (Daniel Alexander Jones, 2019).
4. Audre Lorde, "Eye to Eye: Black Women Hatred and Anger," in *Sister Outsider: Essays and Speeches* (Trumansburg, NY: Crossing Press, 2007).
5. Jones, "Dead & Gone."
6. Jones, "Dead & Gone."
7. Jones, "Revelation."

Sharon Bridgforth

# excerpt from *love conjure/blues*

You are the me i am waiting to be
deep down/i see your Divinity
and i know that we are Free.
free/like the night in flight
free in God's Delight
in the Name of/We are

flesh of the Ocean
the Sun beaming bright
Winds crossing
the Earth's might
we are/your smile
my Heart
with Sight
Free.

no more fighting
i rebuke all fears
no separation/cause we are

the Peace we Pray
the poem we pen
the bridge we make
the song
that dance/is us
and we are

free

          free
          Free.
     cause/We are
     Love.

i                                    i
am the conjure                       am the conjure
sacrificial blood made flesh/i am    sacrificial blood made flesh/i am
sanctified by tears wailing          sanctified by tears wailing
deep in the belly/i am that sound    deep in the belly/i am that sound
released. i am                       released. i am
love remembered                      love remembered
the promise kept                     the promise kept
the should have been                 the should have been
the utterance of hope/i am           the utterance of hope/i am
the Life dreamt                      the Life dreamt


i am the answered Prayer             i am the answered Prayer
the manifested Light                 the manifested Light
i am my Ancestors                    i am my Ancestors
returned                             returned
i am the dead/and the living         i am the dead/and the living
i will carry on                      i will carry on
i will come back                     i will come back
i will grow more powerful            i will grow more powerful
i will remember                      i will remember
i am the one We are waiting for      i am the one We are waiting for
i                                    i
am                                   am
the conjure                          the conjure
come back/to Love.                   come back/to Love.

remember
remember
remember.

# PART V

# RADICAL FUTURITIES

## 1976–2020

We are a people in a quandary about the present. We are a people in search of our future. We are a people in search of a national community.

Barbara Jordan

You know, we are the daughters of Ida B. Wells. We're the daughters of every Black woman who has been a leader—Sojourner Truth, Harriet Tubman, and all the millions of unnamed warriors. All the millions of unnamed ones. We are in a long line. We're just calling it—we're just calling it what it is now—Black feminism is a representation of Black women's power. Black women's agency. Black women's right to look at their material conditions, analyze it, interrogate it, and come away with an analysis that's about empowerment.

Demita Frazier

Our movement must foster transformative conversations among Black folks and Native peoples. Where are we supposed to live? We are not each other's enemies, and we should strive to aid each other's harvest in a world with too much scorched earth. The empire flourishes on our conflict. I believe that we are inherently stronger when we are together, moving in the same direction regardless.

Our collective struggle as Black people is both transnational and local, around the globe and within our hearts. The ongoing project of colonialism lives in each of us and manifests itself in our movement. It shows up in the promotion of disaster capitalism in response to rebuilding Puerto Rico and the U.S. Virgin Islands. It shows up in trials by social media and in the inadequacy of movement institutions to address structural violence and trauma. Therefore, we must take up the work of decolonization, the process of dismantling governmental and cultural systems that control and strip nations, peoples, and groups of self-determination and sovereignty. Independence movements across the Southern Hemisphere may be the most obvious examples of decolonization, but the process doesn't end at declaration of independence. Breaking down what has been learned under colonialism, eradicating internalized colonialism, and disrupting and displacing those who continue to benefit from it—these projects remain long after Independence Day.

**Charlene A. Carruthers**

# Alexis Pauline Gumbs
# The Shape of My Impact

*Sounds to Me Like a Promise: On Survival*
(After the film *Audre Lorde: The Berlin Years* by Dagmar Schultz)
*"I love the word survival, it always sounds to me like a promise. It makes me won-*
*der sometimes though, how do I define the shape of my impact upon this earth?"*
*—reflection cut from an early draft of "Eye to Eye: Black Women, Hatred and*
*Anger" by Audre Lorde (Audre Lorde Papers, Spelman College Archive)*

Survival references our living in the context of what we have overcome. Survival is life after disaster, life in honor of our ancestors, despite the genocidal forces worked against them specifically so we would not exist. I love the word *survival* because it places my life in the context of those who I love, who are called dead, but survive through my breathing, my presence, and my remembering. They survive in my stubborn use of the word *survival* unmodified. My survival, my life resplendent, with the energy of my ancestors, is enough.

Of course *survival* is a keyword in Black lesbian poet warrior mother teacher Audre Lorde's lexicon, and in our memory of her. Ada Griffin and Michelle Parkerson's biographical film about Lorde is called *A Litany for Survival* after her most remembered and recited poem. "A Litany for Survival" is in fact the poem through which Lorde most frequently survives and is often the last shrine of the word *survival* on our tongues.

So it is no surprise that Dagmar Schultz organizes her film, *Audre Lorde: The Berlin Years*, around footage of Audre Lorde powerfully reciting this unkillable poem, stretching the reading through the entire film, but not just because the poem is iconic. The persistence of the poem is appropriate because the film is 100 percent about survival.

The film is the survival of Audre Lorde, her face given back to us through the many portraits interspersed in the film. The film is the survival of the Afro-German women's movement as we watch the living founders of that movement, silver-haired and sleek, comment on their own young gumption more than twenty years ago. The film is the survival of May Ayim, a poet and co-founder of the Afro-German woman's movement, who killed herself at the age of thirty-six, four years after Audre Lorde died. I find it appropriate and moving that Ayim gets the most face time of anyone in the film (besides Audre Lorde) and is also memorialized with a series of portraits, even though viewers who don't know about Ayim's life and death, which the film does not explicitly contextualize, may not understand why her bright face is such a crucial image. The film is the survival of an intergenerational ethos, both in the work of Ayim and other Afro-German women, often raised in white families, to make intergenerational ties, and in Audre Lorde's reminder that "no revolution happens within one lifetime."

The film is about survival. It is Lorde clarifying that "survival is not a theoretical problem and poetry is part of my living," and offering concrete advice for the survival of Afro-German women's groups and literary projects despite the difficulties they face. It is Lorde schooling white women on the urgency of their growth in the face of a 1990s neo-Nazi climate in Germany, explaining that "it is not altruism but survival" that requires them to act.

I appreciate the existence of this survival film, and in the context of our current forum on Black women's health in relationship to the academy I think it offers several lessons. One of course, is the place I start, with the reclamation of the word *survival*. Survival is what some Black women do in the academy, not because they are barely alive, but because we are not supposed to do it, and sometimes we do it anyway. And the way we do it matters.

The survival of Black feminist intellectuals, which happens within or without the academy, is our intentional living with the memory of May Ayim's suicide after being in a mental institution; our living with the knowledge that as Audre Lorde's archival papers prove, she was denied medical leave, had to turn down prestigious fellowships (including the senior fellowship at Cornell) that required residency in places too cold for her to live during her fight against cancer. The English Department at Hunter, which recently honored Lorde with a conference twenty years after her death, rejected her proposals at the end of her life to teach on a limited residency basis that would allow her to teach poetry intensive classes for students during warm weather in New York and to live in warmer climates during the winter based on her health needs.

If Audre Lorde's proposal to teach in a way that allowed her to survive can be denied by the City University of New York, even as she was simultaneously selected as the New York State Poet Laureate, what does that teach us about the value of our bodies in the spaces that tokenize our minds?

And of course this is not unique to Audre Lorde. June Jordan's records show that even as she was battling breast cancer, UC Berkeley would not grant her medical leave or the breaks from teaching that she repeatedly wrote her administration to request in 2001, months before she died, less than two years after her Black feminist Berkeley colleague Barbara Christian died. This is not ancient history. This is twenty-first-century economics, and the austerity measures, scarcity narratives, and exploitative practices of the university have only gotten more severe with time.

Let us be clear. Universities keep huge endowments, money on reserve, because they are supposed to keep money. They will always tell you they cannot afford you. They will not spend their money to save the life of a Black feminist. Poet Laureate though she may be. Let us be clear. The universities that we mistakenly label as our bright quirky only refuge for Black brilliance have worked our geniuses to death, and have denied us help when we asked for it. The universities that employed June Jordan, Audre Lorde, and so many others watched cancer eat away at our geniuses, as they simultaneously ate away at Black women's labor. An institution knows how to preserve itself and it knows that Black feminists are a trouble more useful as dead invocation than as live troublemakers, raising concerns in faculty meetings. And those institutions continue to make money and garner prestige off of their once affiliated now dead faculty members.

The university was not created to save my life. The university is not about the preservation of a bright brown body. The university will use me alive and use me dead. The university does not intend to love me. The university does not know how to love me. The university in fact, does not love me. But the universe does.

Survival is what Audre Lorde calls "a now that can breed futures/like bread in our children's mouths/so their dreams will not reflect the death of ours." But we, Black feminists of my generation navigating our relationships to the academy, are the children. And we must not ignore the lessons of our ancestors, nor the futures that they have made possible to us through their creativity and persistence.

*Should I take a tenure-track job anywhere in the world among any manner of quiet or loud racists just to have the security of a health care plan that will become more useful every year because of the stress and ideological violence I suffer on the job? Does it honor my ancestors for me to uproot myself from the communities that have nurtured me, that are my realest sources of sustenance and that I must also sustain with my presence and my love? Did Audre Lorde and June Jordan teach in prisons, coffee shops, living rooms, and subways so that I could pretend that the university has all the real classrooms and everything else must be a side hustle?*

These are the questions I asked myself as I held those denied requests for medical leave in my hands. And again as I turned down tenure-track jobs.

And I decided that Audre Lorde is right. Survival is a promise. It is not a promise that any university or non-profit organization can make to me. It is a promise that I make with my currently breathing body to the ancestors who move through it. It is a promise I make in honor of the deaths that make this clarity not only possible, but unavoidable. Survival is a promise. Which is why I am living an experimental intellectual life, dedicated to the creation of accessible autonomous school systems (in the living room and on the internet—blackfeministmind.wordpress.com) that bring the work of Black feminist ancestors and elders to our communities directly and commit to creating collective systems of health and mutual support that allow our genius to be accountable to, accounted for, sustained by, and shared by the unendowed oppressed communities that are the source of all genius and transformation. *Survival is a promise. A covenant between my ancestors, my living communities and this body that is 100 percent composed of the love that connects them.*

I am still working it out. I am uninsured and unaffiliated and living a life that overflows with love shared across space and time. I survive, not because I am barely alive, but because I am flagrantly alive in the sight of my ancestors. The universe loves us. And we sell ourselves cheap when we forget. Our ancestors are teaching us what we deserve. May we never sell our legacy for a mess of ego and scholar-styled swag. May we refuse to exploit our legacy in order to earn more exploitation. May we remember who we are. The shape of Audre Lorde's impact includes her achievements, her words, her losses, and everything she went through that we should not repeat as if we did not know.

I love the word *survival*. It sounds to me like a promise worth keeping.

## Audre Lorde

# I Am Your Sister: Black Women Organizing Across Sexualities

Whenever I come to Medgar Evers College I always feel a thrill of anticipation and delight because it feels like coming home, like talking to family, having a chance to speak about things that are very important to me with people who matter the most. And this is particularly true whenever I talk at the Women's Center. But, as with all families, we sometimes find it difficult to deal constructively with the genuine differences between us and to recognize that unity does not require that we be identical to each other. Black women are not one great vat of homogenized chocolate milk. We have many different faces, and we do not have to become each other in order to work together.

It is not easy for me to speak here with you as a Black Lesbian feminist, recognizing that some of the ways in which I identify myself make it difficult for you to hear me. But meeting across difference always requires mutual stretching, and until you *can* hear me as a Black Lesbian feminist, our strengths will not be truly available to each other as Black women.

Because I feel it is urgent that we not waste each other's resources, that we recognize each sister on her own terms so that we may better work together toward our mutual survival, I speak here about heterosexism and homophobia, two grave barriers to organizing among Black women. And so that we have a common language between us, I would like to define some of the terms I use. HETEROSEXISM: A belief in the inherent superiority of one form of loving over all others and thereby the right to dominance. HOMOPHOBIA: A terror surrounding feelings of love for members of the same sex and thereby a hatred of those feelings in others.

In the 1960s, when liberal white people decided that they didn't want to appear racist, they wore dashikis, and danced Black, and ate Black, and even married Black, but they did not want to feel Black or even think Black, so they never even questioned the textures of their daily living (why should flesh-colored bandaids always be pink), and then they always wondered, "Why are those Black folks always taking offense so easily at the least little thing? Some of our best friends are Black . . .

Well, it is not necessary for some of your best friends to be Lesbian, although some of them probably are, no doubt. But it is necessary for you to stop oppressing me through false judgement. I do not want you to ignore my identity, nor do I want you to make it an insurmountable barrier between our sharing of strengths.

When I say I am a Black feminist, I mean I recognize that my power as well as my primary oppressions come as a result of my Blackness as well as my womanness, and therefore my struggles on both these fronts are inseparable.

When I say I am a Black Lesbian, I mean I am a woman whose primary focus of loving, physical as well as emotional, is directed to women. It does not mean I hate men. Far from it. The harshest attacks I have ever heard against Black men come from those women who are intimately bound to them and cannot free themselves from a subservient and silent position. I would never presume to speak about Black men the way I have heard some of my straight sisters talk about the men they are attached to. And of course that concerns me, because it reflects a situation of non-communication in the heterosexual Black community that is far more truly threatening than the existence of Black Lesbians.

What does this have to do with Black women organizing?

I have heard it said—usually behind my back—that Black Lesbians are not normal. But what is normal in this deranged society by which we are all trapped? I remember, and so do many of you, when being Black was considered NOT NORMAL, when they talked about us in whispers, tried to paint us, lynch us, bleach us, ignore us, pretend we did not exist. We called that racism.

I have heard it said that Black Lesbians are a threat to the Black family. But when 50 percent of children born to Black women are born out of wedlock, and 30 percent of all Black families are headed by women without husbands, we need to broaden and redefine what we mean by family.

I have heard it said that Black Lesbians will mean the death of the race. Yet Black Lesbians bear children in exactly the same way other women bear children, and a Lesbian household is simply another kind of family. Ask my son and daughter.

The terror of Black Lesbians is buried in that deep inner place where we have been taught to fear all difference—to kill it or ignore it. Be assured—loving women is not a communicable disease. You don't catch it like the common cold. Yet the one accusation that seems to render even the most vocal straight Black woman totally silent and ineffective is the suggestion that she might be a Black Lesbian.

If someone says you're Russian and you know you're not, you don't collapse into stunned silence. Even if someone calls you a bigamist, or a child-beater, and you know you're not, you don't crumple into bits. You say it's not true, and keep on printing the posters. But let anyone, particularly a Black man, accuse a straight Black woman of being a Black Lesbian, and right away that sister becomes immobilized, as if that is the most horrible thing she could be, and must at all costs be proven false. That is homophobia. It is a waste of woman energy, and it puts a terrible weapon into the hands of your enemies to be used against you to silence you, to keep you docile and in line. It also serves to keep us isolated and apart.

I have heard it said that Black Lesbians are not political, that we have not been and are not involved in the struggles of Black people. But when I taught Black and Puerto Rican students writing at City College in the SEEK program in the sixties I was a Black Lesbian. I was a Black Lesbian when I helped organize and fight for the Black Studies Department of John Jay College. And because I was fifteen years younger then and less sure of myself, at one crucial moment I yielded to pressures that said I should step back for a Black man even though I knew him to be a serious error of choice, and I did, and he was. But I was a Black Lesbian then.

When my girl friends and I went out in the car one July fourth night after fireworks with cans of white spray paint and our kids asleep in the back of the car, one of us staying behind to keep the motor running and watch the kids while the other two worked our way down the suburban New Jersey street, spraying white paint over the black jockey statues and their little red jackets too, we were Lesbians.

When I drove through the Mississippi delta to Jackson in 1968 with a group of Black students from Tougaloo, another car full of redneck kids trying to bump us off the road all the way back into town, I was a Black Lesbian.

When I weened my daughter in 1963 to go to Washington in August to work in the coffee tents along with Lena Horne, making coffee for the marshals because that was what most Black women did in the 1963 March on Washington, I was a Black Lesbian.

When I taught a poetry workshop at Tougaloo, a small Black college in Mississippi, where white rowdies shot up the edge of campus every night, and I felt the joy of seeing young Black poets find their voices and power through words in our mutual growth, I was a Black Lesbian. And there are strong Black poets today who date their growth and awareness from those workshops.

When Yoli and I cooked curried chicken and beans and rice and took our extra blankets and pillows up the hill to the striking students occupying buildings at City College in 1969, demanding open admissions and the right to an education, I was a Black Lesbian. When I walked through the midnight hallways of Lehman College that same year, carrying Midol and Kotex pads for the young Black radical women taking part in the action, and we tried to persuade them that their place in the revolution was not ten paces behind Black men, that spreading their legs to the guys on the tables in the cafeteria was not a revolutionary act no matter what the brothers said, I was a Black Lesbian. When I picketed for Welfare Mothers' Rights, and against the enforced sterilization of young Black girls, when I fought institutionalized racism in the New York City schools, I was a Black Lesbian.

But you did not know it, because we did not identify ourselves, so now you can still say that Black Lesbians and gay men have nothing to do with the struggles of the Black Nation.

And I am not alone.

When you read the words of Langston Hughes you are reading the words of a Black gay man. When you read the words of Alice Dunbar-Nelson and

Angelina Weld Grimké, poets of the Harlem Renaissance, you are reading the words of Black Lesbians. When you listen to the life-affirming voices of Bessie Smith and Ma Rainey, you are hearing Black Lesbian women. When you see the plays and read the words of Lorraine Hansberry, you are reading the words of a woman who loved women deeply.

Today, some of the most active and engaged members of "Art Against Apartheid," which is making visible and immediate our cultural responsibilities against the tragedy of South Africa, are Lesbians and gay men. We have organizations such as the National Coalition of Black Lesbians and Gays, Dykes Against Racism Everywhere, and Men of All Colors Together, all of whom are committed to and engaged in anti-racist activity.

Homophobia and heterosexism mean you allow yourselves to be robbed of the sisterhood and strength of Black Lesbian women because you are afraid of being called a Lesbian yourself. Yet we share so many concerns as Black women, so much work to be done. The urgency of the destruction of our Black children and the theft of young Black minds are joint urgencies. Black children shot down or doped up on the streets of our cities are priorities for all of us. The fact of Black women's blood flowing with grim regularity in the streets and living rooms of Black communities is not a Black Lesbian rumor. It is sad statistical fact. The fact that there is a widening and dangerous lack of communication around our differences between Black women and men is not a Black Lesbian plot. It is a fact that becomes starkly clarified as we see our young people becoming more and more uncaring of each other. Young Black boys believing that they can define their manhood between a sixth grade girl's legs, growing up believing that Black women and girls are the fitting target for their justifiable furies rather than the racist structures grinding us all into dust, these are not Black Lesbian myths. These are sad realities of Black communities today and of immediate concern to us all. We cannot afford to waste each other's energies in our common battles.

What does homophobia mean? It means that high-powered Black women are told it is not safe to attend a conference on the status of women in Nairobi simply because we are Lesbians. It means that in a political action, you rob yourselves of the vital insight and energies of political women such as

Betty Powell and Barbara Smith and Gwendolyn Rogers and Raymina Mays and Robin Christian and Yvonne Flowers. It means another instance of the divide and conquer routine.

How do we organize around our differences, neither denying them nor blowing them up out of proportion?

The first step is an effort of will on your part. Try to remember, to keep certain facts in mind. Black Lesbians are not apolitical. We have been a part of every freedom struggle within this country. Black Lesbians are not a threat to the Black family. Many of us have families of our own. We are not white, and we are not a disease. We are women who love women. This does not mean we are going to assault your daughters in an alley on Nostrand Avenue. It does not mean we are about to attack you if we pay you a compliment on your dress. It does not mean we only think about sex, any more than you only think about sex.

Even if you *do* believe any of these stereotypes about Black Lesbians, begin to practice *acting* like you don't believe them. Just as racist stereotypes are the problem of the white people who believe them, so also are homophobic stereotypes the problem of the heterosexuals who believe them. In other words, those stereotypes are yours to solve, not mine, and they are a terrible and wasteful barrier to our working together. I am not your enemy. We do not have to become each other's unique experiences and insights in order to share what we have learned through our particular battles for survival as Black women . . .

There was a poster in the sixties that was very popular: HE'S NOT BLACK, HE'S MY BROTHER! It used to infuriate me because it implied that the two were mutually exclusive—"he" couldn't be both brother and Black. Well, I do not want to be tolerated, nor misnamed. I want to be recognized.

I am a Black Lesbian, and I *am* your sister.

# Barbara Smith
# Toward a Black Feminist Criticism

*For all my sisters, especially Beverly and Demita*

I do not know where to begin. Long before I tried to write this, I felt that I was attempting something unprecedented, something dangerous merely by writing about Black women writers from a feminist perspective and about Black lesbian writers from any perspective at all. These things have not been done. Not by white male critics, expectedly. Not by Black male critics. Not by white women critics who think of themselves as feminists. And most crucially not by Black women critics who, although they pay the most attention to Black women writers as a group, seldom use a consistent feminist analysis or write about Black lesbian literature. All segments of the literary world—whether establishment, progressive, Black, female, or lesbian—do not know, or at least act as if they do not know, that Black women writers and Black lesbian writers exist.

For whites, this specialized lack of knowledge is inextricably connected to their not knowing in any concrete or politically transforming way that Black women of any description dwell in this place. Black women's existence, experience, and culture and the brutally complex systems of oppression which shape these are in the "real world" of white and/or male consciousness beneath consideration, invisible, unknown.

This invisibility, which goes beyond anything that either Black men or white women experience and tell about in their writing, is one reason it is so difficult for me to know where to start. It seems overwhelming to break such a massive silence. Even more numbing, however, is the realization that so many of the women who will read this have not yet noticed us missing either from their reading matter, their politics, or their lives. It is galling that ostensible feminists and acknowledged lesbians have been so blinded to the implications of any womanhood that is not white womanhood and that they have yet to struggle with the deep racism in themselves that is at the source of this blindness.

I think of the thousands and thousands of books, magazines, and articles which have been devoted, by this time, to the subject of women's writing and I am filled with rage at the fraction of those pages that mention Black and other third-world women. I finally do not know how to begin because in 1978 I want to be writing this for a Black feminist publication, for Black women who know and love these writers as I do and who, if they do not yet know their names, have at least profoundly felt the pain of their absence.

The conditions that coalesce into the impossibilities of this essay have as much to do with politics as with the practice of literature. Any discussion of Afro-American writers can rightfully begin with the fact that for most of the time we have been in this country we have been categorically denied not only literacy, but the most minimal possibility of a decent human life. In her landmark essay, "In Search of Our Mothers' Gardens," Alice Walker discloses how the political, economic, and social restrictions of slavery and racism have historically stunted the creative lives of Black women.[1]

At the present time I feel that the politics of feminism have a direct relationship to the state of Black women's literature. A viable, autonomous Black feminist movement in this country would open up the space needed for the exploration of Black women's lives and the creation of consciously Black woman–identified art. At the same time a redefinition of the goals and strategies of the white feminist movement would lead to much-needed change in the focus and content of what is now generally accepted as women's culture.

I want to make in this essay some connections between the politics of Black women's lives, what we write about, and our situation as artists. In order to do this I will look at how Black women have been viewed critically by outsiders, demonstrate the necessity for Black feminist criticism, and try to understand what the existence or non-existence of Black lesbian writing reveals about the state of Black women's culture and the intensity of *all* Black women's oppression.

The role that criticism plays in making a body of literature recognizable and real hardly needs to be explained here. The necessity for non-hostile and perceptive analysis of works written by persons outside the "mainstream" of white/male cultural rule has been proven by the Black cultural resurgence of the 1960s and '70s and by the even more recent growth of feminist literary scholarship. For books to be real and remembered they have to be talked about. For books to be understood they must be examined in such a way that the basic intentions of the writers are at least considered. Because of racism Black literature has usually been viewed as a discrete subcategory of American literature, and there have been Black critics of Black literature who did much to keep it alive long before it caught the attention of whites. Before the advent of specifically feminist criticism in this decade, books by white women, on the other hand, were not clearly perceived as the cultural manifestation of an oppressed people. It took the surfacing of the second wave of the North American feminist movement to expose the fact that *these* works contain a stunningly accurate record of the impact of patriarchal values and practice upon the lives of women and more significantly that literature by women provides essential insights into female experience.

In speaking about the current situation of Black women writers, it is important to remember that the existence of a feminist movement was an essential pre-condition to the growth of feminist literature, criticism, and women's studies, which focused at the beginning almost entirely upon investigations of literature. The fact that a parallel Black feminist movement has been much slower in evolving cannot help but have an impact upon the situation of Black women writers and artists and explains in part why during this very same period we have been so ignored.

There is no political movement to give power or support to those who want to examine Black women's experience through studying our history, literature, and culture. There is no political presence that demands a minimal level of consciousness and respect from those who write or talk about our lives. Finally, there is not a developed body of Black feminist political theory whose assumptions could be used in the study of Black women's art. When Black women's books are dealt with at all, it is usually in the context of Black literature, which largely ignores the implications of sexual politics. When white women look at Black women's works they are of course ill-equipped to deal with the subtleties of racial politics. A Black feminist approach to literature that embodies the realization that the politics of sex as well as the politics of race and class are crucially interlocking factors in the works of Black women writers is an absolute necessity. Until a Black feminist criticism exists we will not even know what these writers mean. The citations from a variety of critics which follow prove that without a Black feminist critical perspective not only are books by Black women misunderstood, they are destroyed in the process.

Jerry H. Bryant, *The Nation*'s white male reviewer of Alice Walker's *In Love & Trouble: Stories of Black Women*, wrote in 1973:

> The subtitle of the collection, "Stories of Black Women," is probably an attempt by the publisher to exploit not only black subjects but feminine ones. There is nothing feminist about these stories, however.[2]

Blackness and feminism are to his mind mutually exclusive and peripheral to the act of writing fiction. Bryant of course does not consider that Walker might have titled the work herself, nor did he apparently read the book, which unequivocally reveals the author's feminist consciousness.

In *The Negro Novel in America*, a book that Black critics recognize as one of the worst examples of white pseudo-scholarship, Robert Bone cavalierly dismisses Ann Petry's classic, *The Street*. He perceives it to be " . . . a superficial social analysis" of how slums victimize their Black inhabitants.[3] He further objects that:

> It is an attempt to interpret slum life in terms of *Negro* experience, when a larger frame of reference is required. As Alain Locke has observed, "*Knock on Any Door* is superior to *The Street* because it designates class and environment, rather than mere race and environment, as its antagonist."[4]

Neither Robert Bone nor Alain Locke, the Black male critic he cites, can recognize that *The Street* is one of the best delineations in literature of how sex, race, *and* class interact to oppress Black women.

In her review of Toni Morrison's *Sula* for the *New York Times Book Review* in 1973, putative feminist Sara Blackburn makes similarly racist comments. She writes:

> Toni Morrison is far too talented to remain only a marvelous recorder of the black side of provincial American life. If she is to maintain the large and serious audience she deserves, she is going to have to address a riskier contemporary reality than this beautiful but nevertheless distanced novel. *And if she does this, it seems to me that she might easily transcend that early and unintentionally limiting classification "black woman writer" and take her place among the most serious, important and talented American novelists now working.*[5] [Italics mine.]

Recognizing Morrison's exquisite gift, Blackburn unashamedly asserts that Morrison is "too talented" to deal with mere Black folk, particularly those double nonentities, Black women. In order to be accepted as "serious," "important," "talented," and "American," she must obviously focus her efforts upon chronicling the doings of white men.

The mishandling of Black women writers by whites is paralleled more often by their not being handled at all, particularly in feminist criticism. Although Elaine Showalter in her review essay on literary criticism for *Signs* states that "the best work being produced today [in feminist criticism] is exacting and cosmopolitan," her essay is neither.[6] If it were, she would not have failed to mention a single Black or third-world woman writer, whether "major" or "minor" (in her questionable categories). That she also does not even hint that lesbian writers of any color exist renders her purported overview virtually meaningless. Showalter obviously thinks that the identities of being Black and female are mutually exclusive, as this statement illustrates:

Furthermore, there are other literary subcultures (black American novelists, for example) whose history offers a precedent for feminist scholarship to use.[7]

The idea of critics like Showalter *using* Black literature is chilling, a case of barely disguised cultural imperialism. The final insult is that she footnotes the preceding remark by pointing readers to works on Black literature by white males Robert Bone and Roger Rosenblatt!

Two recent works by white women, Ellen Moers' *Literary Women: The Great Writers* and Patricia Meyer Spacks' *The Female Imagination*, evidence the same racist flaw.[8] Moers includes the names of four Black and one Puertorriquena writer in her seventy pages of bibliographical notes and does not deal at all with third-world women in the body of her book. Spacks refers to a comparison between Negroes (sic) and women in Mary Ellmann's *Thinking About Women* under the index entry, "blacks, women and." "*Black Boy* (Wright)" is the preceding entry. Nothing follows. Again there is absolutely no recognition that Black and female identity ever coexist, specifically in a group of Black women writers. Perhaps one can assume that these women do not know who Black women writers are, that they have had little opportunity like most Americans to learn about them. Perhaps. Their ignorance seems suspiciously selective, however, particularly in the light of the dozens of truly obscure white women writers they are able to unearth. Spacks was herself employed at Wellesley College at the same time that Alice Walker was there teaching one of the first courses on Black women writers in the country.

I am not trying to encourage racist criticism about Black women writers like that of Sara Blackburn, to cite only one example. As a beginning I would at least like to see in print white women's acknowledgment of the contradictions of who and what are being left out of their research and writing.[9]

Black male critics can also *act* as if they do not know that Black women writers exist and are, of course, hampered by an inability to comprehend Black women's experience in sexual as well as racial terms. Unfortunately, there are also those who are as virulently sexist in their treatment of Black women writers as their white male counterparts. Darwin Turner's discussion of Zora Neale Hurston in his *In a Minor Chord: Three Afro-American Writers and Their Search for Identity* is a frightening example of the near assassination of a great Black woman writer.[10] His descriptions of her and her work as "Coy," "irrational," "superficial," and "shallow" bear no relationship to the actual quality of her achievements. Turner is completely insensitive to the sexual political dynamics of Hurston's life and writing.

In a recent interview the notoriously misogynist writer, Ishmael Reed, comments in this way upon the low sales of his newest novel:

> . . . but the book only sold 8,000 copies. I don't mind giving out the figure: 8,000. Maybe if I was one of those young *female* Afro-American writers that are so hot now, I'd sell more. You know, fill my books with ghetto women who can *do no wrong.* . . . But come on, I think I could have sold 8,000 copies by myself.[11]

The politics of the situation of Black women are glaringly illuminated by this statement. Neither Reed nor his white male interviewer has the slightest compunction about attacking Black women in print. They need not fear widespread public denunciation since Reed's statement is in perfect agreement with the values of a society that hates Black people, women, and Black women. Finally the two of them feel free to base their actions on the premise that Black women are powerless to alter either their political or cultural oppression.

In her introduction to "A Bibliography of Works Written by American Black Women" Ora Williams quotes some of the reactions of her colleagues toward her efforts to do research on Black women. She writes:

> Others have reacted negatively with such statements as, "I really don't think you are going to find very much written," "Have 'they' written anything that is any good?" and, "I wouldn't go overboard with this woman's lib thing." When discussions touched on the possibility of teaching a course in which emphasis would

be on the literature by Black women, one response was, "Ha, ha. That will certainly be the most nothing course ever offered!"[12]

A remark by Alice Walker encapsulates what all the preceding examples indicate about the position of Black women writers and the reasons for the damaging criticism about them. She responds to her interviewer's question, "Why do you think that the black woman writer has been so ignored in America? Does she have even more difficulty than the black male writer, who perhaps has just begun to gain recognition?" Walker replies:

> There are two reasons why the black woman writer is not taken as seriously as the black male writer. One is that she's a woman. Critics seem unusually ill-equipped to intelligently discuss and analyze the works of black women. Generally, they do not even make the attempt; they prefer, rather, to talk about the lives of black women writers, not about what they write. And, since black women writers are not—it would seem—very likable—until recently they were the least willing worshippers of male supremacy—comments about them tend to be cruel.[13]

A convincing case for Black feminist criticism can obviously be built solely upon the basis of the negativity of what already exists. It is far more gratifying, however, to demonstrate its necessity by showing how it can serve to reveal for the first time the profound subtleties of this particular body of literature.

Before suggesting how a Black feminist approach might be used to examine a specific work I will outline some of the principles that I think a Black feminist critic could use. Beginning with a primary commitment to exploring how both sexual and racial politics and Black and female identity are inextricable elements in Black women's writing, she would also work from the assumption that writings by Black women constitute an identifiable literary tradition. Her familiarity with these writers would have shown her that not only is theirs a verifiable historical tradition that parallels in time

the tradition of Black men and white women writing in this country, but
that thematically, stylistically, aesthetically, and conceptually Black women
writers manifest common approaches to the act of creating literature as a
direct result of the specific political, social, and economic experience they
have been obliged to share. The way, for example, that Zora Neale Hurston, Margaret Walker, Toni Morrison, and Alice Walker incorporate the
traditional Black female activities of rootworking, herbal medicine, conjure,
and midwifery into the fabric of their stories is not mere coincidence, nor
is their use of specifically Black female language to express their own and
their characters' thoughts accidental. The use of Black women's language and
cultural experience in books *by* Black women *about* Black women results in a
miraculously rich coalescing of form and content and also takes their writing
far beyond the confines of white/male literary structures. The Black feminist
critic would find innumerable commonalities in works by Black women.

Another principle which grows out of the concept of a tradition and which
would also help to strengthen this tradition would be for the critic to look
first for precedents and insights in interpretation within the works of other
Black women. In other words she would think and write out of her own
identity and not try to graft the ideas or methodology of white/male literary
thought upon the precious materials of Black women's art. Black feminist
criticism would by definition be highly innovative, embodying the daring
spirit of the works themselves. The Black feminist critic would be constantly
aware of the political implications of her work and would assert the connections between it and the political situation of all Black women. Logically
developed, Black feminist criticism would owe its existence to a Black feminist movement while at the same time contributing ideas that women in the
movement could use.

Black feminist criticism applied to a particular work can overturn previous assumptions about it and expose for the first time its actual dimensions.
At the "Lesbians and Literature" discussion at the 1976 Modern Language
Association convention Bertha Harris suggested that if in a woman writer's
work a sentence refuses to do what it is supposed to do, if there are strong
images of women and if there is a refusal to be linear, the result is innately

lesbian literature. As usual, I wanted to see if these ideas might be applied to the Black women writers that I know and quickly realized that many of their works were, in Harris' sense, lesbian. Not because women are "lovers," but because they are the central figures, are positively portrayed, and have pivotal relationships with one another. The form and language of these works is also nothing like what white patriarchal culture requires or expects.

I was particularly struck by the way in which both of Toni Morrison's novels, *The Bluest Eye* and *Sula*, could be explored from this new perspective.[14] In both works the relationships between girls and women are essential, yet at the same time physical sexuality is overtly expressed only between men and women. Despite the apparent heterosexuality of the female characters I discovered in re-reading *Sula* that it works as a lesbian novel not only because of the passionate friendship between Sula and Nel, but because of Morrison's consistently critical stance toward the heterosexual institutions of male/female relationships, marriage, and the family. Consciously or not, Morrison's work poses both lesbian and feminist questions about Black women's autonomy and their impact upon each other's lives.

Sula and Nel find each other in 1922 when each of them is twelve, on the brink of puberty and the discovery of boys. Even as awakening sexuality "clotted their dreams," each girl desires "a someone," obviously female, with whom to share her feelings (p. 51). Morrison writes:

> . . . for it was in dreams that the two girls had met. Long before Edna Finch's Mellow House opened, even before they marched through the chocolate halls of Garfield Primary School . . . they had already made each other's acquaintance in the delirium of their noon dreams. They were solitary little girls whose loneliness was so profound it intoxicated them and sent them stumbling into Technicolored visions that always included a presence, a someone who, quite like the dreamer, shared the delight of the dream. When Nel, an only child, sat on the steps of her back porch surrounded by the high silence of her mother's incredibly orderly house, feeling the neatness pointing at her back, she studied the

poplars and fell easily into a picture of herself lying on a flow-
ered bed, tangled in her own hair, waiting for some fiery prince.
He approached but never quite arrived. But always, watching
the dream along with her, were some smiling sympathetic eyes.
Someone as interested as she herself in the flow of her imagined
hair, the thickness of the mattress of flowers, the voile sleeves that
closed below her elbows in gold-threaded cuffs.

Similarly, Sula, also an only child, but wedged into a household of throbbing disorder constantly awry with things, people,
voices and the slamming of doors, spent hours in the attic behind
a roll of linoleum galloping through her own mind on a gray-and-
white horse tasting sugar and smelling roses in full view of someone who shared both the taste and the speed.

So when they met, first in those chocolate halls and next through
the ropes of the swing, they felt the ease and comfort of old friends.
Because each had discovered years before that they were neither
white nor male, and that all freedom and triumph was forbidden
to them, they had set about creating something else to be. Their
meeting was fortunate, for it let them use each other to grow on.
Daughters of distant mothers and incomprehensible fathers (Sula's
because he was dead; Nel's because he wasn't), they found in each
other's eyes the intimacy they were looking for. (pp. 51–52)

As this beautiful passage shows, their relationship, from the very beginning,
is suffused with an erotic romanticism. The dreams in which they are initially drawn to each other are actually complementary aspects of the same
sensuous fairy tale. Nel imagines a "fiery prince" who never quite arrives
while Sula gallops like a prince "on a gray-and-white horse."[15] The "real
world" of patriarchy requires, however, that they channel this energy away
from each other to the opposite sex. Lorraine Bethel explains this dynamic
in her essay "Conversations with Ourselves: Black Female Relationships in
Toni Cade Bambara's *Gorilla, My Love* and Toni Morrison's *Sula*." She writes:

I am not suggesting that Sula and Nel are being consciously sexual, or that their relationship has an overt lesbian nature. I am
suggesting, however, that there is a certain sensuality in their
interactions that is reinforced by the mirror-like nature of their
relationship. Sexual exploration and coming of age is a natural
part of adolescence. Sula and Nel discover men together, and
though their flirtations with males are an important part of their
sexual exploration, the sensuality that they experience in each
other's company is equally important.[16]

Sula and Net must also struggle with the constrictions of racism upon their
lives. The knowledge that "they were neither white nor male" is the inherent
explanation of their need for each other. Morrison depicts in literature the
necessary bonding that has always taken place between Black women for the
sake of barest survival. Together the two girls can find the courage to create
themselves.

Their relationship is severed only when Nel marries Jude, an unexcep-
tional young man who thinks of her as "the hem—the tuck and fold that
hid his raveling edges" (p. 83). Sula's inventive wildness cannot overcome
social pressure of the influence of Nel's parents who "had succeeded in rubbing down to a dull glow any sparkle or splutter she had" (p. 83). Nel falls
prey to convention while Sula escapes it. Yet at the wedding which ends the
first phase of their relationship, Nel's final action is to look past her husband
toward Sula:

> . . . slim figure in blue, gliding, with just a hint of a strut, down
> the path toward the road. . . . Even from the rear Nel could tell
> that it was Sula and that she was smiling; that something deep
> down in that litheness was amused. (p. 85)

When Sula returns ten years later, her rebelliousness full-blown, a major
source of the town's suspicions is the fact that although she is almost thirty,

she is still unmarried. Sula's grandmother, Eva, does not hesitate to bring up the matter as soon as she arrives. She asks:

> "When you gone to get married? You need to have some babies. It'll settle you. . . . Ain't no woman got no business floatin' around without no man." (p. 92)

Sula replies: "'I don't want to make somebody else. I want to make myself'" (p. 92). Self-definition is a dangerous activity for any woman to engage in, especially a Black one, and it expectedly earns Sula pariah status in Medallion.

Morrison clearly points out that it is the fact that Sula has not been tamed or broken by the exigencies of heterosexual family life which most galls the others. She writes:

> Among the weighty evidence piling up was the fact that Sula did not look her age. She was near thirty and, unlike them, had lost no teeth, suffered no bruises, developed no ring of fat at the waist or pocket at the back of her neck. (p. 115)

In other words she is not a domestic serf, a woman run down by obligatory childbearing or a victim of battering. Sula also sleeps with the husbands of the town once and then discards them, needing them even less than her own mother did for sexual gratification and affection. The town reacts to her disavowal of patriarchal values by becoming fanatically serious about their own family obligations, as if in this way they might counteract Sula's radical criticism of their lives.

Sula's presence in her community functions much like the presence of lesbians everywhere to expose the contradictions of supposedly "normal" life. The opening paragraph of the essay "Woman Identified Woman" has amazing relevance as an explanation of Sula's position and character in the novel. It asks:

What is a lesbian? A lesbian is the rage of all women condensed
to the point of explosion. She is the woman who, often beginning at an extremely early age, acts in accordance with her inner
compulsion to be a more complete and freer human being than
her society—perhaps then, but certainly later—cares to allow
her. These needs and actions, over a period of years, bring her
into painful conflict with people, situations, the accepted ways of
thinking, feeling and behaving, until she is in a state of continual
war with everything around her, and usually with herself. She
may not be fully conscious of the political implications of what
for her began as personal necessity, but on some level she has not
been able to accept the limitations and oppression laid on her by
the most basic role of her society—the female role.[17]

The limitations of the Black female role are even greater in a racist and sexist
society, as is the amount of courage it takes to challenge them. It is no wonder that the townspeople see Sula's independence as imminently dangerous.

Morrison is also careful to show the reader that despite their years of separation and their opposing paths, Nel and Sula's relationship retains its pri-
macy for each of them. Nel feels transformed when Sula returns and thinks:

It was like getting the use of an eye back, having a cataract
removed. Her old friend had come home. Sula. Who made her
laugh, who made her see old things with new eyes, in whose presence she felt clever, gentle and a little raunchy. (p. 95)

Laughing together in the familiar "rib-scraping" way, Nel feels "new, soft
and new" (p. 98). Morrison uses here the visual imagery which symbolizes
the women's closeness throughout the novel.

Sula fractures this closeness, however, by sleeping with Nel's husband, an
act of little import according to her system of values. Nel, of course, cannot
understand. Sula thinks ruefully:

Nel was the one person who had wanted nothing from her, who had accepted all aspects of her. Now she wanted everything, and all because of that. Nel was the first person who had been real to her, whose name she knew, who had seen as she had the slant of life that made it possible to stretch it to its limits. Now Nel was one of them. (pp. 119–120)

Sula also thinks at the realization of losing Nel about how unsatisfactory her relationships with men have been and admits:

She had been looking all along for a friend, and it took her a while to discover that a lover was not a comrade and could never be— for a woman. (p. 121)

The nearest that Sula comes to actually loving a man is in a brief affair with Ajax, and what she values most about him is the intellectual companionship he provides, the brilliance he "allows" her to show.

Sula's feelings about sex with men are also consistent with a lesbian interpretation of the novel. Morrison writes:

She went to bed with men as frequently as she could. It was the only place where she could find what she was looking for: *misery and the ability to feel deep sorrow.* . . . During the lovemaking she found and needed to find the cutting edge. When she left off cooperating with her body and began to assert herself in the act, particles of strength gathered in her like steel shavings drawn to a spacious magnetic center, forming a tight cluster that nothing, it seemed, could break. *And there was utmost irony and outrage in lying under someone, in a position of surrender, feeling her own abiding strength and limitless power.* . . . When her partner disengaged himself, she looked up at him in wonder trying to recall his name . . . waiting impatiently for him to turn away . . . *leaving her to the postcoital*

*privateness in which she met herself, welcomed herself, and joined herself
in matchless harmony.* (pp. 122–123)[Italics mine.]

Sula uses men for sex, which results not in communion with them, but in her
further delving into self.

Ultimately the deepest communion and communication in the novel
occurs between two women who love each other. After their last painful
meeting, which does not bring reconciliation, Sula thinks as Nel leaves her:

> So she will walk on down that road, her back so straight in that
> old green coat, thinking how much I have cost her and never
> remember the days when we were two throats and one eye and
> we had no price. (p. 147)

It is difficult to imagine a more evocative metaphor for what women can be
to each other, the "pricelessness" they achieve in refusing to sell themselves
for male approval, the total worth that they can only find in each other's eyes.

Decades later the novel concludes with Nel's final comprehension of the
source of the grief that has plagued her from the time her husband walked
out. Morrison writes:

> "All that time, all that time, I thought I was missing Jude." And
> the loss pressed down on her chest and came up into her throat.
> "We was girls together," she said as though explaining something.
> "O Lord, Sula," she cried, "girl, girl, girlgirlgirl."
>      It was a fine cry—loud and long—but it had no bottom and it
> had no top, just circles and circles of sorrow. (p. 174)

Again Morrison exquisitely conveys what women, Black women, mean to
each other. This final passage verifies the depth of Sula and Nel's relationship
and its centrality to an accurate interpretation of the work.

*Sula* is an exceedingly lesbian novel in the emotions expressed, in the

definition of female character, and in the way that the politics of heterosexuality are portrayed. The very meaning of lesbianism is being expanded
in literature, just as it is being redefined through politics. The confusion that
many readers have felt about *Sula* may well have a lesbian explanation. If one
sees Sula's inexplicable "evil" and non-conformity as the evil of not being
male-identified, many elements in the novel become clear. The work might
be clearer still if Morrison had approached her subject with the consciousness that a lesbian relationship was at least a possibility for her characters.
Obviously Morrison did not intend the reader to perceive Sula and Nel's
relationship as inherently lesbian. However, this lack of intention only shows
the way in which heterosexist assumptions can veil what may logically be
expected to occur in a work. What I have tried to do here is not to prove that
Morrison wrote something that she did not, but to point out how a Black
feminist critical perspective at least allows consideration of this level of the
novel's meaning.

In her interview in *Conditions: One* Adrienne Rich talks about unconsum-
mated relationships and the need to re-evaluate the meaning of intense yet
supposedly non-erotic connections between women. She asserts:

> We need a lot more documentation about what actually happened;
> I think we can also imagine it, because we know it happened—
> we know it out of our own lives.[18]

Black women are still in the position of having to "imagine," discover, and
verify Black lesbian literature because so little has been written from an
avowedly lesbian perspective. The near non-existence of Black lesbian literature which other Black lesbians and I so deeply feel has everything to do
with the politics of our lives, the total suppression of identity that all Black
women, lesbian or not, must face. This literary silence is again intensified
by the unavailability of an autonomous Black feminist movement through
which we could fight our oppression and also begin to name ourselves.

In a speech, "The Autonomy of Black Lesbian Women," Wilmette Brown comments upon the connection between our political reality and the literature we must invent:

> Because the isolation of Black lesbian women, given that we are superfreaks, given that our lesbianism defies both the sexual identity that capital gives us and the racial identity that capital gives us, the isolation of Black lesbian women from heterosexual Black women is very profound. Very profound. I have searched throughout Black history, Black literature, whatever, looking for some women that I could see were somehow lesbian. Now I know that in a certain sense they were all lesbian. But that was a very painful search.[19]

Heterosexual privilege is usually the only privilege that Black women have. None of us have racial or sexual privilege, almost none of us have class privilege, maintaining "straightness" is our last resort. Being out, particularly out in print, is the final renunciation of any claim to the crumbs of "tolerance" that non-threatening "ladylike" Black women are sometimes fed. I am convinced that it is our lack of privilege and power in every other sphere that allows so few Black women to make the leap that many white women, particularly writers, have been able to make in this decade, not merely because they are white or have economic leverage, but because they have had the strength and support of a movement behind them.

As Black lesbians we must be out not only in white society, but in the Black community as well, which is at least as homophobic. That the sanctions against Black lesbians are extremely high is well illustrated in this comment by Black male writer Ishmael Reed. Speaking about the inroads that whites make into Black culture, he asserts:

> In Manhattan you find people actively trying to impede intellectual debate among Afro-Americans. The powerful "liberal/radical/existentialist" influences of the Manhattan literary and drama

establishment speak through tokens, like for example that ancient
notion of the *one* black ideologue (who's usually a Communist), the
*one* black poetess (who's usually a feminist lesbian).[20]

To Reed, "feminist" and "lesbian" are the most pejorative terms he can hurl
at a Black woman and totally invalidate anything she might say, regardless of
her actual politics or sexual identity. Such accusations are quite effective for
keeping Black women writers who are writing with integrity and strength
from any conceivable perspective in line, but especially those who are actually feminist and lesbian. Unfortunately Reed's reactionary attitude is all too
typical. A community which has not confronted sexism, because a widespread Black feminist movement has not required it to, has likewise not been
challenged to examine its heterosexism. Even at this moment I am not convinced that one can write explicitly as a Black lesbian and live to tell about it.

Yet there are a handful of Black women who have risked everything for
truth. Audre Lorde, Pat Parker, and Ann Allen Shockley have at least broken
ground in the vast wilderness of works that do not exist.[21] Black feminist
criticism will again have an essential role not only in creating a climate in
which Black lesbian writers can survive, but in undertaking the total reas-
sessment of Black literature and literary history needed to reveal the Black
woman-identified-women that Wilmette Brown and so many of us are
looking for.

Although I have concentrated here upon what does not exist and what
needs to be done, a few Black feminist critics have already begun this work.
Gloria T. Hull at the University of Delaware has discovered in her research
on Black women poets of the Harlem Renaissance that many of the women
who are considered "minor" writers of the period were in constant contact
with each other and provided both intellectual stimulation and psychological
support for each other's work. At least one of these writers, Angelina Weld
Grimké, wrote many unpublished love poems to women. Lorraine Bethel, a
recent graduate of Yale College, has done substantial work on Black women
writers, particularly in her senior essay, "This Infinity of Conscious Pain:
Blues Lyricism and Hurston's Black Female Folk Aesthetic and Cultural Sen-

sibility in *Their Eyes Were Watching God*," in which she brilliantly defines and uses the principles of Black feminist criticism. Elaine Scott at the State University of New York at Old Westbury is also involved in highly creative and politically resonant research on Hurston and other writers.

The fact that these critics are young and, except for Hull, unpublished merely indicates the impediments we face. Undoubtedly there are other women working and writing whom I do not even know, simply because there is no place to read them. As Michele Wallace states in her article, "A Black Feminist's Search for Sisterhood":

> We exist as women who are black who are feminists, each stranded for the moment, working independently because there is not yet an environment in this society remotely congenial to our struggle—(or our thoughts).[22]

I only hope that this essay is one way of breaking our silence and our isolation, of helping us to know each other.

Just as I did not know where to start, I am not sure how to end. I feel that I have tried to say too much and at the same time have left too much unsaid. What I want this essay to do is lead everyone who reads it to examine *everything* that they have ever thought and believed about feminist culture and to ask themselves how their thoughts connect to the reality of Black women's writings and lives. I want to encourage in white women, as a first step, a sane accountability to all the women who write and live on this soil. I want most of all for Black women and Black lesbians somehow not to be so alone. This last will require the most expansive of revolutions as well as many new words to tell us how to make this revolution real. I finally want to express how much easier both my waking and my sleeping hours would be if there were one book in existence that would tell me something specific about my life. One book based in Black feminist and Black lesbian experience, fiction or non-fiction. Just one work to reflect the reality that I and the Black women whom I love are trying to create. When such a book exists then each of us will not only know better how to live, but how to dream.

# Notes

1. Alice Walker, "In Search of Our Mothers' Gardens," in *Ms.*, May 1974, and in *Southern Exposure: Generations of Women in the South* (Winter, 1977): 60–64.

2. Jerry H. Bryant, "The Outskirts of a New City," *The Nation*, 12 (November, 1973): 502.

3. Robert Bone, *The Negro Novel in America* (New Haven: Yale University Press, 1958), 180.

4. Bone, *The Negro Novel* (*Knock on Any Door* is a novel by Black writer Willard Motley).

5. Sara Blackburn, "You Still Can't Go Home Again," *New York Times Book Review*, December 30, 1973, 3.

6. Elaine Showalter, "Review Essay: Literary Criticism," *Signs*, 1 (Winter , 1975): 460.

7. Showalter, "Review Essay: Literary Criticism," 445.

8. Ellen Moers, *Literary Women: The Great Writers* (Garden City, NY: Anchor Books, 1977); Patricia Meyer Spacks, *The Female Imagination* (New York: Avon Books, 1976).

9. An article by Nancy Hoffman, "White Women, Black Women: Inventing an Adequate Pedagogy," *Women's Studies Newsletter* 5 (Spring, 1977): 21–24, gives valuable insights into how white women can approach the writing of Black women.

10. Darwin T. Turner, *In a Minor Chord: Three Afro-American Writers and Their Search for Identity* (Carbondale and Edwardsville: Southern Illinois University Press, 1971).

11. John Domini, "Roots and Racism: An Interview with Ishmael Reed," *Boston Phoenix*, April 5, 1977, 20.

12. Ora Williams, "A Bibliography of Works Written by American Black Women," *College Language Association Journal* (March 1972): 355. There is an expanded book-length version of this bibliography: *American Black Women in the Arts and Social Sciences: A Bibliographic Survey* (Metuchen, NJ: The Scarecrow Press, 1973).

13. John O'Brien, ed., *Interviews with Black Writers* (New York: Liveright, 1973), 201.

14. Toni Morrison, *The Bluest Eye* (New York: Pocket Books, 1976) and *Sula* (New York: Alfred A. Knopf, 1974). All subsequent references to this work will be designated in the text.

15. My sister Beverly Smith pointed out this connection to me.

16. Lorraine Bethel, "Conversations with Ourselves: Black Female Relationships in Toni Cade Bambara's *Gorilla, My Love* and Toni Morrison's *Sula*," unpublished paper written at Yale, 1976, 47. (Bethel has worked from a premise similar to mine in a much more developed treatment of the novel.)

17. New York Radicalesbians, "Woman Identified Woman," in *Lesbians Speak Out* (Oakland, CA: Women's Press Collective, 1974), 87.

18. Elly Bulkin, "An Interview with Adrienne Rich: Part I," in *Conditions: One* 1 (April 1977): 62.

19. Wilmette Brown, "The Autonomy of Black Lesbian Women," ms. of speech delivered July 24, 1976, Toronto, Canada, p. 7.

20. Domini, "Roots and Racism," 18.

21. Audre Lorde, *New York Head Shop and Museum* (Detroit, MI: Broadside, 1974); Lorde, *Coal* (New York: W.W. Norton, 1976); Lorde, *Between Ourselves* (Point Reyes, CA: Eidolon Editions, 1976); Pat Parker, *Child of Myself* (Oakland, CA: Women's Press Collective, 1974). There is at least one Black lesbian writers collective, Jemima, in New York. They do public readings and have available a collection of their poems. They can be contacted c/o Boyce, 1970 University Ave., Bronx, NY 10453.

22. Michele Wallace, "A Black Feminist's Search for Sisterhood," *The Village Voice*, July 28, 1975, 7.

Bettina Love

# A Ratchet Lens: Black Queer Youth, Agency, Hip Hop, and the Black Ratchet Imagination

## Ratchet Binaries

The word *ratchet* has emerged in mainstream culture as a means of describing Black people, particularly Black women, as loud, hot-tempered, and promiscuous. This one-dimensional view of Black women has sparked outrage and debate in social media, historically Black college and university campuses, popular blog sites, and Black feminist communities. Although the hip hop community, particularly in the Southern region of the United States, popularized the term over a decade ago as a slogan to represent the complexities and fluidity of working-class Black life, cultural critic and writer Michaela Angela Davis launched a campaign in 2012 to bury the word *ratchet* because of the portrayal of Black women as "mean, gold-digging women" on reality television shows, such as *The Real Housewives of Atlanta* (Dia, 2012). Yet, Black feminist scholars like Heidi R. Lewis (2013) rejected the idea of burying the word, because, she argues, the term implies binaries about Black women, especially regarding class status. While Lewis contends that the term *ratchet* is used to exclusively describe lower-class Black women and their behavior, she acknowledges that upper-class and professional Black women also enjoy letting loose, dropping respectability politics for a moment in time, and getting "*ratchet*." In Brittney Cooper's (2012) essay, "(Un)Clutching My Mother's Pearls, or Ratchetness and the Residue of Respectability," she offers an important query to interrogating the ways in which Black women's bodies are policed by dominant culture. She asks: "Are any of us winning in a scenario where respectable and *ratchet* are the only two options?" Cooper's question provides a space for researchers to reclaim and reimagine the narrow and superficial binaries of Black womanhood that complicate and humanize working-class Black life and expand these complexities to queer youth of color who consume and create hip hop.

★  ★  ★

Taking up the call offered by the aforementioned Black feminists to interrogate binaries and the policing of Black bodies through a more complex reading of the word *ratchet*, this article attempts to chart new terrain in conceptualizing a *ratchet* methodological perspective for research that studies the unique challenges of Black queer youth who create or engage in the complicated social, emotional, economical, and cultural dimensions of hip hop, working-class Black life, and the fluidity of queerness. This article specifically calls for researchers to approach the study of Black queer youth who create and consume hip hop with a Black *ratchet* imagination lens. A Black *ratchet* imagination lens is a fluid methodological perspective that recognizes, appreciates, and struggles with the agency and knowledge production of Black queer youth who are resisting, succumbing to, and finding pleasure in hip hop by undoing the heteropatriarchal, liberating, queer, homophobic, sexist, feminist, hyper-local, global, *ratchet*, and conservative space of hip hop (Love, 2012, 2016; Rose, 2008). My use of the term *agency* within a queer space is not just about the act of sex. Joan Morgan (2015) argues that "pleasure politics" must include "sexual and non-sexual engagements with deeply internal sites of power and pleasure—among them expressions of sex and sexuality that deliberately resist binaries" (p. 40). This type of methodological perspective is built on a layered definition of agency (Blackburn, 2005; Brockenbrough, 2016; Brockenbrough & Boatwright, 2013; McCready, 2010; Quinn, 2007). Moreover, research findings focused on Black queer youth need to be more complex and intersectional to properly take into account the knowledge production of Black queer youth and how they reimagine spaces and identities to create culturally affirming lives with robust subversive identities and agentive practices, especially within the culture of hip hop (Glover, Galliher, & Lamere, 2009). Black queer youth's subversive identities are messy and disrupt normativity by calling into question fixed terms such as *man* and *woman*, a concept further examined in the following in the context of New Orleans's gender-fluid Black music culture (Duggan, 1992; Jagose, 1996). These complex identities of Black queer youth, as informed by the culture of hip hop, call for an equally intricate framework, thus necessitating messy theoretical orientations that are dynamic, multifaceted, hyper-local, and not generalizable.

In the next section, I define *ratchet* and the need to conduct messy research with Black queer youth. In doing so, I review research literature that reimagines politics of respectability, many of which center Black women's epistemologies and suspend binaries. Following that section is a discussion of the Black *ratchet* imagination, which is a methodological lens that wrestles with the fluidity, precariousness, creativity, and agency of Black queer youth. Agency is highlighted as an affordance of youth in redefining and reimagining established norms. I then bring these ideas together by applying a Black *ratchet* imagination methodological perspective to examining New Orleans's bounce culture. I conclude with a call to humanize Black queer youth through messy, reflective, and localized lenses and practices.

## Defining *Ratchet* and the Need to Conduct Messy Research for Black Queer Youth

The word *ratchet* is messy, meaning it has no straightforward definition; it is contradictory, fluid, precarious, agentive, and oftentimes intentionally inappropriate, which makes it an ideal methodological perspective for exploring how Black queer youth fully participate in Black social spaces and cultural practices to form subversive and creative spaces that humanize. The term's introduction to hip hop first appeared in popular culture in 1999 with the release of "Do the Ratchet" by Anthony Mandigo on his album, *Ratchet Fight in the Ghetto* (Ortved, 2013). Five years later, mainstream hip hop was introduced to the word *ratchet* in the remake "Do Da Ratchet" by Lil Boosie, a rapper from Baton Rouge, Louisiana, who proclaimed: "We all got some *ratchet* in us. Everybody got a lil *ratchet* in them." This provocative statement de-pathologizes Black youth while also blurring the line between classed divisions of respectability and ratchetness (Cooper, 2012). In 2007, Hurricane Chris of Shreveport, Louisiana, released his debut album, *51/50 Ratchet*. In his music, Hurricane Chris generally used the expression *ratchet* in two ways: as a phrase to excite partygoers and as a way to describe reckless behavior. The album's success expanded Shreveport's reach into mainstream popular lexicon. By 2012, household name artists like Beyonce and Lady Gaga were posting pictures on social media wearing earrings inscribed with the word *ratchet*. However, by the height of reality TV's popularity featuring Black women, *ratchet*'s working-class Southern origins were co-opted for popular culture's obsession with debasing Black women.

## Ratchetness and Black Feminism

In response to the media, scholars in the fields of hip hop studies, women's studies, and political science, such as Heidi R. Lewis (2013), Brittney Cooper (2012), Treva Lindsey (2015), L.H. Stallings (2013), Regina Bradley (2013), and Nadia E. Brown and Lisa Young (2015), have interrogated the various meanings of the word *ratchet* and its relationship to Black women. Inevitably, due to the hypersexual and misogynistic visual, sonic, and narrative landscape of popular music, particularly of hip hop, Black women are deemed loud, hostile, reckless, and therefore *ratchet*. For example, Lewis wrote, "Think of ratchet as a combination of Mammy, Sapphire, Jezebel, and the Welfare Queen—every controlling image of black women Patricia Hill Collins taught you about all rolled in to one." Patricia Hill Collins's (2000) earlier work states that "portraying African-American women as stereotypical mammies, matriarch, welfare recipients, and hot mommas has been essential to the political economy of domination fostering Black women's oppression" (p. 147). In contrast, Cooper's reading of ratchetness is one that considers Black women's agency. Cooper suggests that ratchetness provides a pliable framework to challenge the politics of respectability, which shames Black women for their economic status, being single mothers, their sexual choices, and acting on their desires. The shaming further extends to the ways in which Black women reject and challenge dominant norms concerning style of dress and hair, femininity, and body movement (e.g., dance). Within a Southern context, Regina Bradley suggests that the "aesthetic of respectability that continues to dictate southern women" is "an oppositional parallel for black women excluded from this niche of finer womanhood [which] is the highly visible and commodified form of expression that we have come to recognize as (the) ratchet." N.E. Brown and Young shift the interpretation of the word *ratchet* to include institutions invested in heteropatriarchy, white supremacy, and capitalism, thereby enacting violence toward Black women as ratchet. They argue for a shift that allows researchers to ask new questions concerning the rules that govern Black women.

Drawing on the work of these Black feminists and their nuanced readings of the word *ratchet* in response to how Black women are misunderstood, plagued by stereotypical tropes and respectability politics, and living and working in oppressive *ratchet* institutions, I invoke a similar call to utilize the framework of ratchetness to begin imagining a methodological perspective that recognizes and affirms the full humanity of Black queer youth for their sexual desires, multiple identities, economic status, style of dress, language, music, and dance; simply stated, a methodological perspective that acknowledges Black queer youth's precarity but does not blame or shame them for it. It instead asks researchers to center the heritage, community, and audacity of youth to reclaim and make space for cultural practices birthed out of the need for "their imaginations' nourishment for creating a world of freedom where they could be whoever they felt they truly were" (Bell, 1996, p. 1).

## Need for "Messy" and Humanizing Research

The precarity of working-class Black queer youth requires that researchers' methodological perspectives be grounded in a framework that is messy, filled with areas of gray humanization and hyper-locality, to recognize Black queer youth's agency within their precarious conditions. This research approach is not static or linear; it is as fluid as queerness itself and embraces intersections that can lead to messy, incomplete research findings. Within the framework of a ratchet methodological perspective, messiness invites researchers to embrace the interconnections, inconsistencies, and entanglements of qualitative analysis with Black queer youth who learn and live from the edges of society (Roller, 2016). Similarly, hip hop feminism demands a methodological perspective where qualitative analyses lean toward a convening of hypocrisy, contradictions, and intersections and "where those contrary voices meet—the juncture where 'truth' is no longer black and white but subtle, intriguing shades of gray" (Morgan, 2000, p. 62). Equally important, messiness ultimately seeks to humanize Black queer youth who are invisible and hyper-visible at the same time. For example, mainstream America celebrates and commodifies Black queer vernacular (e.g., shade, read, werk) and the dance styles of Black queer youth (e.g., voguing, J-setting) and makes their lives hyper-visible with reality TV shows such as *RuPaul's Drag Race, The Prancing Elites Project,* and *Love & Hip Hop: Hollywood*; however, their day-to-day struggles and agentive practices are notably absent. Agentive practices such as self-determination, negotiating oppressive spaces to survive, reimagining identities, and finding ways to maneuver through precarious conditions to flourish are absent from the literature on Black queer youth (Cruz, 2011; Love & Tosolt, 2013; McCready, 2001, 2004). In 2015, Brockenbrough vehemently called for more education research on queer students of color and new analytical lenses that are deeply concerned with agency and the academic and personal successes of Black queer youth. Multiple studies have shown that Black queer youth find ways to negotiate identities and language practices and connect to familial, communal, and political activism networks while experiencing the intersections of racism, homophobia, sexism, transphobia, poverty, and other oppressive conditions collectively as marginalized queer youth of color (Blackburn, 2005; Brockenbrough, 2016).

However, Huang et al. (2010) and Bartone's (2015) findings suggest that there is a scarcity of research focused on Black queer youth. Bartone argues that much of the research (Glover et al., 2009) focused on queer youth consists of 50 percent white participants and 50 percent racially marginalized groups. Researchers lump Black queer youth into these studies as if they do not face their own unique set of experiences, like homophobia and racism (Dumas & ross, 2016). Research that solely focuses on the sexual identities and experiences of Black queer youth is sporadic at best (Blackburn & McCready, 2009; McCready, 2010). As a research community, we are just starting to understand what we can learn from Black queer youth.

In his article on humanizing research among culturally diverse youth, Paris (2011) writes that "humanizing research is a methodological stance, which requires that our inquiries involve dialogic consciousness-raising and the building of relationships of dignity and care for both researchers and participants" (p. 137). A humanizing research stance is needed because "social science often works to collect stories of pain and humiliation in the lives of those being researched for commodification" (Tuck & Yang, 2014, p. 223). Tuck and Yang (2014) argue that most research is conducted through "the spectacle of the settler colonial gaze" (p. 223). The intensity of that gaze is magnified by research conducted on Black queer youth. As a result, new methodological perspectives are needed not only to recognize the humanity of Black queer youth but also to document and learn from how they create imaginative, pleasurable, and sometimes subversive identities from language, desires, dances, dress, and art forms (i.e., hip hop) to disrupt homophobia, racism, anti-Blackness, and other forms of oppression (Britzman, 1997; Cohen, 1997).

## A Methodological Perspective: Black Ratchet Imagination

The term *Black ratchet* imagination was first introduced by L.H. Stallings (2013) to define an imaginative, agentive, creative, performative, uplifting transitional space established and occupied by queer youth of color in the hip hop community to promote the "performance of the failure to be respectable" (p. 136). Black ratchet imagination should not be viewed as a site where young people come to simply act out but rather as a disruption of respectability politics, particularly for queer youth of color, reclaiming autonomy from middle- and upper-class white male heterosexuality and healing from normalized state-sanctioned violence toward Black and Brown bodies (N.E. Brown & Young, 2015; Cohen, 2004). As a methodological perspective, the Black ratchet imagination affords researchers a lens that is deeply focused on gaining an in-depth understanding of Black queer youth's identity constructions through purposeful and reflective qualitative research questions that are intersectional, seek to understand youth's agency to reclaim space, refuse binary identities, subvert language, create economic opportunities with new economies, and recognize the precariousness of queer youth of color. Within the framework, data collection takes place in youth-centered spaces that are created and/or regulated by youth, and data interpretation is conducted with special responsiveness to youth's Blackness, knowledge production, subversiveness, and self-care practices. Lastly, a researcher utilizing a Black ratchet imagination as a methodological perspective from the onset of the study must embrace messy and incomplete findings, which are not generalizable.

Utilizing a messy and nongeneralizable methodological perspective such as a Black ratchet imagination when investigating queer youth of color allows the researcher to wrestle with the instability and variations of gender and sexuality with queer Black youth who, through hip hop's fluidity, are coming of age in the contested, contradictory, and liberating space of queer hip hop music and culture (Stallings, 2013). As a methodological perspective, the Black ratchet imagination is similar to narrative inquiry, which focuses on "the ways humans experience the world" (Clandinin & Connelly, 2000, p. 2) in relation to their community to tell and retell their lived stories. According to Phillion (2008), narrative in qualitative research "has become more prevalent as researchers draw on critical race theory to bring forward silenced narratives of underrepresented groups" (p. 283). However, while narrative inquiry is concerned with the researcher's experiences and the co-construction of narratives (Phillion, 2008), the Black ratchet imagination centers youth narratives; the researcher is mute, so youth voices cannot be overshadowed.

Equally important, the Black ratchet imagination critiques Western civilization, white supremacy, colonial social order, and positivist research practices (Kelley, 2002). This methodological perspective allows researchers to ask not only new questions but also agentive questions that embrace the knowledge productions of the intersectional articulations that are found when Blackness, hip hop, and queerness are recognized as spaces of agency. Such new agentive inquiries could include how Black queer youth who create and engage with hip hop form intersections of race, religion, gender, sexuality, and class to produce identities that counter narrow and deficit narratives; how Black queer youth through these intersections depart from nationalist ideals and practices (Ferguson, 2004); how practices of self-care and agency are cultivated in Black queer youth–centered spaces; and how young Black masculine-presenting lesbians navigate feminism and misogyny within hip hop in their communities. Furthermore, a methodological perspective of the Black ratchet imagination lens demands that research of Black queer youth be conducted with specificity of local culture and music, historical mappings to examine present-day precariousness, and an examination of how Black queer youth dismantle and disdain "politics of respectability" to breed new categories of human experience, oftentimes through performativity, storytelling, and art making (Kelley, 2002).

## Black Ratchet Imagination Lens as Agency

Morgan's (2000) framing of pleasure politics is through a Black feminist lens; the space she carves out to engage and theorize sexual and nonsexual agency is foregrounded in what L.H. Stallings (2007) describes as an erotic space where an exploitation of sexual desire is "spiritual, intellectual, physical, emotional, and fluid so as to avoid splits or binaries that can freeze Black women's radical sexual subjectivities" (p. 1). Grounded in Black feminisms and hip hop feminism, Black ratchet imagination is necessary to theorize a framework of sexual and nonsexual agency of Black queer youth that pays close attention to the structural inequalities they face while unmasking and acknowledging methods, data, and findings that are messy, complicated, and possibly unable to be triangulated (Morgan, 2000).

## Applying the Black Ratchet Imagination Lens: Hip Hop's Locality and Queerness

Hip hop is a movement with multiple goals and aims; thus, not all hip hop is the same (Stallings, 2013). Hip hop occupies multiple spaces, including its function as the voice of social critique of systemic oppression and the visceral representation that blames and shames Black folks for America's social and economic decay, fueling irrational and undocumented moral panic (Cohen,

2010). Hip hop's innovative aesthetics were not created in a vacuum; America's obsession with brand consciousness, anti-intellectualism, violence, homophobia, sexism, and materialism all frame hip hop (hooks, 2004; Rose, 2008).

Hip hop's complexes, tensions, and desires to love and seek out humility by way of bold and innovative creative expressions is what makes hip hop so enduring to people from all around the globe and what makes it simultaneously queer and imaginative. Hip hop is sonically, vocally, and visually birthed from a "polycultural mix of influences, including the African griot tradition, Caribbean dub music, and loops of black American percussive funk breaks" (Poulson-Bryant, 2013, p. 214). Hip hop's origins and genealogy "wantonly invites queer rumination" (Snorton, 2013, p. vi), which is a composite of many forms of Black cultural expression. Thus, hip hop's roots are stable, but its identity is geographically dependent on distinctive regional sounds and aesthetics that are closely tied to a city's neighborhoods, local allegiances, and territorial rivalries—what Murray Forman (2000) calls the spatial discourse of rap. Within this specificity, there are pockets of hip hop that are queer in theory and practice. Hip hop's queerness is foregrounded by a space of imaginative Black ratchetness. *Freedom Dreams: The Black Radical Imagination*, by Robin D.G. Kelley (2002), contends that a requirement for liberation that refuses victimization is an "unleashing of the mind's most creative capacities, catalyzed by participation in struggles or change" (p. 192). Hip hop's queerness, spatial discourse, and "liberatory pleasure politics" (Morgan, 2015, p. 38), which are radical and ratchet, examined through the methodological perspective of the Black ratchet imagination, provide fertile ground for researchers to conduct studies concerning Black queer youth that reflect how youth understand their intersecting identities to form spaces of agency. Applying this lens, research questions are constructed that seek to make meaning of how hip hop's imaginative and performative space allows for fluidity and interrupts normativity to produce youth-centered spaces generated from local culture that problematizes normative ideas of gender and sexuality. One example of a space robust for data collection for the Black ratchet imagination is New Orleans's bounce music and culture.

# New Orleans and Performativity

Historical mapping is an important component of this methodological perspective. Research should be conducted by examining the past and present-day precariousness of the participants' community with special attention to how Black queer youth undo "politics of respectability" in a quest for dignity (Cooper, 2017). Layers of context are also necessary as hip hop must be examined within its relationship to its local community—how local Black folks resisted oppression and fought for dignity and representation. As an example of historical mappings, hip hop was formed by a polycultural mix of traditions, sonic expressions, African improvisational techniques, and the celebratory performativity of public spectacles. No place embodies this fusion of sonic, vocal, visual, and performative adaptations like New Orleans, whose citizens have created a distinctive African American music and performance that is hyper-local yet borderless. For over 135 years, Blacks were not allowed to participate in the annual Mardi Gras celebrations in New Orleans. In response to this segregation, Blacks formed their own Mardi Gras traditions and festivities (Vaz, 2013a). Clubs such as the Zulu Social Aid and Pleasure Club, the Black Indians of New Orleans, and the Skull and Bones Gang and the district Carnival music tradition soon formed (Vaz, 2013a). These clubs gave birth to jazz funerals and brass band parades known as "second lines" in the historic African American communities of Center City, Mid City, and Treme.

Beyond the Crescent City's elastic sound of fusing African, French, and Spanish music, historically New Orleans is home to some of the most gender-bending public celebration traditions. A subculture of Black Mardi Gras, known as Baby Dolls, developed in the early 1900s in a section called Black Storyville or the Red Light District, a part of town known for bars, gambling, and prostitution. Baby Dolls are African American men and women dressed in short satin dresses, stockings with garters, and bonnets. As Vaz (2013b) states, African American female sex workers of the early 1900s decided to dress up as Baby Dolls because men commonly called women *baby*, but the term also has an ironic "double meaning in it because African-

American women weren't considered precious and doll-like." According to Vaz (2013a), Baby Dolls are "sexy and sometimes raunchy. . . . The Baby Dolls parade in their neighborhoods, singing bawdy lyrics to vaudeville show tunes and Creole songs, playing tambourines and cowbells, chanting and dancing" (p. 8). The best-known group was the Million Dollar Baby Dolls who, accompanied by a male band, paraded the streets holding signs and singing songs that ridiculed and shamed men who paid for sex work, such as, "In the Evening When the Sun Goes Down" and "You Dirty Mutha Fucker, Your Momma Don't Wear No Drawers" (Vaz, 2013a). Within a U.S. context, Baby Dolls are hyper-local to New Orleans and represent a clear example of how subversive techniques through performativity can address communities' sociopolitical concerns and push back on politics of respectability while dancing and singing in the streets for their dignity.

The Big Easy is a site of performance, play, and pleasure, with Black bodies as the main attraction using Black cultural forms of expression that embody a Black radical imagination, and sometimes ratchetness (i.e., intentionally not conforming to respectability politics and gender norms), to disrupt and respond to oppression (Lipsitz, 1998). However, while New Orleans is known as the "city where anything goes," the queer community of the Big Easy has not always been so welcomed. The city has a large conservative Catholic and Christian community that is "focused on containing many of the social practices that one would equate with the American South, for example, proper social etiquette for men and women rather than encouraging sexual freedom" (Thompson, 2011, p. 5). Moreover, New Orleans is subject to racial division within the queer community. According to Monroe (2016), the queer Black communities of New Orleans do not patronize the city's white queer bars or communities.

Thus, the Big Easy is sadly still plagued by racism, regardless of how much Black folks have contributed to the city's culture and social and political economics. Furthermore, New Orleanians experience high levels of concentrated poverty due to heavy segregation and low wages. In 2014, a study conducted by New Orleans–based research group, the Data Center, found low wages to be a major factor crippling the workforce and keeping working-class parents in poverty (Catalanello, 2015). Another report estimated that 39 percent of New Orleans children live in poverty (Catalanello, 2015). However, despite the city's racism, discrimination, lack of resources, or catastrophic natural disasters, New Orleans is still thriving with an abundance of Black creativity, wild queerness, and a history of ratchetness that seeks to disrupt stereotypical tropes and respectability.

The collective memory and energy of New Orleans's music, carnivals, and parades constructs spaces of collective joy, freedom, and pleasure (Miller, 2006, 2012). Another Black Mardi Gras subculture, the Mardi Gras Indians, which features Black working-class men dressed in Native American ceremonial costumes, has inspired the latest New Orleans musical creation: bounce. Mardi Gras Indians are famous for their clever call-and-response chants and spectacular, over-the-top garments. Bounce relies heavily on call-and-response and the chanting style of the Mardi Gras Indians and is molded by the city's local cultural identity. The Black ratchet imagination as a methodological perspective provides a lens to historically map the emotional flexibility and creativity needed to survive the poverty, violence, displacement, and systematic housing segregation with one's soul partially intact to reinvent music and culture that remains fluid, subversive, and agentive. For that reason, bounce is a quintessential space within hip hop for conducting research focused on Black queer youth through the methodological perspective of the Black ratchet imagination. This methodological perspective can only be applied to spaces that have been reclaimed by youth who undo politics of respectability in a quest for dignity, purpose, and pleasure—full humanity.

## Bounce

Bounce music is an up-tempo, dance-oriented, hypersexual, call-and-response, bass heavy, and ratchet form of rap music pioneered by DJ Jubilee. Other notable musicians are Magnolia Shorty (1982–2010), Sissy Nobby, Rusty Lazer, Magnolia Rhome, Nickey Da B, and Baby Erin. Bounce is firmly situated within Black music and Black cultural traditions, which are intricately interwoven through the echoes, tempos, and movements of Black youth. Bounce thrives on undoing and gleefully dismantling the politics of respectability to create spaces of queer performativity that bend, blur, and gyrate a "pleasure politics" that is both sexual and nonsexual for and by Black queer youth. According to Matt Miller (2012), who wrote the book *Bounce: Rap Music and Local Identity in New Orleans*, bounce "emerged from the dynamic relationship between a deeply rooted Afro-Caribbean sensibility and contemporary commodified developments in musical style, practice, and technology" (p. 13). Hobbs (2012) wrote that Bounce's sound is distinctive because of its "strong emphasis on intensely repetitive rhythmic and lyrical sequences, characteristic dances, localized lyrical themes, [and] detailed geographic shout-outs."

The reigning queen of bounce, Big Freedia, is a New Orleans native and a gender-bending queer rapper. Big Freedia, born Frederick Ross, also popularized the dance style of twerking. Growing up, she listened to Patti LaBelle, Michael Jackson, and gospel music; however, her biggest musical influence was a drag queen rapper named Katey Red who lived four blocks away. Before launching her own career, Big Freedia was a backup dancer for Katey Red, the originator of *sissy* bounce. In the context of bounce, *sissy* is a term of endearment that embodies and pays homage to New Orleans's long and influential history of queer entertainers, such as Bobby Marchan, a female impersonator singer, or Pasty Vidalia, born Irving Ale, a cross-dressing hostess of the popular Dew Drop Inn (Dee, 2010). Alison Fensterstock, a New Orleans music writer who focuses on bounce, told *Time* (cited in Dee, 2010),

> Gay performers have been celebrated forever in New Orleans black culture. Not to mention that in New Orleans there's the tradition of masking, mummers, carnival, all the weird identity inversion. There's just something in the culture that's a lot more lax about gender identity and fanciness.

Katey Red and Big Freedia stand on the shoulders of queer New Orleans performers who embraced ratchetness to create a space where Black queer performers are not only accepted but also revered. Big Freedia dresses in stylish men's clothing and prefers the pronoun *she*. A Big Freedia show consists of high-energy, booty-popping, and freeform dancing. Big Freedia's motto is "free your ass, and your mind will follow" (Ross, 2015). Her performances and lyrics are liberating because she ensures that everyone, gay or straight, feels safe at her shows. She told *San Francisco Weekly*:

> I definitely bring some stability to women and let them feel free in their space and let them know that they're protected and can be themselves. That's important to a lot of my fans, and creating that safe space for the women has always been my thing. Even when I started rapping, if boys were trying to touch the girls on their asses or slapping them on their cheeks, I would protect the girls. I will continue to be that way. (Rotter, 2015)

In her book, *Big Freedia: God Save the Queen Diva*, she defines her overall message as self-acceptance (Ross, 2015). Women and men, regardless of their sexuality, attend Big Freedia's shows because they are a safe space that invites and feeds the Black ratchet imagination for pleasure politics and affirms and recognizes Black queer youth's complicated lives of contradictions, agency, liberation, and undoing that can sometimes only be conveyed within a wild and imaginative space that disrupts identities and gets ratchet through cultural modes of expression. For example, in Big Freedia's song "Explore," Freedia raps: "Release ya anger. Release ya mind. Release ya job. Release the time. Release ya trade. Release the stress. Release the love. Forget the rest. Let's go."

The lyrics to the song are freeing and create a moment in time where agency, liberation, and undoing can be explored. For example, the central elements of the Black ratchet imagination—intersectionality, agency, fluidity, and understanding Black youth's precariousness—are present within the song because bounce at its core embodies these elements—they are bounce's foundation. Thus, bounce provides a unique lens for researchers to get a more complex and nonbinary understanding of youth's layered embodiment of ratchetness. When bounce and the Black ratchet imagination meet in the space of education research, researchers unfold how intersectionality is not only multiple identities coming together to showcase youth-centered spaces but also to ensure that Black lives that have been reduced, destroyed, and made illegible matter (Dumas, 2017). For researchers concerned with examining Black queer youth from a strength approach that recognizes life as nonlinear, bounce's subversive healing lyrics and dances are agentive and fluid practices of how Black queer youth define and redefine themselves and reimagine their identities on a continuum of exploration. Lastly, Big Freedia's lyrics highlight the working-class roots of bounce and the precariousness and the stresses of that social construct.

For Black queer youth coming of age in New Orleans, their identities differ greatly from that of a youngster in other American cities because of New Orleans's ratchet and imaginative musical and cultural past. The hyper-locality of the Black ratchet imagination lens provides a space to examine youth's creative agency and resistance that humanize Black queer youth's lived experiences within their particular communities; thus, while data interpretation cannot capture every aspect of Black queer youth's lives, it does free them from victimizing and heteronormative research narratives. To be clear, bounce is not free of sexism, misogyny, capitalism, or patriarchy; these oppressive systems remain fixed to hip hop music and culture as they are fixed to American culture. But bounce from the center to the edges of the music and culture deliberately aims to problematize the limits of identity, confront the tensions of living in a heterosexual capitalist world, and place desires and the imagination alongside the search for humanity (Gang, 2008). The Black ratchet imagination creates a space for data interpretation that categorizes and codes complex identity formations of Black queer youth with special attention to youth's Blackness, knowledge production, and self-care practices. Data collection and methods within a Black ratchet imagination are closely aligned to ethnography, youth participatory action research, portraiture, life history interviews, and narrative inquiry. These methods decenter the researcher's voice while stressing the importance of being respectful when allowed to participate in the cultural practices of Black queer youth; having meaningful conversations, not just interviews, with youth and community members; and recognizing knowledge production of youth. Additionally, youth must play a vital role in data analysis and member checking to ensure the research captures all the textures and layers of their lived experiences. Implementations and findings are pertinent to the community in which the participants live and should be shared with them but should also be disseminated widely to inform and build on research that aims to capture snapshots of the full humanity of Black queer youth.

## Limitations of the Lens

Research conducted using the Black ratchet imagination lens as a methodological perspective is not generalizable; the data are unique to the participants of the study, their subculture of hip hop, and the culture and history of their city. Thus, the in-depth, comprehensive approach to this methodological perspective limits the scope of the study from the onset. Replicability is difficult—if not impossible—outside of the initial research site because a Black ratchet imagination lens approaches research from a hyper-local standpoint. The messy and incomplete findings of the research focused on youth culture are fluid and represent a snapshot into youth's lives; findings do not represent the totality of youth's struggles, accomplishments, and queer identity constructions. Youth culture rapidly changes, so research conducted through a Black ratchet imagination methodological perspective has a short life expectancy, but the research represents a vivid, intersectional, and in-depth understanding of how Black queer youth make sense of the world within their community, culture, and identity constructions at a particular moment in time that draws on the generational knowledge of queer youth of color that came before them. Furthermore, researchers understanding their participants' culture, agentive practices, and community is central to the Black ratchet imagination.

The methodological perspective is heavily dependent on a knowledge base robust in the fields of Black studies, Black queer studies, youth studies, youth cultural movements, hip hop studies, Black feminism, and how white supremacy works to destabilize communities of color and how people of color resist domination. Thus, this methodological perspective should only be used by researchers with a robust historical and present-day understanding of their participants' community and how it has been impacted by racism, capitalism, transphobia, classism, rigid ideas of gender, heteronormativity, and homophobia. The lens necessitates that researchers approach their work through a social justice, intersectional, and anti-racist framework, whereas intersectionality is utilized not just as an analytical tool for recognizing multiple intersecting identities but also as a tool to examine overlapping systems of oppression.

Lastly, it is important to note that not all Black queer youth identify with hip hop; after all, hip hop is just one space of many that supports youth's creativity, imagination, and knowledge production and where Black queer youth have found agency.

## Humanizing Black Queer Youth

One of the major objectives of this article is to chart new methodological perspectives that push researchers to not only investigate the challenges of queer youth of color but also examine how queer youth of color resist one-dimensional, narrow, and objectifying narratives. Patel (2014) argues that too often, humanizing research is disregarded for grand narratives that support the colonizing effect of education research. Thus, methodological perspectives, whether qualitative, quantitative, mixed, or interpretive, that are concerned with Black queer youth, their multiple identities, and how hip hop functions in their lives must be concerned with how Black queer youth create, resist, find joy, build self-efficacy and community, find pleasure, and ultimately construct a "black capacity to desire" (Wilderson, 2008, p. 265). Black queer youth need a methodological perspective that aims to understand how "even in the face of the brutally imposed difficulties of black life, [life] is cause for celebration" (Moten, 2013, p. 742). According to Moten (2013), "celebration is the essence of black thought" (p. 742) because "celebration turns out to be the condition of possibility of black thought, which animates that black operation that will produce the absolute overturning" (p. 742). Methodological perspectives need to recognize the importance of creativity, laughter, joy, love, and innovation to all participants and communities, regardless of race, ethnicity, and gender.

The Black ratchet imagination as a methodological perspective is a humanizing, hyper-local, messy, and unfixed framework that provides more context for research investigating Black queer youth. Its ethos depends on the types of performativity valued in the community, the localized lyrical themes of the neighborhood, the cultural practices that have been passed down from one generation to the next, the celebration that is formed from precarity, and, most important, the researcher's ability to view Black queer youth through their agentive practices as they create ratchet spaces in response to this ratchet world.

# References

Bartone, M. (2015). *Navigating and negotiating identity in the black gay mecca: Educational and institutional influences that positively impact the life histories of black gay male youth in Atlanta* (Unpublished doctoral dissertation). Georgia State University, Atlanta, GA.

Bell, D. (1996). Gospel choirs: *Psalms of survival in an alien land called home.* New York, NY: Basic Books.

Blackburn, M. V. (2005). Agency in borderland discourses: Examining language use in a community center with black queer youth. *Teachers College Record, 107*(1), 89–113.

Blackburn, M. V., & McCready, L. T. (2009). Voices of queer youth in urban schools: Possibilities and limitations. *Theory Into Practice, 48*(3), 222–230. doi:10.1080 /00405840902997485.

Bradley, R. N. (2013, March 19). *I been on (ratchet): Conceptualizing a sonic ratchet aesthetic in Beyonce's "bow down"* [Blog post]. Retrieved from http://redclayscholar .blogspot.2013/03/i-been-on-ratchet-conceptualizing-sonic.html.

Britzman, D. P. (1997). What is this thing called love?: New discourses or understanding gay and lesbian youth. In S. de Castell & M. Bryson (Eds.), *Radical in<ter>ventions: Identity, politics, and differences in educational praxis* (pp. 183–207). Albany, NY: State University of New York Press.

Brockenbrough, E. (2015). Queer of color agency in educational contexts: Analytic frameworks from a queer of color critique. *Educational Studies, 51*(1), 28-44. doi: 10.1080/0013946.2014.979929.

Brockenbrough, E. (2016). Becoming queerly responsive: Culturally responsive pedagogy for Black and Latino urban queer youth. *Urban Education,* 51(2), 170–196. doi:10.1177/0042085914549261.

Brockenbrough, E., & Boatwright, T. (2013). In the MAC: Creating safe spaces for transgender youth of color. In K. Jocson (Ed.), *Cultural transformations: Youth and pedagogies of possibility* (pp. 165–182). Cambridge, MA: Harvard Education Press.

Brown, N. E., & Young, L. (2015). Ratchet politics: Moving beyond Black women's bodies to indict institutions and structures. *National Political Science Review,* 17(2), 45–56.

Brown, R. N., & Kwakye, C. J. (Eds.). (2012). *Wish to live: The hip-hop feminism pedagogy reader.* New York, NY: Peter Lang.

Catalanello, R. (2015, February 26). 39% of New Orleans children live in poverty, well above national average, report says. *The Times-Picayune.* Retrieved from http://www .nola.com/health/index .ssf/2015/02/thirty-nine_percent_of_new_orl.html.

Clandinin, D. J., & Connelly, F. M. (2000). *Narrative inquiry: Experience and story in qualitative research.* San Francisco, CA: Jossey-Bass.

Cohen, C. J. (1997). Punks, bulldaggers, and welfare queens: The radical potential of queer politics? *GLQ: A Journal of Lesbian & Gay Studies,* 3, 437–465.

Cohen, C. J. (2004). Deviance as resistance: A new research agenda for the study of Black politics. *Du Bois Review,* 1(1), 27–45.

Cohen, C. J. (2010). Democracy remixed: *Black youth and the future of American politics.* New York, NY: Oxford University Press.

Collins, P. H. (2000). Black feminist thought: *Knowledge, consciousness, and the politics of empowerment.* New York, NY: Routledge.

Cooper, B. (2012, December 31). *(Un)Clutching my mother's pearls, or ratchetness and the residue of respectability* [Blog post]. Retrieved from http://www .crunkfeministcollective.com/2012/12/31 unclutching-my-mothers-pearls-or-rat chetness-and-the-residue-of-respectablity/.

Cooper, B. C. (2017). *Beyond respectability: The intellectual thought of race women.* Champaign, IL: University of Illinois.

Cruz, C. (2011). LGBTQ street youth talk back: A meditation on resistance and witnessing. *International Journal of Qualitative Studies in Education,* 24(5), 547–558.

Dee, J. (2010, July 22). New Orleans's gender-bending rap. *The New York Times.* Retrieved from http://nytimes.com/2010/07/25/magazine/25-bounce-t.html?page wanted=all&_r=pal.

Dia, H. (2012). *Michaela Angela Davis looks to "bury the ratchet."* Retrieved from http:// newsone.com/2100749/michaela-angela-davis-bury-the-ratchet/.

Dimitriadis, G. (2015). Framing hip hop: New methodologies for new times. *Urban Education,* 50(1), 31–51.

Duggan, L. (1992). Making it perfectly queer. *Socialist Review,* 22, 11–31.

Dumas, M. Timeline [Facebook page]. Retrieved August 2, 2017, from https://www .facebook.com/afrographia.

Dumas, M. J., & ross, K. M. (2016). "Be real Black for me": Imagining BlackCrit in education. *Urban Education,* 51(4), 415–442. doi:10.1177/0042085916628611.

Ferguson, R. A. (2004). *Aberrations in black: Toward a queer of color critique.* Minneapolis, MN: University of Minnesota Press.

Forman, M. (2000). "Represent": Race, space and place in rap music. *Popular Music,* 19(1), 65–90.

Gang, M. N. (2008). *Toward the queerest insurrection* [Zine]. Retrieved from https://itsgoing down.org/wpcontent/uploads/2017/02/toward_the_queerest_insurrection_read. pdf.

Glover, J. A., Galliher, R. V., & Lamere, T. G. (2009). Identity development and exploration among sexual minority adolescents: Examination of a multidimensional model. *Journal of Homosexuality,* 56(1), 77–101. doi:10.1080/00918360802551555.

Hobbs, H. (2012, November 20). A Review of Matt Miller's *Bounce: Rap music and local identity in New Orleans. Southern Spaces.* Retrieved from http://southernspaces .org/2012/review-matt-millers-bounce-rap-music-and-local-identity-new-orleans.

hooks, b. (2004). *We real cool: Black men and masculinity.* New York, NY: Routledge.

Huang, Y. P., Brewster, M. E., Moradi, B., Goodman, M. B., Wiseman, M. C., & Martin, A. (2010). Content analysis of literature about LGB people of color: 1998–2007. *The Counseling Psychologist,* 38(3), 363–396. doi:10.1177/0011000009335255.

Jagose, A. (1996). *Queer theory: An introduction.* New York, NY: New York University Press.

Kelley, R. D. G. (2002). Freedom dreams: *The Black radical imagination.* Boston, MA: Beacon.

Lewis, H. R. (2013). *Exhuming the ratchet before it's buried* [Blog post]. Retrieved from http://www.thefeministwire.com/2013/01/exhuming-the-ratchet-before-its -buried.

Lindsey, T. B. (2015). Let me blow your mind: Hip hop feminist futures in theory and praxis. *Urban Education,* 50(1), 52–77. doi:10.1177/0042085914563184.

Lipsitz, G. (1998). Mardi Gras Indians: Carnival and counternarrative in Black New Orleans. *Cultural Critique,* 10, 99–121. doi:10.2307/1354109.

Love, B. L. (2012). Hip hop's li'l sistas speak: Negotiating identities and politics in the new south. New York, NY: Peter Lang.

Love, B. L. (2016). Complex personhood of hip hop and the sensibilities of the culture that fosters knowledge of self and self-determination. *Equity and Excellence in Education,* 49(4), 414–427.

Love, B. L., & Tosolt, B. (2013). Go underground or in your face: Queer students' negotiation of all-girls Catholic schools. *Journal of LGBT Youth,* 10, 186–207. doi:10.1080 /19361653.2013.799901.

McCready, L. T. (2001). When fitting in isn't an option, or why Black queer males at a California high school stay away from project 10. In K. Kumashiro (Ed.), *Troubling intersections of race and sexuality: Queer students of color and anti-oppressive education* (pp. 37–54). Lanham, MD: Rowman & Littlefield.

McCready, L. T. (2004). Understanding the marginalization of gay and gender nonconforming. Black male students. *Theory Into Practice,* 43(2), 136–143.

McCready, L. T. (2010). Black queer bodies, Afrocentric reform and masculine anxiety. *The International Journal of Critical Pedagogy,* 3(1), 52–67.

Miller, M. (2006). Bounce: Rap music and cultural survival in New Orleans. *HypheN-ation, 1*(1), 15–30.

Miller, M. (2012). *Bounce: Rap music and local identity in New Orleans.* Amherst, MA: University of Massachusetts Press.

Monroe, I. (2016, February 10). Beyonce does justice to New Orleans's rich queer culture. *The Advocate.* Retrieved from http://www.advocate.com/commentary/2016/2/10/beyonce-does-justice-new-orleanss-rich-queer-culture.

Morgan, J. (2000). *When chickenheads come home to roost: A hip-hop feminist breaks it down.* New York, NY: Simon and Schuster.

Morgan, J. (2015). Why we get off: Moving towards a Black feminist politics of pleasure. *The Black Scholar, 45*(4), 36–46. doi:10.1080/ 00064246.2015.1080915.

Moten, F. (2013). Blackness and nothingness (mysticism in the flesh). *South Atlantic Quarterly, 112*(4), 737–780.

Muñoz, J. E. (2009). *Cruising utopia: The then and there of queer futurity.* New York, NY: New York University Press.

Ortved, J. (2013, April 11). Ratchet: The rap insult that became a compliment. *New York Magazine.* Retrieved from http://nymag.com/thecut/2013/04/ratchet-the-rap-insult-that-became-a-compliment.html.

Paris, D. (2011). "A friend who understand fully": Notes on humanizing research in a multiethnic youth community. *International Journal of Qualitative Studies in Education, 24*(2), 137–149. doi:10 .1080/09518398.2010.495091.

Patel, L. (2014). Countering coloniality in educational research: From ownership to answerability. *Educational Studies, 50*(4), 357–377. doi:10.1080/00131946.2014.924942.

Phillion, J. (2008). Multicultural and cross-cultural narrative inquiry into understanding immigrant students' educational experience in Hong Kong. *Compare, 38*(3), 281–293.

Poulson-Bryant, S. (2013). "Put some bass in your walk": Notes on queerness, hip hop, and the spectacle of the undoable. *Palimpsest: A Journal on Women, Gender, and the Black International, 2*(2), 214–225.

Quinn, T. M. (2007). "You make me erect!": Queer girls of color negotiating heteronormative leadership at an urban all-girls' public school. *Journal of Gay & Lesbian Issues in Education, 4*(3), 31–47. doi:10.1300/J367v04n03_04.

Roller, M. (2016). Qualitative analysis: *The biggest obstacle to enriching survey outcomes* [Blog post]. Retrieved from https://researchdesign-review.com/2016/03/28/qualitative-analysis-the-biggest-obstacle-to-enriching-survey-outcomes.

Rose, T. (2008). The hip hop wars: *What we talk about when we talk about hip hop and why it matters.* New York, NY: Basic Books.

Ross, F. (2015). Big Freedia: *God save the queen diva.* New York, NY: Gallery Books.

Rotter, J. (2015, June 25). Big Freedia bounces his way to pride. *The San Francisco Weekly.* Retrieved from http://www.sfweekly.com/shookdown/2015/06/25/big-freedia-bounces-his-way-to-pride.

Snorton, C. R. (2013). As queer as hip hop. *Palimpsest: A Journal on Women, Gender, and the Black International, 2*(2), vi–x.

Stallings, L. H. (2007). *Mutha is half a word: Intersections of folklore, vernacular, myth, and queerness in Black female culture.* Columbus, OH: The Ohio State University Press.

Stallings, L. H. (2013). Hip hop and the Black ratchet imagination. *Palimpsest: A Journal on Women, Gender, and the Black International*, 2(2), 135–139.

Thompson, J. (2011). *You make me feel: A study of the gay rights movement in New Orleans* (Unpublished honors thesis). The University of Southern Mississippi, Hattiesburg, MS.

Tuck, E., & Yang, K. W. (2014). R-words: Refusing research. In D. Paris & M. T. Winn (Eds.), *Humanizing research: Decolonizing qualitative inquiry with youth and* communities (pp. 223–247). Thousand Oaks, CA: Sage.

Vaz, K. M. (2013a). The "baby dolls": *Breaking the race and gender barriers of the New Orleans Mardi Gras tradition*. Baton Rouge, LA: Louisiana State University Press.

Vaz, K. M. (2013b, February 16). *The "baby dolls" of Mardi Gras: A fun tradition with a serious side*. Retrieved from http://www.npr.org/2013/02/16/172165237/the-baby-dolls-of-mardi-gras-a-fun-tradition-with-a-serious-side.

Wilderson, F. B., III. (2008). Incognegro: *A memoir of exile and apartheid*. Cambridge, MA: South End.

# Cathy J. Cohen

# Deviance as Resistance: A New Research Agenda for the Study of Black Politics

This article is motivated by a series of conversations I have had and observations I have made about the study of Black politics, African American Studies, and the condition of African American communities.[1] At the heart of such concerns has been what I believe to be a fundamental contradiction between the crises facing Black communities and the passive routinization of much of what passes for the academic study of Black people. As both the discipline of African American Studies and the sub-field of Black politics become more enmeshed in the curriculum and structures of colleges and universities, research in these areas seems to mirror the increasing specialization of disciplines and distancing between researcher and worldly experience that characterize the academy at this moment. It is the observation of disconnect between me and my colleagues and the communities from which many of us hail and purport to study that has motivated my interest in building a field of inquiry others have labeled Black queer studies.[2]

I must admit to being a skeptic of the transformative potential of anything we might label Black queer studies, especially as such efforts begin to resemble a recovery project of the lost tribe of Black gay exceptionals. It is, of course, a worthwhile undertaking to include as part of the canon of African American Studies, for example, those Black gay writers of the Harlem Renaissance or Black gay activists of the Civil Rights Movement who for too long have been hidden and silenced by those who would police the representation of such critical periods and events. Furthermore, I, like other scholars concerned with the future of African American Studies, believe that the full inclusion of gay, lesbian, and queer lives would not only open up new realms of research in African American Studies, but should also lead to the reconsideration and reconceptualization of now standard narratives in the field. For example, John D'Emilio, in his book *Lost Prophet: The Life and Times of Bayard Rustin* (2003), not only rightly inserts Rustin into African American and American history, establishing him as an architect of the Civil Rights Movement, but also helps us to interrogate the concept of leader and the standards used to construct public leaders both in and outside of Black communities. Barbara Ransby, in her book *Ella Baker and the Black Freedom Movement: A Radical Democratic Vision* (2003), makes a similar intervention around the issues of gender, sex, and leadership. However, in spite of the insights to be gained from a project of inclusion, the approach to queering African American Studies that I advocate is one based in an expansive understanding of who and what is queer and is, therefore, rooted in ideas such as deviance and agency and not exception and inclusion.

Queer theorists and queer activists since the 1980s, in an effort to challenge seemingly stable and normalizing categories of sexuality, introduced or reintroduced the analytic concept of queer. Individuals such as Judith Butler (1990), Eve Sedgwick (1990), Diana Fuss (1991), and Michael Warner (1993) produced what are now thought of as some of the grounding texts to the field of "queer theory." Working from a variety of postmodernist and poststructuralist theoretical perspectives, these scholars focused on identifying and contesting the discursive and cultural markers found within both dominant and marginal identities and institutions that prescribe and reify "heterogendered" or normalized understandings and behavior. These theorists presented the academy with a different conceptualization of sexuality, one which sought to replace socially named and presumably stable and natural categories of sexual expression with an understanding of the constructed and fluid movement among and between forms of sexual behavior.

Despite complicating our understanding of sexuality, heterosexism, and heteronormativity, some queer theorists, and more queer activists, write and act in ways that unfortunately homogenize everything that is publicly identifiable as heterosexual and most things that are understood to be lesbian, gay, bisexual, and transgender or "queer" (Cohen 1997). Further diminishing the returns from this very important theoretical work has been the incredible silence in many of the writings by queer theorists on the subject of race, in particular the structural access to power that results from the designation of Whiteness in a relatively persistent racial order where White and Black root opposite poles of at least one dimension (Kim 2000). Disappointingly, left largely unexplored has been the role of race and one's relationship to dominant power in constructing the range of public and private possibilities for such fundamental concepts or behaviors as desire, pleasure, and sex.[3] So while we can talk of the heterosexual and the queer, these labels/categories tell us very little about the differences in the relative power of, for example, middle-class White gay men and poor heterosexual Black women and men.

For me, this serious shortcoming in queer theory is not the end of my interest in or use for this field of scholarship. Instead, in spite of noted absences in queer theory as it is currently constituted, there are still important insights to be gained from this literature that will enhance the study of sex and race in many disciplines including African American Studies.[4] If, for example, we use the theoretical insights into the construction and malleability of categories as well as the work of processes of normalization found in queer theory in tandem with the detailed understanding of power, in particular as it is structured around and through axes such as race, gender, and class found in African American Studies, we have the possibility of reconstituting both African American Studies and queer theory with an eye toward recognizing and transforming how people live and the desperate conditions they too often face.

A focus, for example, on poor single Black women with children, whose intimate relationships and sexual behavior are often portrayed as directly in conflict with the normative assumptions of heterosexism and the nuclear family, but who also often live under the constant surveillance of the state through regulatory agencies such as welfare offices, courts, jails, prisons, child protective services, and public housing authorities, might do much to advance the work of both those who locate themselves exclusively in African American Studies or queer theory. In contrast to many privileged gay, lesbian, and queer folks, poor single Black women with children, structurally unable to control an exclusive "ghetto" or area of a city where their dealings with the state are often chosen and from an empowered position, are reminded daily of their distance from the promise of full citizenship. Their lives are indicative of the intersection of marked identities and regulatory processes, relative powerlessness and limited and contradictory agency. It is here that Black queer studies must be rooted and a politics of deviance must begin.

Thus, I continue to be interested in the possibility of constructing a field of investigation based in African American Studies and borrowing from queer theory and Black feminist analysis that is centered around the experiences of those who stand on the (out)side of state sanctioned, normalized White, middle- and upper-class, male heterosexuality. I am talking about a paradigmatic shift in how scholars of Black politics and more broadly African American Studies think and write about those most vulnerable in Black communities—those thought to be morally wanting by both dominant society and other indigenous group members. The reification of the nuclear family, the conformity to institutionally prescribed and informally regulated gender roles and intimate sexual relations are but the tip of the normative moral super structure they confront daily.

Sadly, while the moral prescriptions of this normative structure pervade nearly every aspect of our lives and have been used consistently to marginalize African Americans further, little attention has been paid, at least in the social sciences, to how the normalizing influences of the dominant society have been challenged, or at least countered, often by those most visible as its targets. Reflecting Michel Foucault's idea of simultaneous repressive and generative power, individuals with little power in society engage in counternormative behaviors, having babies before they are married, structuring their relationships differently from the traditional nuclear family, or rejecting heterosexuality completely. These so-called deviants have chosen and acted differently, situating their lives in direct contrast to dominant normalized understandings of family, desire, and sex. It is these instances of deviant practice, resulting from the *limited agency* of those most marginal in Black communities, that are the heart of this work.

Scholars, especially those interested in the evolving nature of Black politics, must take seriously the possibility that in the space created by deviant discourse and practice, especially in Black communities, a new radical politics of deviance could emerge. It might take the shape of a radical politics of the personal, embedded in more recognized Black counter-publics, where the most marginal individuals in Black communities, with an eye on the state and other regulatory systems, act with the limited agency available to them to secure small levels of autonomy in their lives. Ironically, through these attempts to find autonomy, these individuals, with relatively little access to dominant power, not only counter or challenge the presiding normative order with regard to family, sex, and desire, but also create new or counter-normative frameworks by which to judge behavior.

And while these choices are not necessarily made with explicitly political motives in mind, they do demonstrate that people will challenge established norms and rules and face negative consequences in pursuit of goals important to them, often basic human goals such as pleasure, desire, recognition, and respect. These visible choices and acts of defiance challenge researchers to identify how we might leverage the process people use to choose deviance to choose political resistance as well. It just might be that after devoting so much of our energy to the unfulfilled promise of access through respectability, a politics of deviance, with a focus on the transformative potential found in deviant practice, might be a more viable strategy for radically improving the lives and possibilities of those most vulnerable in Black communities.

Finally, it is important to remember, as theorists of stigma and deviance have written, that understandings of what is respectable and stigmatized or normal and deviant are constructed and relational. Erving Goffman (1963) in his book *Stigma* writes, "Society establishes the means of categorizing persons and the complement of attributes felt to be ordinary and natural for members of each of these categories. . . . We lean on these anticipations that we have, transforming them into normative expectations, into righteously presented demands" (p. 2). Howard Becker (1973) in his study of the sociology of deviance continues along this line of reasoning and suggests that scholars be attuned to the distinction between rule-breaking behavior and the labeling of such behavior as deviant. He writes, "Deviance is not a quality of the act the person commits, but rather a consequence of the application by others of rules and sanctions to an 'offender.' The deviant is one to whom that label has successfully been applied; deviant behavior is behavior that people so label" (p. 9).[5]

In the rest of this article I will explore the feasibility of a politics of deviance in Black communities. I begin this investigation with a brief review of the major frameworks for studying Black politics. I then recount the ways deviance has been examined in some of the canonical texts in African American Studies. Finally, I detail how we might build an analytic model detailing the relationship between deviance, defiance, and resistance.

## Twentieth-Century Obsessions: A Black Politics of Respectability, Elites, and Public Opinion

A review of much of the recent scholarship exploring the politics of African Americans reveals at least three dominant analytic frameworks of study: mobilization, respectability, and public opinion. While each of these approaches to investigating Black politics allows for the inclusion of those most vulnerable and seemingly "deviant" in Black communities, absent in each approach is a serious examination of the potential for politics in the everyday decisions and actions of these individuals and groups. For example, possibly the most widely read form of analysis of Black politics has been scholarship documenting and analyzing the organized efforts, formal and informal movements, and less structured uprisings originating in Black communities, meant to alter hierarchies of power and resources based at least partially in racial distinctions (Horne 1995; Kelley 2002; Marable 1991; Morris 1984).

Work ranging from an analysis of Black revolts under slavery to the nationalist efforts of leaders like Marcus Garvey to the election of Black politicians to the mass mobilization defining the Civil Rights and Black Power Movements are all part of this tradition. However, more often than not, such scholarly analyses have sought to highlight those structured, coordinated, and seemingly purposeful acts assumed to comprise meaningful political struggle. Furthermore, these studies have at times been so consumed with the actions of leaders, usually male leaders, and well-established political organizations that they have ignored the everyday contests over space, dress, and autonomy that may pervade the lives of average Black people. Most of this literature, even when presumably exploring the work of "everyday" people, looks to those clearly defined political spaces like churches, civil rights organizations, and unions to find politics and political work, negating social spaces where most politics is lived (Harris-Lacewell 2004; Kelley 1994; Scott 1990).

Of course, a politics of mobilization has not been the only lens through which African American politics has been explored and described. A second dominant framework used to understand Black politics has been that of respectability. In this approach, respectability is used to categorize a process of policing, sanitizing, and hiding the nonconformist and some would argue deviant behavior of certain members of African Americans communities (Carby 1987, Gaines 1996, Higginbotham 1993). In this literature, respectability is understood as a strategy deployed primarily by the Black middle class but also by other individuals across the Black class strata to demonstrate their adherence to and upholding of the dominant norms of society. It is hoped and expected that such conformity will confer full citizenship status, bringing with it greater access, opportunities, and mobility. And while some recent scholarship has cast a critical eye on the exclusionary processes associated with a political strategy of respectability, it is important that we not trivialize or demean this vehicle to political advancement since for many African Americans it was not only a mechanism to leverage dominant power but also a means to demonstrate the basic humanity and equality of Black Americans (Carby 1987, Gaines 1996, Higginbotham 1993, McBride 1998). It is, however, important to underscore, as critics of respectability remind us, the relative positioning necessary to prove that one is respectable and acceptable compared to other less fortunate "souls" who compromise the excluded.

Historian Evelyn Brooks Higginbotham (1993), in her examination of Black women's involvement and leadership in the Baptist church in the early twentieth century, describes the use of a politics of respectability to counter the dominant racist constructions of Blackness and gender. She writes, "While adherence to respectability enabled Black women to counter racist images and structures, their discursive contestation was not directed solely at White Americans; the Black Baptist women condemned what they perceived to be negative practices and attitudes among their own people. Their assimilationist leanings led to their insistence upon Blacks' conformity to the dominant society's norms of manners and morals. Thus the discourse of respectability disclosed class and status differentiation" (p. 187).

Thus, another approach to studying the politics of African Americans, an approach first deployed by scholars in the humanities, has been an interrogation of the extra-institutional, some might say, social and cultural actions of Black Americans. Through the framework of respectability the researcher is primarily concerned with the actions of those who would regulate, most often middle-class Black Americans and working-class Blacks with middle-class aspirations. Again, lost in this analysis are the agency and actions of those under surveillance, those being policed, those engaged in disrespectable behavior. Missing from this understanding of Black politics is what Robin Kelley calls "a politics from below" (1994, p. 5).

The third and final approach to the study of Black politics I will mention briefly is the overwhelming focus on the public opinion of Black Americans found in the social sciences today, especially in the field of political science. Increasingly, as researchers in the social sciences became committed to the use of large N datasets to map out the political attitudes and behaviors of ordinary people, so too did scholars in the field of Black politics demonstrate increasing expertise in the use of statistical analysis in conjunction with newly developed datasets such as the National Black Election Study and the National Black Politics Study to explore the declared politics of Black respondents. The work of scholars such as Michael Dawson (2003, 1994), Larry Bobo (2000), Katherine Tate (1998), and many others has provided new insights into the ideological and behavioral dimensions of African American politics in the late twentieth century.

Unfortunately, while this literature often includes close analysis of differences in political attitudes and behavior based on class and in some cases sex and gender, the in-depth exploration of how such differences might be molded into a new politics for the twenty-first century has largely been ignored. This scholarship tends to excel in identifying and explaining differences found among African Americans and between African Americans and other members of racial and ethnic groups, most often White Americans. Left for a later day has been any sustained discussion of how the differences identified manifest themselves in the everyday lives and politics of Black people. Similarly, scholars of this orientation seem to shy away from more theoretical and normative discussions of what should be done to change the patterns of inequality, alienation, and anger evident in their data.

Thus, while all three of these approaches to analyzing politics and political work in Black communities have generated important insights, illuminating the multiple forms of resistance and ideas about politics found among Black Americans, there exists an inherent bias in each framework toward the recognition and study of a politics that is declared and traditionally organized. I am not suggesting that the political activity of poor, working-class, and marginal Black people has not made its way into our published accounts of Black politics. Instead, I contend that the politics of those most marginal in Black communities are usually discussed when they conform to traditional understandings of what constitutes legitimate politics, ranging from engagement with formal political institutions to the traditional, extra-systemic politics of riots, boycotts, and protests, to the adherence to dominant norms and expectations regarding behavior. Again, missing is an examination of the possibility of oppositional politics rooted outside of traditional or formal political institutions and, instead, in the daily lived experiences of those most marginal in Black communities.

Given these absences, those of us concerned with the lives and politics of Black people might do well to recalibrate our lens of examination toward those deemed "deviant" in Black communities, for here lies not only understudied populations but, more important, groups engaging in behaviors that I believe hold the potential for new understandings of how Black politics might once again become radically transformative for Black communities and the country at large. By transformative I am not arguing merely for better policies or a slight shift in the distribution of wealth and power, important as these advances are. Instead, I am suggesting that through a focus on "deviant" practice we are witness to the power of those at the bottom, whose everyday life decisions challenge, or at least counter, the basic normative assumptions of a society intent on protecting structural and social inequalities under the guise of some normal and natural order to life. However, not only do these individuals daily act in opposition to dominant norms, but they also contradict members of Black communities who are committed to mirroring perceived respectable behaviors and hierarchal structures.

I am urging scholars to take a critical and respectful look at such behavior, instead of the instinctive reaction of rushing to pathologize such acts. With careful investigation we might begin to understand why the same people who daily "reject" formal and informal incentives for conformity, choosing instead alternative and oppositional lifestyles, are most often not engaged in the kind of mass mobilization that organizers and academics contend would significantly improve their lived condition. It is time for a new generation of scholars to put forth a new analytic framework for the study of Black politics, that of deviance. This, of course, means hearing from and listening to those who many would silence and make invisible in Black communities, individuals like single Black mothers, including those on welfare and/or teenagers; gay, lesbian, bisexual, transgender, and queer members of Black communities; Black men on the "down-low" having at times risky sex with both men and women; and young Black men and women who are currently or have been incarcerated and who seem to engage uncritically in unlawful behavior with knowledge of the growing consequences of such behavior. Only by listening to their voices, trying to understand their motivations, and accurately centering their stories with all of their complexities in our work can we begin to understand and map the connection between deviant practice, defiant behavior, and political resistance.

## Pathologizing Black Deviance: African American Studies and Beyond

I am not suggesting that the topic of deviance has not found its way into the work of those studying and commenting on Black communities. The observance of and fascination with those labeled deviant has long existed in the social sciences and in African American studies. By now we have all become accustomed and well equipped at pointing out the constant pathologizing of Black communities. The researchers of the Eugenics period, the Moynihan Report in 1965, work on the underclass, and the publishing of *The Bell Curve* (1996) have all been rightly incorporated into our understanding and narrative about the continued marginalization and attack on Black people. Less familiar, however, may be the pathologizing, in particular of the poor, women, lesbian and gay, and young Black people, that is part of the multiple traditions, to borrow a phase from Rogers Smith (1993), that comprise the field of African American Studies.

Beginning with W.E.B. Du Bois's *The Philadelphia Negro* and extending through St. Clair Drake and Horace R. Cayton's *Black Metropolis* to more recent Black community studies, like those authored by Elijah Anderson and William Julius Wilson, there has always been a tradition of pathologizing the behaviors of the African American poor and working class, especially women. In defense of these authors and other similar texts, the fundamental objective of such studies, I believe, is to describe the contours of Black communities and to mount a rigorous examination of the systemic discrimination experienced by these subjects. However, far too often, as the researcher works to differentiate the lived conditions of segments of Black communities, internalized normative judgments about the proper and natural structure of family, intimate relationships, and forms of social interaction creep into the analysis and prescriptions about what must be done. It is here, under the guise of objectively studying Black communities, that the assumed importance of the nuclear family, appropriate gender relations, and the efficiency of the capitalist system imposes an understanding of difference that results in the pathologizing of all those who would choose differently on such fundamental and often assumed truths. The result can be the textual presentation of the Black poor and other Black "deviants" as not only suffering from the systemic discrimination experienced by all Black Americans, but also as allowing cultural deficiencies to lead one down a deviant path. It thus becomes the duty of an enlightened Black elite to rescue this wayward group of Blacks,

modeling for them the appropriate modes of behavior: those that will lead
to assimilation, acceptances, and access. Briefly, let me offer two examples of
work in this mode.

If we begin with Du Bois's groundbreaking work in *The Philadelphia
Negro* (1899), we find an astonishing piece of research emblematic of the
ideals of objective social science study, but driven ever so forcefully with
a mission of proving the respectability of the Negro race. With the help
of his assistant Isabel Eaton, Du Bois sets out to survey the conditions of
the seventh ward of Philadelphia, mapping the lived condition of Black
Americans as no scholar had before him. By the end of his work, Du Bois
had visited or talked with nearly five thousand individuals. Through his
travels he observed the wide range of experiences and lived conditions
thought to make up the Black experience. Throughout the book, Du Bois
reminds the reader of the historical and continued discrimination that has
shaped the lives of Black Americans. He does, however, also present what
some have called the "ugly facts" of some Black communities, including the
high levels of crime, pauperism, and family disorganization. For Du Bois
such behaviors could not be explained merely by discrimination and so it
was incumbent on the author to offer what he believed to be a complex
explanation for such occurrences, one that made visible discrimination,
agency, and difference among the Negro classes. This complex or contradictory tone is apparent throughout the book, as is evident in this discussion of crime:

> It would, of course, be idle to assert that most of the Negro crime
> was caused by prejudice; the violent economic and social changes
> which the last fifty years have brought to the American Negro,
> the sad social history that preceded these changes, have all con-
> tributed to unsettle morals and pervert talents. Nevertheless it is
> certain that Negro prejudice in cities like Philadelphia has been
> a vast factor in aiding and abetting all other causes which impel a
> half-developed race to recklessness and excess . . .

Thus the class of Negroes which the prejudices of the city have distinctly encouraged is that of the criminal, the lazy and the shiftless; for them the city teems with institutions and charities; for them there is succor and sympathy; for the educated and industrious young colored man who wants work and not platitudes, wages and not alms, just rewards and not sermons—for such colored men Philadelphia apparently has no use (pp. 351–52).

It was in the end differences among Black Americans, in particular class differences among Black Americans, where Du Bois rooted his argument against grand racial theories of the inferiority of the Negro. How could a biological concept of race account for behavior and ability when such diversity in each attribute was evident in Philadelphia's seventh ward? Du Bois was especially intent on noting the variations in family structure as an indication of the profound differences among the multiple classes and characters of Black Americans. It was the absence of a strong nuclear family and its corresponding bourgeois sexual mores that aided systemic discrimination in destroying Black communities.

Kevin Gaines, in his writing on Du Bois's *The Philadelphia Negro*, reiterates this point about the importance of family structure to Du Bois's understanding of the Black condition and the limits of Black progress. He writes,

> Bourgeois sexual morality provided Du Bois with a crucial means of articulating class differences among blacks, facilitating in his study a problematic linkage of poverty and immorality, and equating the disturbing presence of unmarried black women with promiscuity. He associated unemployment with idleness and sin, but his vision of lower-class status especially faulted all signs of the absence of the patriarchal black family . . .
>
> Du Bois's discussion of the weakness of the family stemmed from the uplift assumption of the home and family as signs of progress and security, and sources of strength. Indeed much

commentary on urban poverty targeted the status of the family as
the barometer of social health or pathology. (p.166)

While Du Bois's unflinching adherence to the assumption of the necessity and inherent preference of the nuclear family might be accepted as an
indication of the times in which he was writing, we should be suspect of
those writing today who continue to demonstrate uncritical allegiance to
such assumptions. Unfortunately, such is the case of most recent writing on
poor Black urban communities, especially those classified under the title the
"underclass." Beginning largely in the 1960s, researchers began to categorize what they perceived as more severe indicators of destructive behaviors
and characteristics found in poor urban communities. While scholars had
always noted the escalated rates of out-of-wedlock and teenage births, crime,
welfare dependency, female-headed households, joblessness, and drug use
in poor urban communities compared to other geographical areas, in the
1960s such behaviors were increasingly described as common-place, persistent, and disproportionate, especially among a sub-population of the urban
poor deemed the "underclass."

As we might suspect, there are varied approaches to explaining these behaviors and exploring these communities in the literature of the "underclass."
The point of this essay is not to survey the range of texts available. Instead, I
want to examine briefly one of the most structurally based interrogations of
the idea of an underclass to see how patriarchal and gender norms limit the
analysis, prioritizing a move toward respectability in thinking about something as concrete as policy prescriptions. To that end, I believe a brief review
of William Julius Wilson's The Truly Disadvantaged (1987) will be helpful.
Regarded by many in the academy and the Clinton administration as one
of the most important scholars writing on the subject of the urban poor,
Wilson seeks to provide a more rigorous and "balanced public discourse on
the problems of the ghetto underclass" (p. 19). Wilson centers his analysis
on the structural changes faced by the Black urban poor, highlighting in
particular the shift in available jobs for members of the Black urban poor
from living-wage manufacturing jobs to low-wage service employment.

While job opportunities were shrinking for the urban poor, middle-class and working-class African Americans experienced economic access and, thus, allowed some Black Americans to exit the inner city for neighborhoods with better schools, services, and security. This exit has meant greater social isolation for the urban poor, resulting in a concentration of all ill effects associated with poverty and sustained marginalization.

While Wilson's concern with the exit of the Black middle class has been problematized by numerous scholars, with one of the most hard-hitting treatments being that penned by Adolph Reed (1991), for this article I want to draw the reader's attention to the normative assumptions of Wilson's analysis and, more specifically, the prominent framing of a politics of respectability in Wilson's policy prescriptions to address the needs of the underclass. Continually in this work one is struck by the importance of the nuclear family structure and dominant gender relationships for the author. For example, after detailing the increased probability of living in poverty for female-headed households, Wilson does not urge a policy intervention that would focus on raising the wages of women, including single women and teenagers who are heads of households. Instead, Wilson locates the remedy for the poverty experienced by women and children in the reemergence of viable families, specifically expanding women's marriageability pool of employed men. He writes, "The black delay in marriage and the lower rate of remarriage, each associated with high percentages of out-of-wedlock births and female-headed households, can be directly tied to the employment status of black males. Indeed, black women, especially young black women, are confronting a shrinking pool of 'marriageable' (that is economically stable) men" (p. 145).

*The Truly Disadvantaged*, in the tradition of *The Philadelphia Negro*, is a well-researched and often insightful work into the structural and demographic changes confronting poor Black communities. And while Wilson does not offer explicit normative judgments about the inherent deficiencies of poor Black people that other "underclass" scholars promote, he does question many of the assumed standards of respectability thought to be shared among enlightened and appropriate people, independent of race or class. For

example, never in the text does Wilson fundamentally question the importance of, nor does he raise the possible negative consequences of, the dominant and imposed nuclear family structure. Never does he openly worry
about the impact of strict gender relations on the lived experience of young
Black males—no doubt some of them gay—at the center of his analysis.
Moreover, never does he attempt to explore the creativity, adaptability, and
transformative possibilities that exist in the alternative family, intimate, and
social relationships and behavior thought to distinguish the underclass. He
never explores what Ted Gordon calls the "cultural range" of Black communities where "there appears a repertoire of practices and meanings which,
when seen in relation to the dominant culture, extends from resistant to
accommodative" (1997, p. 40).

For example, is it possible that the socialization of young boys to believe
that they have not fulfilled their manly obligations unless they are able to
provide for their families means that young men who have no access to
the low-skilled, high-wage jobs of past years and thus no legal means of
"providing" for their children, partners, and other family members decide
to engage in dangerous and illegal activity to meet or appear to meet such
norms? Furthermore, is it possible that traditional narratives of masculinity
encourage men who are structurally unable to meet such ideas to detach
from any engaged role with their children and partners? Similarly, is it possible that the shared caretaking strategies of young, single women with children, where both family and friends aid in the "raising" of children—often
because their help is required in light of limited resources—could help us
better understand and appreciate the benefits to be gained from communal
practices in child rearing?

I am not suggesting that norms of masculinity explain all of the counter-
normative behavior with regard to family structure that Wilson outlines in
his book. I do believe, however, that we must examine such ideas, norms,
and processes of socialization as both part of the cause and possible "solution"
to these phenomena. In the same way that scholars develop and advocate new
economic programs they believe will create living-wage jobs for both men
and women who are under- and unemployed, so too must we explore and

put forth new ways of defining and teaching what it is to be a contributing and healthy man or woman in this society and in Black communities. Structural interventions, while critically important, will never provide sufficient solutions to normative and structurally constituted crises.

Clearly Du Bois and Wilson do not represent the breadth of approaches and the body of literature that has developed on the Black poor. They do, however, represent the general complacency found among those who study such communities, leaving unexamined the normative structure that is used to pathologize certain choices and demonize specific communities. I offer their work as a lesson to us all about the instinctive move, even among some of our most dedicated and respected scholars, to judge and pathologize the lives of those most vulnerable in Black communities. At the root of such judgments sits an unexamined acceptance of normative standards of association, behavior, and even desire that limits our ability to respect the subjects under consideration and to explore their lived decisions with an eye toward their transformative and oppositional potential.

It would be disingenuous of me to suggest that those studying the Black poor have only engaged in the pathologizing of those communities. There is a contrasting literature on the Black poor that has explained their seemingly deviant behavior as reflecting the limited and adaptive choices of a marginalized group. Whether it is ethnographies like Carol Stack's *All Our Kin* (1997) or Mitch Duneier's *Slim's Table* (1994), these works have stopped short of demonizing the actions of the Black poor, seeking instead to understand the reasons for such choices and the functions they serve. However, still left unexplored in these texts are the possibilities for broader and more radical transformation. No doubt the political potential of these acts is ignored, in part because the intent of these and other ethnographic studies is to detail what exists and offer reasoned explanations of why these patterns are maintained. Rarely is an ethnographic work focused on the question of what might be, especially in the political realm and especially beyond the neighborhood or community under study. Thus, because of past limitations in focus, question, and method, I believe a new focus on the relationship between deviant practice, discourse, and politics is necessary.

# Deviance, Agency, Autonomy, and Resistance

Throughout this article I have argued for a renewed focus on those acts of perceived deviance in Black communities, not to explain their functional or dysfunctional characteristics, but instead to investigate their potential for the production of counter-normative behaviors and oppositional politics. As I stated earlier, I am interested in why individuals with little access to and protection from dominant power choose to engage in behaviors that are largely deemed, at least by dominant narratives, to be outside the realm of acceptable behavior. These choices can threaten or call into question one's status within Black communities, but more often they jeopardize the formal standing of already marginal individuals in relation to the state.[6] In addition to these individual acts of deviance, I am also interested in how deviant choices that are repeated by groups or subgroups of people can create a space where normative myths of how the society is naturally structured are challenged in practice (the decision to have a baby before one is married) and in speech (the statement "I don't need a man" by the same single mother). While I accept the warning of Dorian Warren that cumulative acts of individual agency are not the same as collective agency, I do believe that in this counter-normative space exists the possibility of radical change, not only in the distribution of resources, but also definitional power, redefining the rules of normality that limit the dreams, emotions, and acts of most people.

Observing and probing the agency of people who, understanding the expectations of the larger society and their communities, choose differently from what is prescribed must be the point from which we start to build a new research agenda for African American Studies in general and the study of Black politics in particular. The centering of those most marginal in Black communities is, for me, the real work of queering Black studies. Using a theoretical framework closely associated with the commitments of Black feminists, queer theorists, and students of Black politics, where the counter-normative behavior and marginal position of different segments of Black communities are highlighted, not with an eye toward pathologizing or even justifying such behavior, but instead with an eye toward recognizing and understanding its possible subversive potential, we can reorient our respective fields to focus on the potential libratory aspects of deviance.

I am not suggesting that researchers ignore the deviant positioning of the choices and behaviors of individuals relative to normative standards. In fact, it is their diminished position that makes such choices in part worthy of study. My hope, however, is that our research does not stop there, merely noting their deviant status and the seemingly self-destructive "nature" of such acts. Instead, I am suggesting that we also explore why people believe they made these decisions; did they understand, expect, and experience negative consequences from these choices; and does such behavior demonstrate some degree of agency on the part of marginalized individuals that can be mobilized for more explicitly political goals? These deviant choices, which are by no means chosen freely in the liberal sense, have the ability to help us delineate the relationship between agency, autonomy, and opposition that has been missing in many of our most insightful analyses of oppositional politics by oppressed people.

Specifically, I hypothesize that many of the acts labeled resistance by scholars of oppositional politics have not been attempts at resistance at all, but instead are the struggle of those most marginal to maintain or regain some agency in their lives as they try to secure such human rewards as pleasure, fun, and autonomy. In no way is this statement meant to negate the political potential to be found in such behavior. It does underscore, however, my stance that the work marginal people pursue to find and protect some form of autonomy is not inherently politicized work and the steps leading from autonomy to resistance must be detailed and not assumed. We must begin to delineate the conditions under which transgressive behavior becomes trans-formative and deviant practice is transformed into politicized resistance.

For example, Jim Scott in both the *Weapons of the Weak* (1987) and *Domination and the Arts of Resistance* (1990) implores the reader to look beyond the public transcript of formal interactions between the dominant and those much less powerful to understand the full range of political acts of resistance being pursued by those dominated. Scott writes:

Until quite recently, much of the active political life of subordinate groups has been ignored because it takes place at a level we rarely recognize as political. To emphasize the enormity of what has been, by and large, disregarded, I want to distinguish between the open, declared forms of resistance, which attract most attention, and the disguised, low-profile, undeclared resistance that constitutes the domain of infrapolitics . . .

Taking a long historical view, one sees that the luxury of relatively safe, open political opposition is both rare and recent. . . . So long as we confine our conception of the *political* to activity that is openly declared we are driven to conclude that subordinate groups essentially lack a political life or that what political life they do have is restricted to those exceptional moments of popular explosion. To do so is to miss the immense political terrain that lies between quiescence and revolt and that, for better or worse, is the political environment of subject classes (1990, pp. 198–99).

Similarly, Robin Kelley in *Race Rebels* (1994) argues that if we expand where we look for political acts and what counts as politics, one can find numerous everyday acts of resistance in the lives of "ordinary" people. Extending this line of reasoning, Kelley argues that independent of the intended effect, marginal people can and do resist daily, through acts ranging from the outright challenge to those in power to participation in cultural forms thought to be deviant. He writes:

Like Scott, I use the concept of infrapolitics to describe the daily confrontations, evasive actions, and stifled thoughts that often inform organized political movements. I am not suggesting that the realm of infrapolitics is any more or less important or effective than what we traditionally understand to be politics. Instead I want to suggest that the political history of oppressed people cannot be understood without reference to infrapolitics, for these

daily acts have a cumulative effect on power relations. While the
meaning and effectiveness of various acts differ according to the
particular circumstances, they do make a difference, whether
intended or not (p. 8).

While I, too, believe that an expanded frame for recognizing resistance or
more generally political acts would reveal daily examples of what Scott calls
infrapolitics, I worry that both Scott and Kelley collapse important and necessary distinctions that exist in the choices and intent of those labeled marginal and deviant. Specifically, while I believe that some choices that are
labeled deviant, such as the choice to live one's life as an out gay, lesbian,
bisexual, transgender, or queer person, may be driven by a conscious inten-
tionality to resist the heteronormativity of the society and the second-class
position of gay subjects, surely not all acts of deviance are examples of politicized resistance to either larger or local manifestations of domination and
oppression. Some acts labeled deviant are defiant in nature, where individuals make a conscious decision to go against established rules either publicly
or through hidden means. However, every counter-normative defiant act
is not political, either in intent, result, or both, where political resistance is
the intent to defy laws, interactions, obligations, and normative assumptions
viewed as systematically unfair. Thus, one of the significant challenges facing scholars is to determine how to differentiate deviant practice, defiance,
and resistance.

It is the distinction I make among deviance, defiance, and resistance and
the significant role I assign to *intent* in marking politicized resistance that I
believe helps us to build on the important insights provided by Scott and
Kelley while offering more analytic precision to our efforts to identify and
understand the political potential contained in deviant behavior. Again, I
am not suggesting that Scott and Kelley do not recognize the difference
between, for example, cultural expression and political resistance, but in
their writings there exists less clarity about the boundaries between these
categories. For example, in describing the work and pleasure of "dance halls,
blues clubs and 'jook joints'" in the South, Kelley writes,

In darkened rooms ranging in size from huge halls to tiny dens, black working people of both sexes shook and twisted their over-worked bodies, drank, talked, engaged in sexual play, and—in spite of occasional fights—reinforced their sense of communi-ty . . .

I am not suggesting that parties, dances, and other leisure pur-suits were merely guises for political events, or that these cultural practices were clear acts of resistance. Instead, much if not most of African American popular culture can be characterized as, to use Raymond Williams's terminology, "alternative" rather than oppositional. Most people attend those events to escape from the world of assembly lines, relief lines, and color lines, and to leave momentarily the individual and collective battles against racism, sexism and material deprivation . . .

Knowing what happens in these spaces of pleasure can help us understand the solidarity black people have shown at politi-cal mass meetings, illuminate the bonds of fellowship one finds in churches and voluntary associations, and unveil the conflicts across class and gender lines that shape and constrain these collec-tive struggles. (pp. 46–47)

Again, while I agree with Kelley's call to study nontraditional sites of social gathering in Black communities, it is his claims about the creation of com-munal bonds in social spaces that transfer to more explicitly political and civic formations that I believe demand greater elaboration and empirical investigation. I hypothesize that most acts labeled deviant or even defiant of power are not attempts to sway fundamentally the distribution of power in the country or even permanently change the allocation of power among the individuals involved in an interaction. Instead, these acts, decisions, or behaviors are more often attempts to create greater autonomy over one's life, to pursue desire, or to make the best of very limited life options. Thus, instead of attempting to increase one's power *over* someone, people living with limited resources may use the restricted agency available to them to create autonomous spaces absent the continuous stream of power *from* outside authorities or normative structures. And while an act of defiance can be misinterpreted as having political intent and a direct challenge to the distribution of power and may result in the actual redistribution of power, I would contend that the initial act was not one of resistance. Thus, understanding the distinction between deviance, defiant acts, and acts of resistance lies in recognizing the perspective or intent of the individual. It is my emphasis on understanding intent as it relates to the agency of marginal individuals where I believe I part ways with Kelley and Scott.

I want to be clear. I am not suggesting that acts somehow deemed as deviant or defiant have no relationship to the category of acts I label resistance or are devoid of political consequence. Instead, I am suggesting that such acts cannot be read as resistance independent of some understanding of the intent and agency of the individual. While there may be political possibilities in the deviant or defiant acts of marginally positioned people, that potential has to be mobilized in a conscious fashion to be labeled resistance. This distinction is not arbitrary, but one that signals the need for intervening mechanisms to transform deviant and defiant behavior into politically conscious acts that can be used as a point of entry into a mobilized political movement. Of course, the following question logically is, what type of intervening mechanisms are necessary? While I believe there exists multiple possibilities of effective interventions, from a relatively traditional approach to politics, one such intervention might be an increase in the number of grassroots organizations focused on talking to and organizing young people, including the so-called "deviants" of Black communities. For example, organizers that will listen to the stories of young people, who can relate to the cultural vehicles of this group, who recognize the counter-normative potential that exists in their non-traditional living and sexual arrangements, and who can aid in developing and articulating a political agenda that speaks to their lived condition are one example of an intervening mechanism I would recommend. In fact, some of the most interesting political work around the country is happening among organizations trying to mobilize those segments of society too often deemed deviants—young people who are unemployed, not in school, and possibly struggling with children; people incarcerated and now reentering their communities; and undocumented workers.

Unfortunately, too often scholars concerned with the politics of marginal communities have ignored the distinction of defiant or resistant acts and acts of politicized resistance, misdiagnosing the resources that exist and the resources needed for political mobilization. It might be that marginal subjects with a politicized consciousness choose localized attempts at control and autonomy because they have no mobilized outlet to confront the larger political context. Or they reject politics because they believe that the mobilized organizations that do exist have no interest in and commitment to the issues that animate their lives; those disrespectable life and death issues in hiding in Black communities. These are empirical questions waiting for study.

It is possible that eventually the cumulative impact of individual deviant choices may indeed have an effect on power relations as Kelley suggests, creating spaces or counter-publics, where not only oppositional ideas and discourse happen, but lived opposition, or at least autonomy, is chosen daily. And through the repetition of deviant practices by multiple individuals, new identities, communities, values, and politics may be created where seemingly deviant, unconnected behavior was thought to exist. And to go one long step further, it might also be that in those counter-normative choices lie the seeds for challenging many of the normative structures that have defined some in Black communities as deviant. Thus, it is possible that through deviant choices individuals open up a space where public defiance of the norms is seen as a possibility and an oppositional worldview develops. But again, while this newly created space of autonomy and difference may in fact change the incentive and norm structure for that subgroup, the original choice was not one of resistance even if the continued practice of deviant behavior has long-lasting political consequences. Of course, this example suggests that intended political resistance is not the only way to achieve political results, although it may be a necessary and effective component to protect and maintain newly created spaces and norms. My instinctive move toward collective mobilization leads me to believe that the modeling of public defiance and the opening up of new counter-normative space is not enough. Organizations, networks, and groups have to be mobilized that will engage those making deviant decisions in a sustained discussion about opposition, agency, and norms in and out of Black communities. Consciousness must be raised as processes and institutions of regulation are exposed.

## Conclusion

It is my belief that a new focus on those previously understood as deviant in Black communities opens up important research questions for social scientists, different from the work of earlier scholars like Du Bois, reflecting the changing political and racial landscape of the twenty-first century. The benefit of a new approach to Black politics with a focus on deviance is not that we arrive at some unexamined position of support for every counter-normative and seemingly self-destructive behavior that exists in Black communities. Instead, at its best, questions about the construction of Black deviance should lead us first to an engagement with the normative assumptions that structure Black politics and the lives of Black people, interrogating whose rule-breaking will be labeled deviant, altering significantly their political, social, and economic standing.

Second, a focus on deviance, different from Du Bois's attempt to mask those seen as culturally inferior, should lead to the inclusion of previously silenced and absent members of our communities, expanding our understanding of who constitutes Black communities and reconstructing the boundaries of membership and identity. This means that we must pay attention to power within our communities, something Black feminists have demanded for some time. For me this is the process of the queering of Black studies: making visible all those who in the past have been silenced and excluded as full members of Black communities—the poor, women, lesbians, and gays—those people on the margins of society and excluded from the middle-class march toward respectability. But we must remember that reconstituting and expanding the membership of Black communities is not enough; we must also understand and detail the work of power that constructs and disseminates the idea of outsider or deviant within and outside of Black communities.

Third, a centering of deviance should also generate new theories and models of power, agency, and resistance in the lives of largely marginal people, cognizant of the different intents involved in defiant acts and acts of politicized resistance. Despite my disagreement with some of his analysis, I see the work of Robin Kelley, in particular in *Race Rebels*, as taking on this charge in exceptional fashion, providing the reader with a much more complicated understanding of the work, politics, and leisure habits of the Black working class. Kelley attempts to demonstrate how behavior previously deemed as deviant, decadent, or even self-destructive was driven in part by a politics of resistance or infrapolitics, as James Scott has labeled such processes. While I believe that both Kelley and Scott at times see and impose an oppositional motive in the lives of the poor and oppressed where it does not exist, I hold both scholars in very high esteem for their attempt to interrogate the assumptions of what constitutes resistance, opposition, and agency, broadening how we think about politics and the possibility for transformational politics from below.

Fourth, a focus on acts of deviance in Black communities should also direct our attention to the power and oppression being imposed on Black lives from structures and institutions outside of Black communities. We must all remember that the normative categories of "respectable" and "deviant" have significant political consequences beyond the academy in determining one's access to needed resources. If we take, for example, the idea of the family, specifically the ideal of the nuclear family, we find its continued prominence, or at least one's conformity to it, as a standard in determining the distribution of political, economic, and social resources. Not too unlike the policing of intimate relationships of women on welfare by caseworkers in the 1960s and 1970s, there has emerged a new commitment on the part of the government to compulsory marriage among the poor.

Anyone familiar with the Bush administration's policies toward women's reproductive rights both here and abroad has seen up close the use of normative ideals of the family and the "unborn child" to structure a policy agenda. The promotion of fatherhood programs and paternity requirements that seek to tie funding for the poor to being married is now a common standard by which agencies and organizations are judged with regard to funding. Even

President George W. Bush's recently passed AIDS initiative to provide money to treat AIDS in Africa and the Caribbean was stalled in Congress as other conservatives sought to restrict HIV and AIDS prevention and education funds from those international organizations and agencies providing integrated family planning—including counseling around abortion. Continually, the Bush administration has used family structure as a litmus test for the allocation of needed resources both here and abroad. In line with this move have been efforts to restrict everything from Head Start to welfare assistance based on conformity to the nuclear family structure.

However, the diminished political status of those defined as deviant is not only the result of right-wing politics. As I noted earlier, within established Black political organizations there is also reluctance to embrace those issues and sub-populations thought to be morally wanting or ambiguous (Warren 2000). Despite the feelings of some in Black communities that we have been shamed by the immoral behavior of a small subset of our community some would label the underclass, scholars must take up the charge to highlight and detail the agency of those on the outside, those who through their acts of nonconformity choose outsider status, at least temporarily. It is an intentional deviance given limited agency and constrained choices. These individuals are not fully or completely defining themselves as outsiders or content with their outsider status, but they are also not willing to adapt completely or conform. The cumulative impact of such choices is possibly the creation of spaces or counter-publics, where not only oppositional ideas and discourse happens, but lived opposition, or at least autonomy, is chosen daily. Furthermore, it may be that through the repetition of deviant practices by multiple individuals new identities, communities, and politics are created and a space emerges where seemingly deviant, unconnected behavior might evolve into conscious acts of resistance that serve as the basis for a mobilized politics of deviance. Only through serious and sustained examination can we begin to understand what is possible through deviance. I hope that this new space of possibility is at the center of studies of Black politics in the twenty-first century.

# References

Anderson, Elijah (1992). *Streetwise: Race, Class and Change in an Urban Community*. Chicago: University of Chicago Press.

Becker, Howard S. (1973). *Outsiders: Studies in the Sociology of Deviance*. New York: The Free Press.

Bobo, Lawrence D. (Ed.) (2000). *Prismatic Metropolis: Inequality in Los Angeles*. New York: Russell Sage Foundation.

Brody, Jennifer DeVere (2000). Theory in motion: A review of black queer studies in the millennium conference. *Callaloo*, 23: 1274–1277.

Butler, Judith (1990). *Gender Trouble*. New York: Routledge.

Carby, Hazel (1987). *Reconstructing Womanhood: The Emergence of the Afro-American Woman Novelist*. New York: Oxford University Press.

Cohen, Cathy J. (1997). Punks, bull daggers and welfare queens: The real radical potential of 'queer' politics, *GLQ*, 3: 437–485.

Cohen, Cathy J. (1999). *The Boundaries of Blackness: AIDS and the Breakdown of Black Politics*. Chicago: University of Chicago Press.

Dawson, Michael C. (1994). *Behind the Mule: Race and Class in African-American Politics* Princeton, NJ: Princeton University Press.

Dawson, Michael C. (2003). *Black Visions: The Roots of Contemporary African American Political Ideologies*. Chicago: University of Chicago Press.

D'Emilio, John (2003). *Lost Prophet: The Life and Times of Bayard Rustin*. New York: Free Press. Drake, St. Clair and Horace R. Cayton (1993). *Black Metropolis: A Study of Negro Life in a Northern City*. Chicago: University of Chicago Press.

DuCille, Ann (1990). "Othered" matters: Reconceptualizing dominance and difference in the history of sexuality in America. *Journal of History of Sexuality*, 1: 102–127.

Duneier, Mitchell (1994). *Slim's Table: Race, Respectability and Masculinity*. Chicago: University of Chicago Press.

Foucault, Michel (1980). *The History of Sexuality, Volume I: An Introduction*. New York: Vintage Books.

Fuss, Diana, (Ed.) (1991). *Inside/Outside*. New York: Routledge.

Gaines, Kevin K. (1996). *Uplifting the Race: Black Leadership, Politics, and Culture in the Twentieth Century*. Chapel Hill, NC: University of North Carolina Press.

Goffman, Erving (1963). *Stigma: Notes on the Management of Spoiled Identity*. New York: Touchstone Books.

Gordon, Edmund T. (1997). Cultural politics of black masculinity. *Transforming Anthropology*, 6: 36–53.

Guttman, Herbert (1976). *The Black Family in Slavery and Freedom, 1750–1925*. New York: Pantheon.

Harper, Phillip Brian (1998). *Are We Not Men? Masculine Anxiety and the Problem of African-American Identity*. New York: Oxford University Press.

Harris-Lacewell, Melissa (2004). *Barbershops, Bibles and BET: Everyday Talk and Black Political Thought*. Princeton, NJ: Princeton University Press.

Hebdige, Dick (2001). *Subculture: The Meaning of Style*. New York: Routledge.

Hernstein, Richard J. and Charles Murray (1996). *The Bell Curve: Intelligence and Class Structure in American Life*. New York. Free Press.

Higginbotham, Evelyn Brooks (1993). *Righteous Discontent: The Women's Movement in the Black Baptist Church, 1880–1920*. Cambridge, MA: Harvard University Press.

Horne, Gerald (1995) *Fire This Time: The Watts Uprising and the 1960s*. New York: DeCapo Press.

Kelley, Robin D. G. (1994). *Race Rebels: Culture, Politics, and the Black Working Class*. New York: The Free Press.

Kelley, Robin D. G. (2002). *Freedom Dreams: The Black Radical Imagination*. New York: Beacon Press.

Kim, Claire Jean (2000). *Bitter Fruit: The Politics of Black-Korean Conflict in New York City*. New Haven, CT: Yale University Press.

Jewell, K. Sue (1993). *From Mammy to Miss America and Beyond: Cultural Images and the Shaping of US Social Policy*. New York: Routledge.

Ladner, Joyce (1971). *Tomorrow's Tomorrow: The Black Woman*. New York: Doubleday.

Lubiano, Wahneema (1997). Black nationalism and black common sense: Policing ourselves and others. In *The House That Race Built: Black Americans, U.S Terrain*, Q. Lubiano (Ed.), pp. 232-252. New York: Pantheon Books.

Marable, Manning (1991). *Race, Reform and Rebellion: The 2nd Reconstruction in Black America, 1945–2000*, 3rd Edition. Jackson, MI: University Press of Mississippi.

McBride, Dwight (1998). Can the queen speak? Racial essentialism, sexuality and the problem of authority. *Callaloo*, 21: 363–379.

Morris, Aldon D. (1984). *The Origins of the Civil Rights Movement: Black Communities Organizing for Change*. New York: The Free Press.

Moynihan, Daniel (1965). *The Negro Family: The Case for National Action*. Washington, DC: Government Printing Office.

Mullings, Leith (1996). *On Our Own Terms: Race, Class and Gender in the Lives of African-American Women*. New York: Routledge.

Ransby, Barbara (2003). *Ella Baker and the Black Freedom Movement: A Radical Democratic Vision*. Durham, NC: University of North Carolina Press.

Reed, Adolph L., Jr. (1991). The 'underclass' as myth and symbol: The poverty of discourse about poverty. *Radical America*, Summer.

Rose, Tricia (2003). *Longing to Tell: Black Women Talk about Sexuality and Intimacy*. New York: Farrar, Straus and Giroux.

Scott, James C. (1987). *Weapons of the Weak: Everyday Forms of Peasant Resistance*. New Haven, CT: Yale University Press.

Scott, James C. (1990). *Domination and the Arts of Resistance: Hidden Transcripts*. New Haven, CT: Yale University Press.

Sears, David, Jim Sidanius, Lawrence Bobo, and James Sidanius (2000). *Racialized Politics: The Debate about Racism in America*. Chicago: University of Chicago Press.

Sedgwick, Eve (1990). *The Epistemology of the Closet*. Berkeley: University of California Press. Smith, Rogers M. (1993). Beyond Tocqueville, Myrdal, and Hartz: The multiple traditions in America. *The American Political Science Review*, 87: 549–566.

Somerville, Siobhan (1994). Scientific racism and the emergence of the homosexual body. *Journal of the History of Sexuality*, 5: 243–255.

Stack, Carol B. (1997). *All Our Kin*. New York: Westview.

Staples, Robert (1973). *The Black Woman in America: Sex, Marriage and the Family*. Chicago: Nelson-Hall.

Tate, Katherine (1998). *From Protest to Politics: The New Black Voters in American Elections*. Cambridge, MA: Harvard University Press.

Thomas, Kendal (1997). Ain't nothin like the real thing: Black masculinity, gay sexuality, and the jargon of authenticity. In W. Lubiano (Ed.), *The House That Race Built: Black Americans, U.S. Terrain*, pp. 116–135. New York: Pantheon Books.

Warner, Michael (1993). *Fear of a Queer Planet: Queer Politics and Social Theory*. Minneapolis, MN: University of Minnesota Press.

Warren, Dorian T. (2000). The intersection between voting rights and criminal justice: The national black organizational response to felon disenfranchisement. Unpublished Manuscript.

White, E. Frances (2001). *Dark Continent of Our Bodies: Black Feminism and the Politics of Respectability*. Philadelphia: Temple University Books.

Wilson, William Julius (1987). *The Truly Disadvantaged: The Inner City, the Underclass, and Public Policy*. Chicago: University of Chicago Press.

## Notes

1. This paper was originally prepared for the conference "The Ends of Sexuality: Pleasure and Danger in the New Millennium," Northwestern University, April 4–5, 2003. My thinking has evolved since its first inception because of the helpful comments of Brandi Adams, Alan Brady, Michael Dawson, Victoria Hattam, Sheldon Lyke, Patchen Markell, Barbara Ransby, Beth Richie, Dorian Warren, Deva Woodly, Iris Marion Young, and the participants of the University of Texas, Center for African and African American Studies' Race, Gender, and Sexuality Series. Of course, any and all shortcomings in the argument and the article are the responsibility of the author.

2. I am lucky to be a part of an amazing community of scholars in Chicago committed to the development of a field of research we might call Black queer studies. Some of the members of this intellectual and social family include Jennifer Brody, Jackie Goldsby, Sharon Holland, Lynette Jackson, E. Patrick Johnson, Waldo Johnson, Dwight McBride, Darrel Moore, and Beth Richie.

3. The recent revelations of mixed-race children by racist and prominent White men such as Thomas Jefferson and Strom Thurmond as well as the recent hysteria of purported "down-low" sexual behavior by some unknown number of Black men underscores the possible disjuncture between one's expressed public and lived private sexual behavior and power.

4. See for example, the work of Tricia Rose (2003); E. Frances White (2001); Jennifer DeVere Brody (2000); Dwight McBride (1998); Philip Brian Harper (1998); Kendal Thomas (1997); and Siobhan Somerville (1994) and Ann DuCille (1990).

5. Throughout the paper when I use the term *deviant* I am referring to those groups of people who have been constructed as engaging in substantial rule- or norm-breaking behavior, whose counter-normative social behavior is attributed not only to individual choice but also to deficiencies in their fundamental or inherent character, making such behavior predictable or inevitable. Among such individuals, deviant behavior in one social realm, such as in the composition of family, is seen as connected to deviant behavior in other realms, such as norms around work. I am not talking about, for example, individuals who have a pattern of rolling through stop signs instead of coming to a complete stop—rule-breaking behavior. Instead, I am focused in this paper on those individuals thought to break the assumed agreed upon norms of socially acceptable behavior. See, for example, Becker (1973) for an extended discussion of deviance.

6. It is important here to note that normative structures around things such as family, work, or sex can vary between their macro or dominant articulation and their micro, group-based articulation and practice. Thus, having children before one is married may result in harsh consequences from the state with regard to financial support for example, but be largely accepted and seemingly embraced in Black communities.

doris diosa davenport

# Never Mind the Misery/ Where's the Magic?

## A Self-interview*

My perceptions and experiences of the world have been permanently influenced by my initial or childhood experiences. That is, i grew up in one of the most beautiful parts of this country, northeast Georgia. Cornelia (& Gainesville) Georgia, at the "foot" of Appalachia. Surrounded by pines, oaks, lakes, rivers, azaleas, honeysuckles, sweet peas and distant mountains. Devastatingly sensuous summer heat and invigoratingly cool autumns. And always, in every form, shape, and season, red dirt.

My mother and father (who called himself "El Diablo") were separated, so i grew up surrounded by Ethel Mae's (my mother) family, one of the largest in town. That meant 10 aunts and uncles (ranging from 3 years older than i to 4 years older than my mother), my grandparents, "M'evie & Daddie John"; and at least 30 first, second, or third cousins. As if that wasn't enough, i had 5 younger sisters and a brother. Even when i was considered "too young" by some of these relatives (or vice versa) i had lots of company, always. Yet, increasingly, age seemed unimportant, since we all partied together, and "telling lies" (cf. Hurston) was a primary source of entertainment, and a highly valued skill.

Apart from all this, or, along with all this, my sister Dolores, my cousin Jimmy, and i were uncontestably the smartest in school, from the time we started, to the time we quit. Dolores left first, but me and Jimmy carried on our "tradition" of being the best, period. Increasingly, it seemed to me that between myself and Jimmy, we knew *everything*. We sure *did* everything, between us. This world was magical, beautiful and in fact, "rich." (Oh yes—

---

* First published in 1981.

Cornelia was and is segregated, but that and poverty were things i took for granted, just as being a womon and being black were natural to me, & even desirable and enviable.) So i am constantly amazed at the "world's" expectations that since i am from the "lower" class (economically-speaking, ONLY), a womon, and black, i am/was expected to feel (be) impoverished, inadequate, and "triply" oppressed! (Or, in other words, altogether shitty). Fortunately, i also grew up defying or rebelling against anyone's "sposed-to-be's/"

For example, as i keep (unfashionably) saying, the first oppression that i consciously noticed was definitely sexism, and at that, from my precious black community. Their general consensus was that since i was so "pretty," and so "wild," i would get pregnant and quit school by age 13 (partly, perhaps, to spite them, i'm still in school, working on a Ph.D in English, and if somewomon invents another degree, i might work on that one too). My response to this was to laugh, and do what i wanted.

Like, i started some serious drinking (white lightning) at age 14, and still made the honor roll, played basketball, sang in the choir, and worked on the school yearbook. i "committed adultery" at age 14, (it was a failed rape, so i went back and requested him to finish the job) but did not get pregnant, just notorious. Simultaneously, i also took care of my younger sisters and brother, and then, went to college at 16, from the eleventh grade. i don't remember feeling any kind of insecurity about my worth or abilities on any level, in spite of people's efforts to the contrary. It didn't work, because i had the natural beauty of the town, the support of Ethel Mae & Jimmy, plus a newly-discovered alternative reality in art, writing, and dreams. i'd developed a habit, too, of taking long walks alone, late at night, especially if there was a thick fog. i'd developed, also, a loud unladylike laugh which startled and ridiculed peopled. For all this, i was called things like weird, perverse, disrespectful, and crazy. In other words, i was considered "other," by a community that was itself quite "other," due to its many eccentricities. . . . As a result, my perceptions as a 2-5 time "outsider," differ from the "norm," (whatever that is) especially in those volatile areas of sex/race/class. To quote Alice Walker, "Because I'm black and a woman and because I was brought up poor and because I am a Southerner, I think the way I see the world is quite different from the way many people see it. And I think that I could not help but have a radical vision of society, and that the way I see things can help people see what needs to be changed" (*Southern Exposure*, Festival Issue, 1981).

## II

The last time i was home, i was saying something to Momma that she mildly objected to, so i said, "Momma, you sposed to tell the truth, and 'the truth shall make you free.'" Ethel Mae responded, "Yeah, but you ain't got to free me all the time." We both laughed, but the fact is, i have to at least try to "free" folk all the time, or to tell the truth. This truth is "radical," especially since it is sifted through a "lesbian-feminist world view," to quote Terry Wolverton.

What i saw, and see, is how "others" attempt to limit, define, and thereby dismiss, un-categorizable wimmin (like me, especially). i see clearly, as many sisters do, that most folks try to use black wimmin as a means to a quite neurotic end. (Like, wimmin of *any* race from the middle class "need" to see me as less-than.) For example, this "strong black womon" label is a mis-nomer and catchall for what (in other people/races) would be called brilliance, genius, humanism, or even, mysticism. Einstein, Martha Graham, Van Gogh, Joan of Arc, Cleopatra, Martin Luther King and others were all "strong," but that is not the primary adjective attached to their names. (It sounds stupid: "Gee, that Gandhi, he sure was a strong man.") Every black womon i know is an unacknowledged genius in one way or another, AND each one is a true "feminist," without the necessity for the theory or misapplied practice. i am a feminist because I always have been. That means that i think *all* people should be free.

So one day i thought about it, and realized that "freedom" really means that the more free a person is, the more s/he can leave alone, or the less that person needs to oppress anyone else. This led to a more significant revelation: the oppressive/repressive forces directed at black wimmin is in direct proportion to those folk's fear or sense of threat/inadequacy. Which also applies to *all* folks who are threatened by lesbianism. Which is a negative testimony to just how "powerful" we are perceived to be. So there. Now, if and when folk start to deal with the *truth*, there might be a few positive and powerful changes in the world.

Immediately, this fact would have "revolutionary" potential in the feminist/lesbian communities. For example, the current fad consists of the roles of "strong black struggling womon" or "triply oppressed womon-of-color" vs. the "privileged white womon" or the "white-and-therefore-powerful womon." By now, this is simply corny. We all know, or should know, better. These two roles simply mirror each other. They reinforce the devaluation of third world wimmin, while at the same time they prevent an evaluation of white wimmin. But what's worse, these roles keep us all enervated and obsessed with pettiness. It seems silly to argue about the relativity of past oppressions, when the real debate is whether we, or anyone else, has a *future*.

As far as i am concerned, we *do* have a future, BUT to realize it requires a lot of hard work, honesty, dedication, and visionary transcendence. That is, if there is going to be a future, it will be because of the commitment and work of feminists (male and female, of all races). Personally, i resent having to do all this work: since i didn't have a hand in this current fucked up situation, why should i give my *back*, brain, and energy (not to mention hands) to this horrendous cleanup job? Personally, i'd just as soon write poetry, about that visionary, magical world that i knew and intend to know. Obviously, to do that, i have to alter this world.

Even now, with the perceptions and persecutions of a lifelong "outsider," i still see a potential for beauty and meaning, a perception which seems lacking in many people, these days. Even as i daily struggle to achieve a more positive reality, i see people becoming, daily (hourly), more isolated, hostile, bestial, and lost. (In L.A., it ain't really safe for me to go outside by day, much less by nite.) i also see a second "civil war" about to start. This civil war, as i keep saying to anyone who will listen, will be quite tricky: males against wimmin, "lower" class against *any* class, and of course, whites against all colored folk. Now, with a scenario like this, where will we be, or rather, how can anyone know how to choose sides? i *know* this much: we had all better think about it, and soon. More importantly, we ought to concentrate on ways to STOP IT.

This is one of my ways of stopping it: to write this & try to share some of my "radical" perceptions. Since i have, it seems, inherited a "legacy" of survival. i'd like to live up to it, and pass it on. Clearly, i did not survive by being the "mule of the world." Besides, mules are mute and basically passive. i survived because of mental agility and deliberate verbosity or in short, "talking shit/ & taking none." More importantly, i survive, because of a stubborn dedication/commitment to another vision, which i try hard to get others to see. Yes—by now, i am quite weird, crazy, and honest enough to believe that *my* perceptions and definitions can positively enhance the world. Furthermore, now git to this: not only am i "rich," i am also a philanthropist. Am presently "giving away" truth and freedom. Because in spite of the "world's" attempts to negatively define or "cripple" me, i still believe/i can fly. And i also believe other folk have the potential to at least/grow wings . . .

*This essay, now. Forty years later, i am amazed by the energetic language, and exuberant style, impressed yet dismayed by some of its claims. Writing this note now, in July 2020, in the midst of this worldwide pandemic(s), i am amazed because when i wrote this in 1981, at the request of Virginia Scott, the editor of* Sunbury Literary Magazine, *i was a part of a wimmin's literary movement that truly meant to be world changers. And one of my personal goals, then and now, is to provide corrective "truth" and insight. i still refuse to play "victimized-object" to anyone's insecure neediness and self-definition. Since 1981, socio-linguistic innovations provide sharper analytical tools than those i used here. That omnibus (portmanteau) of "heteronormative-patriarchal-whyt-male-supremacist" plus "toxic/(rape) male culture" are extremely useful. "Misogynoir" is priceless, in its accuracy; i am so grateful to that term's inventor! Still, the definer "lesbian" is a rich, delightful, and very real concept (albeit often politicizing or polarizing) like "womon-loving-womon." On the other hand, it is not white or male "privilege" that is so dominant and destructive in the world, but rather, "pathology." It's not "privilege," it's pathology. (Spread the word.) Most people are really not interested in the truth, and will resent, attack, punish and annihilate, in vengeful (often petty yet ongoing) retaliation. So, dismayed (and enraged) and unemployed and homeless. (IJS/shrug) We sought a cleansing revolution, in the 1980's. What we have here in this country right now is a "hot mess" of vileness, an opposition to even the concept of basic decency. i remain, however, optimistic and am energized by this essay's style. i still like it. i still "stand by it." And i am so very grateful to have it re-published here.*

# Kate Rushin

# At Another Crossroads

You leave this place with the same gifts you brought with you. Your questions. Your laughter. Your actions. Your anger. Take this charge with you. Past through the gate to widen the gate. Then, storm the gate. Dismantle the gate. Build the gate. Be a gateway. Then, storm the gate. Dismantle the gate, and so on.

For your journey, I remind you of Audre's gift. Audre Lorde. Poet Laureate. Change agent. Itinerate. Courageous gate keeper. Glorious gate crasher. She left this question for all of us to use: *Are you willing to use the power you have in the service of what you say you believe?* For your journey, I give you poetry. The delicious, unpredictability of love and living things. For your journey, I give you this mirror reflecting your own sweet eyes.

# SDiane Bogus

# The Myth and Tradition
# of the Black Bulldagger

There is really no such thing as a Black lesbian; well not in the African-American past anyway. The word lesbian is a derivation of the Greek word *Lesbos*. Lesbos was an isle of Mytilene, Greece, where sixth-century songstress and poet Sappho was supposed to have trained, loved, and instructed young ladies in the arts of music, composition of verse, and love.

Like the ideal of the Black woman as immemorial African queen in the high literature of Black poets and writers, Sappho has arrived in the twentieth century royally imagined and adored as an ideal lesbian by contemporary women-loving women of all colors. The fact is, if one calls herself a lesbian at all it is because Sappho was from Lesbos, and hence the circumlocutions of etymology.

Although she is heralded in countless lesbian poems, essays, books, artistic representations, rituals, and conversations—in which she is portrayed as a fair-skinned nymph whose genteel and aesthetic woman-loving woos women to visions of lyre music and nimble-footed dancing under nature's fullest moons—Sappho is not our highest, truest or best representation.

Sappho doesn't have enough historical, romantic, or physical substance to make her as rich as our own culture makes the Black Bulldagger (whom I distinguish from the Black lesbian). Sappho isn't American or African-American. This is a distinction of nationality and culture, not of race, for Sappho, as a Greek, was probably a woman of color. Judy Grahn, in *Another Mother Tongue*, has described her as "small and dark." Obviously this is not well-disseminated information; in fact, it is ignored, as is the obvious dark skin of the historical Jesus, who nonetheless hangs on the cross lily white, stained with red, red blood. As in Jesus's case, Anglo-heterosexual and homosexual culture has created Sappho in the image of a white deity much like Venus or Artemis (Diana) whom Sappho and the girls of Mytilene worshipped. I can respect this lesbian past and understand the necessity of bringing it forward to these times, times in which any historical evidence of homosexual lives is (for all of the visibility of gays and lesbians) still rejected or denied. We must be fastidious about preserving lesbian and gay history, but as a Black lesbian feminist, I am annoyed by the ethnocentric racism inherent in advocating for the symbol of One Lesbian. In this the herstory of Black lesbians is made invisible by omission.

The images that are put forth of women-loving women, Amazon women, are rarely women of color. Yet we accept these images as symbolic of our loving; we often subscribe, whether consciously, resignedly, or willingly, to the idealism of these images, all the while being defined by them. This essay is an attempt to revitalize the sense of self and history that the Black lesbian must maintain, develop and nurture if she is to survive as a reality and as a teacher for the next generation of women-loving Black women.

African American lesbians have, in our ancient lesbian past, the fierce Dahomean Amazons of West Africa who were, during the Songhai influence over that region (1464–1591), the most learned, the richest, and the most sought-after people on the planet, if not for their knowledge and riches, then for their slaves. These were Amazons, as Audre Lorde wrote in *The Cancer Journals* who severed their right breasts in order to free their bow arms for the fight against enslavement. We also have Queen Califia, namesake of California who, according to legend, was a thirteenth-century leader of a tribe of Black Amazons who ruled the land without the presence of a single man.

The Black Bulldagger is a link to our ancient and recent Black woman-loving past, and the predecessor of today's Black lesbian. She is a character, an idea, a woman who loved women but was heavily male identified more often than not. She was the unattractive girl, the tomboyish teen, the independent woman, or any Black sister who repulsed the advances of men.

Moreover, the Black Bulldagger, unlike the Black lesbian, was a loner in both myth and reality. She had no politic other than her daily life. She had no community other than that which she discovered. She had no women-loving role models other than men. She had no books, no records—save those that she hid—no café (unless you include the out-of-the way bar or the house party), and she had no festivals. But the Black Bulldagger survived in our language, in our imaginations, and in our lives. If we were to assign her an era, that era would begin in the 1880s and extend through the 1950s. The 1920s were her best years.

The Black Bulldagger's American antecedents were women such as gun-toting Mary Fields (1832) or Cora Anderson (1840) who passed as male and married a woman. She even had intellectual counterparts who were less assertive Black women-loving women than she. They include Alice Dunbar-Nelson and Angelina Weld Grimké, the artistic branch of the women-loving line. But the Black Bulldagger is not an artist in our imaginations. She is a creature made in the image of man. She is the doorway through which many of today's conveniently labeled Black lesbians have passed as studs, as "sweet-men."

The Black Bulldagger has also been women like Ma Rainey and Bessie Smith, Mabel Hampton, and Annie Lee Grant, a Mississippi bulldagger who lived as a man for fifteen years. Through eight decades, the presence of the Black Bulldagger has waned but has never disappeared.

Know that we come to the Black Bulldagger with some confusion. She has existed and does exist; she is both a folk myth and a genuine article. She has been a transvestite, a bisexual, and always an identifiable lover of women. We've seen her and have not seen her; we've heard about her or whispered about her. The Black Bulldagger has been what our girlhoods abhorred: we the ribbons; she the hat. We the dolls; she the jack. We the prom; she the bar. We the wife—the protectorate of man, his mistress, girlfriend, or date; she the woman-made-woman, her self's own escort, her own self's counsel and chief, the equal of men.

In this she is very unlike Sappho, for Sappho, in the end, is an ambiguous figure, very distant in time and very much the image men most prefer in Woman: the delicate beauty in silks, harmless, hardly man's equal even if she knows a million thrusts of the *olispo* (dildo). Sappho is the lesbian men want to watch in movies. They want to see airy-fairy, wispy strokes and caresses between women, the imagined frustration of penis-less tribadism.

They want to see breast sucking and cunt tickling because, to them, therein lies no consummation. The Black Bulldagger would never give them a show, and no one would ever know the ways of her loving. What skills she had with women, what art, what pleasures in her hands, what practice in her tongue, whatever augmentations to her desire, she never told. She kept her own council. She went for bad.

The strength of the Black Bulldagger lies in the self-asserting herstory of our pasts. Any Black woman with character enough to cry, "Look at my arm! I have ploughed, and planted, and gathered into barns, and no man could head me! And ain't I a woman?" has the same power or potential for power as the Black Bulldagger. She, like Sojourner Truth, has had to struggle for her place in our minds, against our weakness and fear, our fuzzy sense of our lesbian past, our Black history, and against internalized homophobia. But because we have not seen her humanity, nor her loving, and have only begrudged her strength, power, and woman-loving nerve—we cried out "Bulldagger! Bulldagger!" hardly knowing the words were an incantation to our own hidden Black histories.

Bulldagger. Just what does this word mean? Where does it come from? It is related, as Judy Grahn speculates in *Another Mother Tongue*, to Boudica (*Boo-dike-a*), the Iceni Queen of Celtic history who rode on Rome against the colonization. In AD 61 she reigned as priest-goddess and queen, performing ceremonial rites wherein bulls were regularly killed on the altar of sacrifice. The blood ran down into an embankment or "dike" that drew it away. In any case, her descendants and others like them gave to lesbians a character rebellious, armed, masculine, warrior-like, and dangerous. Boudica's name, like her wondrous but infamous defiance of Rome, was driven underground, not to be spoken, not to be remembered except with derision: "bulldiker, bulldagger, Boudica"

The name Boudica and the business with bulls and dikes accounts nice-ly for the associative transposition to bulldiker, but Boudica's name doesn't quite account for the use of it in Black culture. Our Bulldagger is said to have sexual prowess beyond the wildest dreams of a man, and certainly beyond his damnedest capabilities. How did this Iceni legend arrive in Black culture? Or is bulldagger some wild concoction of the Black imagination?

Before the Roman Empire was that of ancient Egypt. Subduing bulls or sacrificing them is as old as Horus, the bull, Egyptian ruler, consort to (Black) queen Tyre. It is in our blood. Come from northern Africa as certainly as the Black and female sovereignty of Nefertiti, Hatshepsut or Cleopatra.

Ancient Egypt the land of the Great Sphinx, of hieroglyphics, mummification, treasures, and unknowable mysteries. All that is in our blood if not in our accessible memories. Our reverence for, fascination with, interest in the bull is as honest as the day we were born; it is as old as the word "God" or "El," which, according to *The Woman's Encyclopedia of Myths and Secrets*, means "bull god or Father of Men." And it was Bill Pickett, Black cowboy extraordinaire, whose magnificent and creative rodeo feats with bulls reminded us of our connection to the ancient relations of Blacks and bulls.

In the 1920s, Black people who had migrated from the Midwest farm and southern part of the United States to the North had the rare and uplifting treat of seeing Bill Pickett in the one and only movie of its Black kind, *The Bulldogger*. There he was on the great silver screen, larger than life, leaping from horses with the greatest of ease, wrestling bulls and calves to the ground in record time, manhandling them in the most rope-fangled fashion, and creating for the new American West a rodeo event that lives on today. His feats credited him with the origin of the word "bulldogger." The word was then appropriated by other cowboys who had observed the behavior of bulldogs who'd get a hold of something and refuse to let it go.

Once we had seen that movie, we talked about Bill Pickett, and we talked about his exotic life, and we said "bulldogger" whenever we could. We used it as a term of reference for any man's prowess, especially if he was bullish about women; we created similes using "like a bulldogger" to describe how fiercely, adroitly, or strongly a task was performed. The word "bulldogger" had its way with our imaginations. Then somewhere, at some time, somebody crossbred that admiration with hate, or with comedy, when he saw one bull mount another and go heigh-ho in forceful stabling motions, or when some woman did a thing with the unabashed aptitude of a bulldogger. In the twinkling of an eye, or perhaps, in the time it takes to spread gossip, the word "bulldogger" became "bulldagger."

Bulldagger. Just what has it come to mean? Ask any contemporary Black lesbian, and she'll tell you. It mean ridicule; it means you act like a man, that you go for bad, that you're some kind of freak, and that you hate men. She is a hellish "It," a supernatural "he" or at the very least, an "unnachel" woman. And she was, even to herself, the most despicable beast in the hell of a man's world. In Black oral tradition, especially in old wives' tale, the Black Bulldagger is and has always been a creature of enormous power to those who were terrorized by the tales of her knife-toting ways, her smooth charm, her exceptional and extraordinary sexual parts. Her clitoris was called "a hammer" or "a pertongue" (or pearl tongue). It was thought to be elongated, a very different organ between her legs which could hook onto a woman's libido and enslave her heart or ruin her health. Once taken from a man, a Bulldagger's woman would never go back again. These are the myths, but the reality was that the Black Bulldagger believed she had a right to love women, and she lived that right fearlessly. She believed she had the right to walk the streets day or night unmolested, and she did—conquering the fear in her heart. She believed she had the right to defend herself and her chosen, to assert herself, to govern herself.

The Black Bulldagger did not lack the courage of her convictions. She was self-defining, self-escorting, self-reliant; she was proud, manly, possessive, and strong; she was streetwise and recognized for herself when she wanted to be. The attributes of the Black Bulldagger are not all complimentary or worthy of emulation; not all are applicable to the evolved Black lesbian. To distinguish ourselves, to distinguish our way of woman-loving, we must begin to ask ourselves what there is to be saved in the model of the Black Bulldagger. At present we lose much by our estrangement from her. It is true that our woman-loving style may be less possessive, less maleidentified, more equal in sexual exchange and in the power dynamic, but are we as well-defined, as relentlessly public (i.e. free), or are we still constrained by the horrors of being called "bulldagger!" Is it easier to be called a dyke or to be enveloped in someone else's image of ourselves?

As Black lesbians who are on the threshold of the twenty-first century, we must repossess as much as we can of our woman-loving past to shore us up for the future. We can no longer allow our lesbianism to be defined for us by popular ideology, by the non-Black lesbian ideal—though some non-Black heroines may embody our values. As Black lesbians we are certainly less threatening and threatened than ever a Bulldagger was. We have a freedom of being that she never had. I propose we find ways to repossess the model, the lessons, and the power of this unlikely matriarch.

Savannah Shange

# Play Aunties and Dyke Bitches: Gender, Generation, and the Ethics of Black Queer Kinship

## Gender Judo: Desire as a Weapon

Using the weight of my whole body, I pushed Kairo into the empty computer-lab-cum-library and shut the door behind me. Her[1] gleaming red-and-white Jordans[2] paced back and forth, baby dreads bouncing between her razor-sharp line up and the collar of her oversized white Polo. Having broken up my fair share of scuffles during a decade of youth work, I knew the drill: separate, de-escalate, reflect, repair. This one caught me by surprise, because La'Nea and Kairo were more likely to be seen cuddling than scrapping. Thinking they were playfighting when I heard their voices crescendo in the hall, I came out of my classroom to chastise them. I arrived just in time to see the rage on La'Nea's face and grabbed Kairo to separate them.

Down the hall, I could hear the thump-thump of La'Nea's sparkly Fuggs[3] running toward us, her voice echoing epithets. I worked on the de-escalation phase, sitting down with Kairo and reminding her of the stakes she faced while on probation. "Kairo—it don't matter what she said, you don't never put your hands on a woman. Plus you can't afford to be doing this shit—she is just . . . upset." I tried not to divulge my own suspicions about why La'Nea provoked a confrontation with Kairo in the hallway of San Francisco's Robeson Justice Academy minutes earlier, goading her into hitting her in the face.

La'Nea crammed her cocoa face into the tiny glass window of the computer lab. She punctuated her barrage of language with claps and head swivels so fierce that her high ponytail threatened to tumble off of its tightly brushed foundation.

"Dyke bitch! You wanna be a man, come out here and whoop my ass then! Always tryna look like a dude—you ain't no fuckin' dude!"

La'Nea's latter epithet almost lands heavier than the first: "bitch" is an attempt to melt away every meticulous inch Kairo had carved out between herself and the inherited image of womanhood. *You ain't no fuckin' dude.* La'Nea advertises her own learned equivalence between masculinity and violence when she tells Kairo, "You wanna be a man, come out here and whoop my ass then!" Here, to be a man is to beat a woman, laying bare the range of antagonisms that lie within the frame of The Black Family, and the constrained set of choices masquerading as the "agency" available to Black girls and women surviving the war at home. La'Nea renders masculinity—or perhaps more precisely, manhood—as a weapon always already formed against her. I knew well enough how La'Nea had to survive the men she loved; I was there when she came back to school crying and enraged one evening after her brother hit her with a hanger in her own home. Knowing that teachers were mandatory reporters, but not wanting to call the police on her own blood, she used the school bureaucracy as a self-defense tactic. Both La'Nea's invocation of intimate violence in the halls of her high school, and her ways of using that school as a strategy for protection, point to the flimsiness of the line between public and private space, particularly for Black women.[4]

After being called a dyke, Kairo ran up on the door that I narrowly beat her to (dammit, how did I always forget this lock was broken?!), bellowing and grabbing her crotch. "Oh, but you want the dick though! You want the dick though!" callously referencing La'Nea's long-time crush on her. Kairo fought back with gender judo, weaponizing the force of La'Nea's proto-femme desire against her while reasserting a sovereign form of masculinity.

By now I was out of breath, sandwiched between the two kids fighting to open the door I was leaning against to keep shut. Tears ambushed me as I shoved Kairo away from the door and shouted at my co-workers to get La'Nea back to her own space—this was too close, too raw, too much of our collective business in the street. As a baby gay, I too was outed by a peer as a form of retaliation, and the sense-memory of that social exposure overwhelmed me. I felt La'Nea's betrayal as my own in the midst of the fight, and probably pushed Kairo back with more force than necessary, a self-defense once removed.

# Through the Wormhole: Methods in Motion

Our three bodies, compressed against a janky wooden threshold at the top of a hill in Frisco,[5] formed a portal of Black queer life—a sort of wormhole that captures a series of slippages between girlhood and grownness, dykes and dudes, masculinity and manhood, public and private, then and now, me and you, love and war.

I reflect on our entanglement in the pages that follow, using autoethnographic narrative as a lens into the production of Black queer common sense across gender and generation. I am reticent to reduce the fleshy dimensions of my kinship with Black children to something "clear" or transparent. Instead, I write in collusion with queer scholars who engage autoethnography as a fugitive epistemology, one that escapes the ruse of de-raced objectivity by including the lived experience of the researcher as a central data point.[6] For instance, in the autoethnographic film *It Gets Messy in Here*, scholar-artist Kai M. Green "attempted to create a documentary film that refused a will to know or pin down for the sake of knowledge. . . . I made my film with hopes of creating space for the unknowable to exist as we do."[7] This essay is written another register of his refusal; it is a missive from the Black queer *space that demands to be thought, but refuses to be known.*

My methodological approach is also guided by fellow Black anthropologist Jafari Allen, who reminds us that

> to follow the routes of black/queer/diaspora is to interrogate dynamic, unsettled subjects whose bodies, desires, and texts move. Our methodologies must therefore be supple, our communication polyglot, our outlook wide and open, and our analysis nuanced. This multiple, luxuriant, and subtle approach is intellectually generative (if not also a bit unsettling for some).[8]

If the methodological demand of a Black/queer/diaspora anthropology is to *move*, write in transit, shuttling between times and places, first and third persons, academic and AAVE registers. A text in motion seeks to unsettle the stability of our inherited relation to language itself, even as it dances around scholarly convention. I invite readers to move with me, our intellectual gestures syncopated but never synchronized.

## Black Queer Common Sense

The contradictory choreography performed by Black genders is rendered intelligible through Kara Keeling's work on Black femme gender and the cinematic, and I engage her conceptualization of "common sense" throughout this essay. For Keeling,

> common sense is a shared set of memory-images and a set of commonly habituated sensory-motor movements with the capacity to enable alternative perceptions and, hence, alternative knowledges.[9]

While Keeling examines the sensory-motor dimensions of Blackness on screen, the kinesthetics of common sense bleed into the visual field of everyday life. Her analytic work of perceiving and producing alternative knowledges at the site of the body is also necessary labor for me as an anthropologist—the particularly queer "epistemology of ethnography."[10] The technologies of self-making and other-making at work between me, La'Nea, and Kairo point to the infrastructure of Black queer common sense, and signal the queer-ness of Blackness writ large.

If we are to engage "[B]lack gender as an infinite set of proliferative, constantly revisable reiterations figured 'outside' of gender's established and establishing symbolic order,"[11] then we might imagine both the fight between Kairo and La'Nea and their ensuing reconciliation as sites of the proliferation of Black gender. At the same time, while each of our queer subjects are indeed figured "outside" of the order of normative gender, the coordinates of our outsideness are still mapped onto the languages and logics of normative gender: *you want the dick tho'*. We outchea, but we ain't outside the realm of common sense, queer or otherwise.

Keeling reminds us of the fractious, partial, and complicit nature of common sense, insofar that

> common sense contains elements that consent to dominant hegemonies, as well as to aspects that are antagonistic to them. It can be understood as a record of a group's survival, incorporating compromises to dominating and exploitative forces while retaining challenges to those forces.[12]

This dance between incorporating and rejecting the forces of domination is instructive as we try to make sense of all this callous talk of bitches and dicks, not to mention the very Black and very queer capacity to forge kinship in one of the most highly surveilled sites of neoliberal statecraft. As a place to revel in Black queer common sense, we slip back through the wormhole to the halls of a high school in Frisco.

## Frisco Geographies: Mapping a Research Context

Undergirding the tussle between La'Nea and Kairo over the boundaries of Black masculine practice are the broader penal technologies that work to confine and expunge unruly Blackness in school settings. I came to know both of them through my twin roles as volunteer teacher and ethnographer at Robeson—the year this fight happened, I was conducting research for a book project on anti-Blackness and the failures of progressive politics. Kairo, whose given name Juanita was ignored by peers and school staff alike, was one of several studs—or masculine-presenting people assigned female at birth[13]—who had attended Robeson over the past decade. In reflection of the interlocking violences of gender normativity, toxic masculinity, and the carceral state, young studs of color in Frisco were hypercriminalized, and Kairo was no exception. At sixteen, she was on probation for the felony theft of an iPhone, and any formal write-up of the fight could mean her going back to jail. Even though Kairo was first to put hands on La'Nea, the staff specifically decided not to suspend Kairo or call her PO[14] in an attempt to protect her from the tributaries of the school-to-prison pipeline. No such accommodation was made for La'Nea: her disciplinary file was too thin to merit an exception. The discrepancy between the disciplinary consequences for La'Nea and Kairo reveals the confluence of high risk and high reward that masculinity entails: the criminalization associated with Black boys and men stretched beyond those assigned male at birth to ensnare Kairo in the penal system, even as the hypervisibility of Black boys as victims of the system earned her protection within the anti-carceral logics of the progressive school. La'Nea's putatively unremarkable performance of Black girlhood afforded her no protection in the eyes of the state; no self to defend, indeed.[15]

The tension between district-mandated discipline policy and the day-to-day practices of school staff is just one of an ensemble of contradictions through which the school operates. Robeson is a small, in-district public high school serving about 250 students. It has an explicit social justice vision of "liberation," and yet is funded by the austerity-driven carceral state of California. Frisco is gentrification's endgame, its Black-less diversity a progressive mecca for the 1 percent. For most of the past ten years, Robeson was the Blackest high school in the least Black city in America, and functioned as one of the few remaining Black-serving institutions in the city. In this context, the school also served as a homeplace of sorts, its four hallways repurposed by Black students and staff alike as we stole away from class and meetings to create spaces of Black social life. From local rap songs sung in harmony at the top of our lungs in the hallway, to impromptu classroom dance sessions after school, to a standing weekly lunch date for Black staff to commiserate and conspire, the school was littered with pockets of Black joy.

Because of its social justice theme, Robeson appears to be the complete inverse of the "paradigm of overt homophobic discourse and the removal of race"[16] that one might find at a typical urban California high school. This is a school where the white administrator has asked police to park down the hill instead of in the parking lot whenever they have business in the building, so as not to create a militarized environment. Freshman humanities classes analyze Huey Newton's speech about solidarity with gay struggle and are assigned Carla Trujillo's lesbian coming-of-age novel, *What Night Brings*, as required reading. Robeson is the best-case scenario for progressive state reform, and yet is still governed by the logics of anti-Blackness and heteronormativity, as revealed by its gender-biased and racially disproportionate disciplinary practices. However, the specific institutional context of the school still radically shifts the terrain on which Black cultural labor is performed, and shaped how I showed up in that space as a Black queer femme educator.

My presentation of self as a pedagogue deeply resonates with the one described by gender and race scholar Kaila Story; for Story, the femmehood she brings into her classroom is "a Black and queer sexual identity and gendered performance rooted in embodying a resistive femininity. It is one that transcends and challenges White supremacist, homonormative, and patriarchal ideas of femininity and queerness as white."[17] However, rather than the toxic combination of invisibility and hypervisibility that Story faced in her predominantly white university setting, the majority people-of-color staff at Robeson was relatively gender- and sexuality-affirming. Trans-identified students were given a key to the teacher's bathroom if they felt uncomfortable in any of the student restrooms, and one year a Xicanx stud was crowned prom king. I was one of several out gay teachers at Robeson—the visibility of queerness at Robeson is part of the matrix of sexual politics in neoliberal San Francisco, where rainbow flags seem to fly on every corner, welcoming the new wave of settlers to a safe space.[18] Amidst the desperately needed wave of recent research about queer teachers, mentors, and students of color in K–12 settings, they are usually discussed separately[19]—what happens when we find each other? The context of Robeson allows us to examine schools as not just hostile territories to queer teachers or students in isolation, but also potentially as sites of the collaborative, contested production of queer communities of color.

# An Intimacy at War:
# Conflict as Mode of Kinship

It took fifteen more minutes to defuse the conflict, in part because neither young person was finna back down off a fight, and partly because the
gendered and eroticized ammunition they chose was so volatile. It's not for
nothing that a story about queer Black kinship is also the story of a fight. To
be queer is to pick a fight—not necessarily in the way that La'Nea did, but
to choose to fight for the space to love and live autonomously. Too often,
though, the web of inherited trauma and structurally shortened fuses means
we as racialized queer folks end up *fighting against* one another instead of *alongside* one another, or perhaps even worse, internalizing the warrior impulse in
a spiral of self-harm and self-sabotage.

For many of us, particularly those who have traveled by will or by force
under the sign of "woman," family is a double helix of trauma and repair.
Kairo and La'Nea were most certainly performing family as I know it. Their
kinship was the kind that bruises, transforming secrets into vulnerabilities,
truths into weapons—an intimacy at war. In the makeshift homespace of an
alternative high school, "their" is a euphemism for "our." As La'Nea's critique demonstrates in this section, I was also woven into the queer intimacy
of growing up, and failed her in ways that hurt.

My relationship with La'Nea was in some ways reflective of what Mel
Michelle Lewis found in her research on Black lesbian professors who embodied a "femme 'auntie' performance," in which "there is this familiarity, but at
the same time, it's very authoritative."[20] La'Nea and other students actually
called me "play auntie"—I wasn't warm enough to be a "school mom," as my
co-worker Amma was often referred to; nor was I wise enough to be "everybody Grandma," like the elder dean of students, Ms. Watkins. As La'Nea's
play auntie, I was the one who drove her to the public health clinic when she
had a false STI alarm, and consoled her when Kairo started publicly dating
a perfectly fine Xicanx[21] girl, even though she and La'Nea had been lightweight talking.[22] La'Nea (probably rightfully) felt wronged, and sitting on
the couch in my classroom we sifted through layers of loyalty, colorism, and

what I like to call "deep 17"—good old-fashioned teenage ennui. It was on that same couch that La'Nea checked me for my failures as a femme auntie.

"How could you choose her over me?"

Steely-eyed and wet-faced, La'Nea demanded to know my answer as she stuffed notebooks into her backpack. It was the end of our Advisory period,[23] and I had known something was up when she refused to speak or make eye contact for the whole forty minutes. Turns out that when I pulled Kairo out of the hall and away from her, La'Nea experienced my departure as a betrayal: I chose to prioritize Kairo's needs over hers. Despite my intentions to keep La'Nea safe, she was right, and I failed in the femme4-femme imperative to destabilize heteropatriarchy by elevating the feminine-of-center—*hoes before bros*.[24]

What does La'Nea's righteous anger teach us about how to interrupt Black masculinity's function as the centrifugal force of care? Certainly, when an intense event is occurring, we act on instinct, but those instincts are shaped by somatic rankings of value and danger. When I chose to grab Kairo, some part of me was aware of her criminal record, and the stakes of getting in trouble for her. At best, it was care work, at worst it was coddling. At the same time, I had faith in La'Nea's maturity and ability to self-regulate, and trusted that she could handle this. I left La'Nea to fend for herself, as I was left so many times at that age, and that ain't right. Why do Black folks who are feminine-of-center have to always be handling business? We know this to be true, as Ruthie Gilmore, Beth Richie, and Mariame Kaba have shown us time and again: Black women and girls bear the brunt of the labor associated with state violence and captivity,[25] from making sojourns to visit loved ones in prison to covering bills and working triple time to fill the financial pit left by mass incarceration. The activist hashtag #sayhername is a crucial intervention in this dynamic, calling upon Black organizers to address gendered violence against all Black women, trans and non-trans.[26] La'Nea called me out when I let her down, and in doing so invited me to reflect on my own complicity in this uneven distribution of labor. As non-masc Black people, we are called upon to self-regulate and take up less space, use less resources, to make room for the crises of Black masculinity.

Ours was a queered scene of Black gender socialization—no Black male to fret about or blame, and yet the array of state and social resources were still oriented toward masculinity. Kairo's proximity to state violence warranted protection, and La'Nea called me on the ways my femme auntie self perpetuated the same hierarchy of care as the school that I critique. Rebuilding trust between us took time and care, both of which were sorely needed. At the same time, I still had to reckon with La'Nea's [internalized] homophobia. By challenging Kairo's right to embody boyhood, La'Nea struck at the tenderest place she could find—manifesting the intimacy she so desired with a curse instead of a caress. She had weaponized gender and sexuality in an attempt to mend her own heartbreak, and in doing so had violated the first principle of Black liberation, queer or otherwise: self-determination.

# Failing Femme: On the Production of a Fucknigga

Kairo's was a [counter] hegemonic masculinity perfected—twice as many trips to the barber shop, sneakers that cost more and were worn less, romantic trysts that were trifling and extractive. What I tried to convey to both of them in the aftermath of this incident was that while Kairo's nigganess [her Black masculinity] was unassailable, the unfortunate thing was that the nigganess she had so assiduously crafted was that of a fucknigga.[27] As an archetype, "fucknigga" is related to, but distinct from the carcerally-derived pejorative "fuckboy." In this context, a fucknigga is a Black masculine person with all of the patriarchal trappings that spark desire in the beloved, and none of the ethics that make loving such a person sustainable. Indeed, it was that very fuckniggadom that sowed the seeds of the beef at the heart of this tale. Kairo and I struggled over the nature of our relationship, and over what it meant for her to stand fully in her masculine self. I was part caseworker, part mediator, and part antagonistic gay godmother—I often defused beef between her and male teachers caught in pissing contests with a stud teenager. We bumped heads over the way she talked about Sofia, her new girlfriend. While my observations of their interactions were relatively egalitarian, without the red flags of possessiveness and silencing that I saw too often among adolescent relationships, Kairo braggingly referred to Sofia as "my bitch." I gave her the tired, but maybe true, trope of stud gentlemanliness: *What does it look like for dudes to see studs calling women bitches?! Ain't we supposed to be setting an example for what it looks like to love women?* She insisted that she would never call Sofia "a bitch," but that calling her "*my* bitch" was an expression of affection and value—classic fucknigga shit.

Bitch is not an honorific—at least in spaces where it is the given, rather than repurposed, gender appellation.[28] I told Kairo as much, and that I expected more of her as a member of our community; whether it sank in, or she was just tired of hearing about it, Kairo stopped using "bitch" so casually around me, and if it slipped out, she would tack on a sheepish "my bad, Ms. Shange." The aftermaths of this fight, and the larger constellation of relationality between myself, Kairo, and La'Nea, point to the maternal dimensions of my role as femme auntie. Beyond socialization, there was a reproductive capacity embedded in our kinship, in which I trained each of the young people up in the Black queer common sense of stud-femme sociality. C. Riley Snorton offers us a spatial analytic, whereby "the [B]lack mother's gender is vestibular, a translocation marked by a capacity to reproduce beings and objects."[29] In this instance, my femme auntie persona is one such maternal vestibule, a hallway or passage through which studs, femmes, and stud-femme sociality itself are not only reproduced, but disciplined.

## Period Pedagogy

Femme is a verb and a vocation—we midwife [fuck]niggas even as we mother ourselves. The queer maternal function of the Black femme auntie was thrown in relief one afternoon when I was grading essays in my classroom. Kairo came boppin' in, hall pass swinging from her wrist.

"Eyy, you got something?" she asked expectantly.

It took me a beat, but I reached in my desk and handed her a slender capsule-shaped tampon. Kairo cocked her head and gave me a quizzical look. My expectation collided with experience—she must know what to do with this. All the studs I knew used applicator-less tampons, and more than a couple had responded to questions about menstruation with "what period?"[30] She was still standing next to my desk, and even with years of experience trotting out bananas and condoms for ninth-grade sex-ed classes, I was flustered. I stammered through a short speech on the importance of using organic cotton tampons and the convenience of their small size. I removed the plastic wrapper, and showed her how to spread the cotton base apart with the string before, um, inserting it. "You good with that part?" I asked, dazed by the surreality of talking about self-penetration at school with a baby stud. I sent Kairo on her way, and she popped her head in on the way back to class, giving me a head nod to secure the transaction.

The tampon tutorial surfaces the unexpected intimacies of youth work, and the inchoate ways everyday tasks become gender pedagogies. I explicitly taught Kairo that applicatorless tampons were the preferred studly blood-catching method—*see, it fits in the small pocket of your jeans.* Whether or not that is true, my stating that from a "familiar, yet authoritative" femme auntie positionality *produces it as true.* Our deeply de-sexualized, yet also disorientingly intimate, encounter reiterated the same tired homonorms that I railed against in my dating life, while at the same time holding the too-rare space for a Black kid to grow up in multi-generational queer community. We know about the reproduction of stud-femme sociality in the intimate pair, whether long-form (romantic relationships) or fleeting (dance-floors, too-long-stares across rooms)—my kinship with Kairo and La'Nea pushed me to think about the cross-generational production of Black queer social life, and my role as a relative elder in their lives. Queer kinship as an intellectual and interpersonal practice nourishes an expansive Black queer common sense that can serve as a bulwark against creeping homonationalism, the deadly promise that It Gets Better when queers contort their politic aspirations to fit rainbow stripes on the American flag.[31] I opened this essay with one wormhole formed by Black bodies—the three of us mashed into a classroom door—and close with another: a "sister circle" of young women of color, gathered in the chilly lounge of a seaside hostel.

# "I was a lil' nigga": Girlhood, Stud-Femme & Queer Coalition

A month or so after the fight, scabs were falling off of hearts and things were almost back to normal. La'Nea and Kairo were both part of a group of a dozen girls enrolled in "The Journey Within" yoga intersession that I co-taught with another Black Robeson teacher, Zahra. Intersessions were held at the end of every school year at Robeson—students selected from ten differently themed three-week intensives focused on physical activity that both helped support community building and provided a workaround for the mandatory PE credits that Robeson didn't have the capacity to offer year-round. Zahra and I had chosen to offer a gender-specific intersession in order to create a body-positive environment for self-identified young women to try out yoga, meditation, and other wellness practices. Part of the course was an overnight retreat to the Marin Headlands, and that evening we gathered: a cipher of ten Black, Latina, and Filipina girls and two grown-ass women cuddled on a sectional couch on the first floor of an old Victorian boarding house overlooking the Pacific. We had a "sister circle" of advice and sharing, centered on anonymous questions that we each wrote on index cards like "Should age matter for going out with somebody?" or "Where do you go clear your head when shit gets to be too much?" Zahra unfolded and read aloud the last question—the only one that mentioned a name: "Ms. Shange—when did you first know you liked girls?"

I gave my usual spiel about playing doctor as a kid, being serially outed by my "friends," fucking other girls as a teenager in Philly but without a vision for a queer future; I settled for dudes until I moved to the Bay, where I found a robust queer community replete with mentorship and models of middle-aged lesbian women of color. After I spoke, I looked around tentatively: "Does anyone else wanna speak on this one?" Kairo laughed. "Why y'all all lookin at me tho'?! If you want me to speak, just say it's on me!" She shared:

> When I was younger, I still dressed like a boy, so girls would always think I was a boy, so, yeah. I mean like, they was likin' me,

so I liked the attention—I like that attention. So I was like aite, I just kept it going. But I don't like this attention, so stop it. . . . I never seen nobody else gay except for my cousin. I grew up with hella boys—when I was younger I didn't mess with dolls, none of that. So I was like—aouno—I'm a boy. I was a lil' nigga.[32]

Key here is the way Kairo narrates the development of her queerness as a communal, rather than a solitary, process. Kairo's intermeshing of desire and identity flummoxes Diversity 101 notions of sexuality and gender as both completely distinct and individual identities. Her testimony also challenges unidirectional conceptions of femme labor; for example, in her work on femmes in relationships with FTM partners, Jane Ward defines gender labor as "the affective and bodily efforts invested in giving gender to others, or actively suspending self-focus in the service of helping others achieve the varied forms of gender recognition they long for."[33] In this service-based model of labor, queer femmes pour work into their intimate others at the expense of their own needs. When she challenged me for abandoning her during the fight, La'Nea demanded that I account for this inherited imbalance. An ethical witnessing of my maternal failure means trying to imagine a femmeness otherwise: what if, as opposed to only "giving gender to others," folks might also co-produce stud-femme sociality as a mutually beneficial site of Black praxis?

The hyphen that links stud-femme is a bridge that carries more than a strap on its back—it is a weight-bearing social infrastructure that both destabilizes and jerry-rigs the gender binary. We who live in the house Black lesbians built make our lives in relation to the duality of stud-femme, even (or especially) when we create other formulas of gendered intimacy like femme4femme and stud4stud. Seen from this angle, stud-femme is not a rule to be followed or broken, but a cultural grammar that reveals the deviance encoded in every performance of queer Black gender, whether masculine, feminine, or gendered in ways that defy binarism. The gag is that instead of reveling in our fluid inter-relation, we have been convinced that masc folks are somehow both more valiant and more vulnerable than their femme kin.

For Kairo, her "boy" gender was induced and stabilized by the desire of Black girls, one of whom was sitting right across the circle from her as she shared her story of growing up. Rather than transgressive gender as something that is centered on the defiantly masculine body, Kairo's studness was made coherent by the desire of ostensibly non-queer girls—they were why she "kept it going." This erotic potentiality, too, is femme labor, performed in ephemeral spaces like first-grade classrooms and middle school locker rooms. The sister circle is one such space—Kairo and I may have answered the question, but who asked it? It's possible that La'Nea wrote it; but she and I had had that conversation so many times over, it seemed unlikely. Among the crew of young women, there was another unnamed erotic subject peeking into the possibility of being In the Life.[34] Her presence, and her desire to hear and be heard, was the impetus for the sharing of queer life stories.

She called me forth as "the genuine article," what Lewis calls "an embodied text that counters campus beliefs about 'what a feminist looks like.'"[35] In the case of The Journey Within, the scales of power are reversed from what Lewis observed at white universities: I was a genuine article that provided a glimmer of what a grown, queer, colored life could be like for kids who live in the homonationalist capital of the United States, my body a countergeography to the white-on-white bourgeois men's space that the Castro has become.[36] However, I was not the only genuine article to speak. Kairo and I both shared a story, and in so doing we labored together against the absence of other lived models of queerness that linked our experiences across geography, gender, and generation. Boy or nah, this lil' nigga belonged in the circle. Lounging on those couches, there was space for each of us to speak as experts of our own experience, while also co-presencing girlhood as a queer coalitional space that made good on the imperative Cathy Cohen issued two decades ago.[37] In the sister circle, and in the broader set of relations held by the school and The City, we queered kinship and forms of intimacy—we were the vessels of repetition with a difference, teaching each other how to be with and for ourselves.

# On the Shoreline:
# A Portal to Black Queer Kinship

Stud-femme sociality produces a Black queer common that exceeds the limited expectations of the intimate coupling, and also shapes "straight" performances of girlhood, as we see in the sister circle. In my academic and community work, there are no straight kids. Young people's sexuality is by definition an open set, and queer (or at least queered) from the gate. Even as Kairo steps (one leg limp) agentically into stud-hood, that doesn't produce the non-studs around her as femme. Rather, the Black femme function capacitates that which we understand as queer post-lesbian sociality, even if the agent who enacts it isn't necessarily a femme herself, or a "her" at all. It is here, too, that we see the overlaps between being non-trans and being gender defiant—just because "woman" is put upon me and I assent, it is not the same thing as picking up femme as a weapon in the world. Over the course of The Journey Within, we learned a bit about each other's social arsenals and how we were surviving the afterlives of slavery and settlement, not to mention puberty. Ours was an armistice of sorts, where we took a breather from the wars going on between and around us to experiment with peace.

After the sister circle, we headed out into the chilly night for a hike to the beach. In the Headlands, there are no streetlights, and the only rule Zahra and I set for the walk was that none of us could use a flashlight. Lit by the moon, the half-mile walk along a brackish pond was not technically difficult, but required a wholly different skill set than making your way home though streets of the Mission or Bayview at midnight. We had to trust the land to hold us, and lean into the intimacy between each other as we held over-grown brush aside for the person behind us and quelled titters of fear and tiredness. Once we reached the beach, a tender silence blanketed our crew. Kids spread out solo or in pairs far enough to have some privacy, but close enough to keep the energetic container of our circle intact. Kairo and La'Nea sat in front of me on the sand staring at the Pacific, shoulders touching, but otherwise still. Another pair of girls, whose silhouettes I could not quite make out, held each other's waists and tossed stones in the water, each one landing farther than the last.

The fullness of the moment sent me back though the wormhole to my own adolescence, and I felt the bite of how badly I had needed a space like the one we co-created on The Journey Within—I had been living the Lorde's litany, "seeking a now that can breed / futures / like bread in our children's mouths."[38] Unlike me, these beloved children wouldn't have to travel this journey by themselves. If, as Keeling proposes (riffing on Lorde), "the black femme is a figure that exists on the edge line, that is, the shore-line between the visible and the invisible, the thought and the unthought,"[39] our posse tiptoed on that literal shoreline, peering from the sand into the expanse of Black, liquid possibility. We were in the darkness, cold but not alone. Not only did the kids have me and Zahra there to hold a container for emergent affections, we also had them. Across genders and generations, sand and sea, we held the sacred intimacy of girlhood as queered kinship.

# Notes

1. Kairo used she/her/hers pronouns, and that is how she is referred to throughout this essay. Beyond reflecting Kairo's lived practice, the textual use of "she" is also in generative tension with "they" as the current socially respectable queer pronoun for when one doesn't know the pronouns of a person who appears gender non-conforming.

2. Kairo wore Retro Air Jordan X's, kiddie size to be exact.

3. "Fuggs" refers to "fake" or knock-off Ugg brand snow boots. Both the name-brand and generic versions are marketed to women and feature a thick shearling lining that made them popular among youth who had to commute to school on foggy, cold San Francisco mornings.

4. For more on the interrelationships between intimate partner violence and the state-driven war against Black people, see Dána-Ain Davis, *Battered Black Women and Welfare Reform* (Albany, NY: SUNY Press, 2012) and Beth Richie, *Arrested Justice* (New York: NYU Press, 2012).

5. Frisco is a contested nickname for the city of San Francisco used by generations of working-class residents and in communities of color.

6. Jafari S. Allen, "For 'the Children': Dancing the Beloved Community," *Souls* 11, no. 3 (2009): 311–26; Marlon M. Bailey, *Butch Queens Up in Pumps: Gender, Performance, and Ballroom Culture in Detroit* (Ann Arbor: University of Michigan Press, 2013); Shaka McGlotten, "A Brief and Improper Geography of Sexpublics and Queer-spaces in Austin Texas," *Gender, Place & Culture* 21, no. 4 (2013): 471–88. In terms of Black queer scholars who engage autoethnographic methods, see Allen, "For 'the Children': Dancing." For a

rich discussion of the relationship between queer scholarship and autoethnographic methods, see Tony E. Adams and Stacy Holman Jones, "Telling Stories: Reflexivity, Queer Theory, and Autoethnography" *Cultural Studies ↔ Critical Methodologies* 11, no. 2 (April 2011): 108–16.

7. Green, "The Essential I/Eye in We: A Black TransFeminist Approach to Ethnographic Film," *Black Camera* 6, no. 2. (2016): 189–90.

8. Allen, "Black/Queer/Diaspora at the Current Conjuncture," *GLQ* 18, nos. 2–3 (2012): 215.

9. Kara Keeling, *The Witch's Flight: The Cinematic, the Black Femme, and the Image of Common Sense* (Durham, NC: Duke University Press, 2007), 20.

10. Margot Weiss, "The Epistemology of Ethnography: Method in Queer Anthropology," *GLQ* 17, no. 4: 650.

11. C. Riley Snorton, *Black on Both Sides: A Racial History of Trans Identity* (Minneapolis: University of Minnesota Press, 2017), 74.

12. Keeling, *Witch's Flight*, 20–21.

13. *Stud* is a racialized and classed term used to describe people assigned female at birth who have a masculine-of-center gender presentation. While *butch* could be seen as an analogous term, *stud* and its East Coast variants (*AG, dom, aggressive*) invoke a Black/ened "female masculinity." Particularly in the Bay Area, *stud* is a multiracial formation that includes Latinx, Polynesian, Filipinx, Native, Arab, and Asian folks, and even the odd working-class white stud, but they cohere in their studness through their participation in and improvisation upon the cultural lexicon of Black style.

14. PO is an abbreviation of parole or probation officer; in Kairo's case, it was the latter.

15. Mariame Kaba, ed., *No Selves to Defend* (zine), https://noselves2defend.files.wordpress.com/2016/09/noselvestodefend_v5.pdf.

16. Damien Schnyder, "Masculinity Lock-down: The Formation of Black Masculinity in a California Public School," *Transforming Anthropology* 20, no. 1 (2012): 5–16.

17. Kaila Story, "Fear of a Black Femme: The Existential Conundrum of Embodying a Black Femme Identity While Being a Professor of Black, Queer, and Feminist Studies," *Journal of Lesbian Studies* 21, no. 4 (2017): 412–13.

18. Christina Handhart, *Safe Spaces: Gay Neighborhood History and the Politics of Violence* (Durham, NC: Duke University Press, 2013).

19. See Ed Brockenbrough, "Agency and Abjection in the Closet: The Voices (and Silences) of Black Queer Male Teachers," *International Journal of Qualitative Studies in Education* 25, no. 6 (2012): 741–65; Bettina Love, "'She Has a Real Connection with Them:' Reimagining and Expanding Our Definitions of Black Masculinity and Mentoring in Education through Female Masculinity," *Journal of Lesbian Studies* 21, no. 4 (2017): 443–52; Kevin Kumashiro, ed., *Troubling the Intersections of Race and Sexuality: Queer Students of Color and Anti-Oppressive Education* (New York: Rowman & Littlefield, 2001).

20. Mel Michelle Lewis, "A Genuine Article: Intersectionality, Black Lesbian Gender Expression, and the Feminist Pedagogical Project," *Journal of Lesbian Studies* 21, no. 4 (2017): 422.

21. *Xicana* is a political term developed from the "Chicano" movement of the mid-twentieth century that mobilized Mexican-descended people in the United States against Eurocentrism and systemic oppression. The beginning "X," advocated by recent generations of activists, marks a break from the colonial Spanish language, and revives the "x"

used by Mayan and Aztec languages. The ending "x" is an intervention of feminist and queer cultural workers as a form of linguistic resistance to the binary gendering of the Spanish language. Earlier neologisms included Xican@ and Chican@, but with the advent of "@" being used as a key command in online spaces, new adaptations were required. For more on the racial and political implications of the "x," see Jessica Marie Johnson's "Thinking About the 'X'," *African American Intellectual History Society* (blog), December 12, 2015, http://www.aaihs.org/thinking-about-an-x/ (accessed January 24, 2016).

22. "Talking" is a Black English vernacular referent for a non-exclusive, exploratory stage of dating in which there is mutual romantic interest but no obligation to escalate commitment or manage the other's emotional investment. Its usage here, along with the modifier "lightweight," signals my investment in using Black English as a theoretical language.

23. Advisory period is an organizational structure common to small progressive secondary schools; similar to a homeroom in that it meets every day. Advisory is a time when all members of the school community meet in small, intimate groups of twelve to eighteen students with the same teacher, or advisor. The advisor–student relationship is the nucleus of schools using this model, and functions as a hub for academic support, wellness services, family collaboration, and discipline. For more on Advisory, see Debbie Meier, *The Power of Their Ideas: Lesson for America from a Small School in Harlem* (Boston, MA: Beacon Press, 2002).

24. Femme4femme derives from a romantic shorthand used in lesbian personals ads to indicate one femme-identified person seeking another for a sexual or romantic liaison. The erotic impulse of femme4femme has since been politicized and is used in social media and other public intellectual work to index a (sometimes reductive) femme centrism. For instance, the Femme4Femme track of the 2015 Allied Media Conference offered an intersectional, power-sensitive approach to femme politics. Co-written by track organizers Megan Robyn Collado, Noreen Khimji, Caleb Luna, and Cortez Wright, the description of the subtheme read more like a manifest: "Femme is a concept of femininity that draws its power from the queer, trans, Black, immigrant, indigenous, fat, poor, and disabled survivors of this world. Femme is a queer-of-color identity that is centered around embodying a femininity that transcends and challenges white supremacist patriarchal ideas of femininity as white, of femininity as weakness, of femininity as not innovative. Our femme challenges these notions and embraces femme as power, as survival, as cutting-edge and as community. The Femme4Femme Media Track will explore media that makes femme brilliance visible and irresistible."

25. Gilmore, *Golden Gulag: Prisons, Surplus, Crisis, and Opposition in Globalizing California* (Berkeley: University of California Press, 2007); Richie, *Arrested Justice*; Kaba, *Prison Culture: How the PIC Structures Our World* (blog, 2010–present), http://usprisonculture.com/blog (accessed December 3, 2017).

26. I use *non-trans* here as a racially appropriate alternative to *cisgender*, which means that (a) the gender that you feel inside, (b) the gender that you perform outside, and (c) the gender you were assigned at birth all line up and "match." However, everything we know about dominant genders—both masculinity and femininity—are based on white bourgeois normativity. As Cathy Cohen ("Punks, Bulldaggers, and Welfare Queens: The Radical Potential of Queer Politics?," *GLQ: A Journal of Lesbian and Gay Studies* 3, no. 4 (1997): 437–65) and Hortense Spillers ("Mama's Baby, Papa's Maybe: An American Grammar Book." *Diacritics* 17, no. 2 (1987): 65–81) teach us, there is no way for Black women to ever achieve "real" or legitimate womanhood, from Serena to Saartje to anyone on

WIC—this dynamic holds for Black men, just with different stereotypes. Thus, to call us cisgender is to act like we have the privilege of dominant gender when we don't. At the same time, that doesn't make all Black folks trans either—trans Black people experience another kind of material risk in their daily lives, and thus have another toolkit for survival, as well as a whole 'nother space of fire and brilliance that I as a non-trans person do not have access to. *Non-trans* tries to center transness as a site of epistemic privilege while also not fronting like non-trans Black women wield structural power.

27. For an excellent cinematic rendering of a fucknigga, see "Hella Open," a 2017 episode of Issa Rae's *Insecure* (S02E03), directed by Marta Cunningham and broadcast on HBO.

28. *Bitch* is used frequently among gay men of color and between women of all gender assignments and sexualities as a term of gender affirmation and affection. However, the frequency of its usage does not rinse *bitch* of its misogynoiristic valence. For more on misogynoir and the term *bitch*, see Antonia Randolph, "Why Bitch Isn't Nigger: Misogynoir and the False Equivalences of Hip Hop" (paper presented at the annual meeting for the National Women's Studies Association, Baltimore, MD, November 16–19, 2017).

29. Snorton, *Black on Both Sides*, 107.

30. Jane Ward, "Gender Labor: Transmen, Femmes, and the Collective Work of Transgression," *Sexualities* 13, no. 2: 236–54. Ward specifically identifies the masquerade of non-menstruation as a type of femme labor.

31. Jasbir Puar, "Rethinking Homonationalism," *International Journal of Middle East Studies* 45, no. 2 (2013): 336–39—"a facet of modernity and a historical shift marked by the entrance of (some) homosexual bodies as worthy of protection by nation-states, a constitutive and fundamental reorientation of the relationship between the state, capitalism, and sexuality" (337).

32. "Aite" is used here as an utterance of assent, while "aouno" is a Black English demurral of certainty. These terms are cognatic with, but irreducible to, "alright" and "I don't know."

33. Ward, "Gender Labor," 237.

34. Here, I reference both the vintage term for being gay and the title of the pathbreaking and life-saving anthology of Black gay men's literature.

35. Lewis, "A Genuine Article," 430.

36. Homonationalism here refers to a conservative political move that positions LGBT people as ideal citizens and legitimizes the white supremacist, capitalist, imperial U.S. state through efforts like military inclusion and marriage equality. For more on homonationalism, see Jasbir Puar, *Terrorist Assemblages* (Durham, NC: Duke University Press, 2007).

37. Cohen, "Punks, Bulldaggers, and Welfare Queens."

38. Audre Lorde, "Litany for Survival," in *The Black Unicorn* (New York: W.W. Norton, 1995).

39. Keeling, *Witch's Flight*, 2.

Shawn(ta) Smith-Cruz

# Archiving Black Lesbians in Practice: The Salsa Soul Sisters Archival Collection

At the CUNY Graduate Center, I have the honor of serving as the head of reference, supplying direct service to the varied members of the GC community. At CUNY and other universities across the country, although there are administrative librarians, many librarians are appointed faculty. Departmental faculty and students alike are often unclear of the role library faculty perform for the university in addition to the service functions of their positions. Yet, our scholarship informs our service. As a woman, a person of color, and a lesbian, I am no stranger to the expended labor of clarifying my role in any given interaction (even to well-meaning colleagues aiming to add my voice to the conversation). As an assistant professor at the Graduate Center, with the challenge of engaging in scholarship alongside library service, I find it efficient to apply my archival training in a method that places my research in the real world, thereby affecting and serving people outside of the academy. My work with the Lesbian Herstory Archives (LHA) over the past ten years has led me to coordinate with, and participate in, the processing of a very vital archival collection: the Third World Women: Salsa Soul Sisters Special Collection, the archival material of the first known "black" or African ancestral or "third world women" lesbian organization in the country, which includes an array of Latina lesbians and other lesbians of color. CUNY has supported this work in three ways: 1) structurally, by employing librarians as faculty, allowing for our scholarship to extend outside of an academic community; 2) personally, by supplying me with a PSC CUNY grant for the 2018–2019 academic year to fund archiving that engages community and requires a peer-based dissemination of archival material, and 3) incidentally, by keeping archivist positions vacant at some campuses, like the GC, thereby supplying a gap in the offerings, enabling librarians such as myself to respond as our expertise allows.

Although we do not have an archivist on staff at the Mina Rees Library, I am prompted to respond to the archival research questions that approach the reference desk. Whether it pertains to digital repositories, archival exhibitions, or special collections, I and each of the librarians at the Mina Rees Library have the expertise to share and contribute to the scholarly pulse as it pertains to primary source material and archival dissemination.

The radical nature of this specific archiving story is enmeshed in my personal narrative and unveils the multitudinous culling of the Salsa Soul Sisters archival materials—a practice that spanned time and space. In 2010 I sat on a panel at a town hall meeting held at the NYC Lesbian and Gay Center (now the LGBTQ Services Center) sponsored by the African Ancestral Lesbians United for Societal Change (AALUSC), an organization that was the spinoff of the Salsa Soul Sisters. The town hall meeting was meant to cover AALUSC's history: how she began and why, the history of the LGBTQ communities, women of color and Black lesbian communities, and the current state of Black lesbians. A panelist, Cassandra Grant, an elder, announced herself as the arbiter of the *Third World Women: Salsa Soul Sisters* archival collection. She noted that the Salsa Soul contents predated 1980 (which marked the year of the first black lesbian conference), thereby making the collection the first known black lesbian organization in the country, and likely the world. At this meeting, Grant pleaded with the community that someone of this current generation take the collection and care for its contents.

African Ancestral or third-world lesbians were present and at the table of lesbian and gay agendas since the marking of the gay liberation movement. In 1976, for example, Salsa published an invitation and statement to the world staking their claim in the lesbian and gay community. Versions of this statement can be found in the *Salsa Soul Gayzette*, their serial literary publication and newsletter, but for ready reference, listed below is the 1976 version published as an advertisement in the popular periodical, *The Lesbian Feminist,* discoverable online as a result of a digitization project of Lesbian Herstory Archives newsletters. Their platform begins:

> The necessity for third world gay women to organize in our own interest is paramount. Existing gay organizations have neither welcomed our participation nor championed our concerns. Out of this reality, the Salsa Soul Sisters was organized and continues to grow. We function as a loosely structured collective, recognizing the varied age, academic class, and economic differences that exist in the group. We see this diversity as enriching our experiences and contributing to the emotional and intellectual growth of the organization (1976).

In 2010, employed part-time as memberships and fellowships coordinator of CLAGS, the Center for LGBTQ Studies at the CUNY Graduate Center, led me to be on the steering committee for the CLAGS Lesbians in the '70s conference. I authored *The Black Lesbians in the '70s* zine, which led the spring series event and brought over one hundred community members, many of whom were black lesbians, into the Lesbian Herstory Archives. This event began the dialogue of connecting myself to the Salsa Soul women, who recalled the *Keepin' On* exhibit that already included their contents from its previous board member and LHA volunteer Georgia Brooks. LHA held a consistent presence in Black lesbian lives and culture and became accepted as a space noteworthy for future archiving of their work.

On the closing panel of the second national Black Lesbian conference, *Beyond Bold and Brave*, held at Barnard College in March 2016, Cassandra Grant sat beside me once again, alongside journalist and publisher Linda Villarosa and acclaimed Black Lesbian scholar Alexis Pauline Gumbs. On the panel, titled, "Black Lesbian Organizing and Activism: 1970s to Now," we called to our foremothers and paid homage to women who found the courage to participate in and at times initiate these global conversations of inclusion and representation. It was at this conference in front of a public audience that Cassandra announced that the collection would be placed in the Lesbian Herstory Archives.

Since this date, in 2018, a zine has been published by Endless Editions, and a public exhibition on the Salsa Soul materials was showcased at the Robert Blackburn Printmaking Workshop.

The zine was co-coordinated by Essye Klempner, program and exhibitions manager of the Robert Blackburn Printmaking Workshop, using a Risograph printing technique. Its intricate design with illustrations by Jaz Smith-Cruz and Krystal C. Johnson, two lesbians of color, was meant to embody an intimate texture of herstory combined with a current flow of movement and connection toward the future. Its contents represented an overview of the process for exhibiting this material through its collaborations and efforts over the past ten years.

The Blackburn Printmaking Workshop hosted the exhibition, *Salsa Soul Sisters: Honoring Lesbians of Color at the Lesbian Herstory Archives,* as a celebration showcasing the recent donation of Salsa Soul Sisters: Third World Women archival materials to the Lesbian Herstory Archives (LHA). Members Cassandra Grant, Imani Rashid, Nancy Valentine, and Brahma Curry were responsible for this generous donation made in November 2016. It includes photographs, monthly newsletters, event flyers, discussion schedules, meeting minutes, financial papers, correspondence, pamphlets, and other materials documenting years of activism. It greatly expands the pre-existing holdings of LHA, furthering its positioning as the most comprehensive archive of lesbian materials in the world. The CUNY PSC research grant was granted to continue the exhibition and archiving of this herstoric resource.

# Reference

*The Lesbian Feminist.* "Third World Gay Women's Organization Salsa Soul Advertisement," December 1976. Newsletters. Lesbian Herstory Archives. From Archives of Sexuality & Gender, http://tinyurl.galegroup.com/tinyurl/8PtWWX. Accessed November 20, 2018.

Susana Morris

# More Than Human: Black Feminisms of the Future in Jewelle Gomez's *The Gilda Stories*

In her collection of essays *The Black Interior*, poet and critic Elizabeth Alexander sks two important questions about the nature of Black cultural practice: "What do we learn when we pause at sites of contradiction where black creativity complicates and resists what blackness is 'supposed' to be? What in our culture speaks, sustains, and survives, post-nationalism, post-racial romance, into the unwritten *black future we must imagine*?"[1] Alexander answers these questions by mining the fertile fields of African American art, literature, and film, teasing out the ways in which Black artists from Langston Hughes to Denzel Washington create vibrant, transgressive images of Black experience in their works. I too want to respond to Alexander's query, particularly in regard to her concern about what in our culture (re)imagines a Black future with Black folk—and Black women, in particular—actively centered and thriving. More specifically, I want to illuminate black women's engagements with Afrofuturism and feminism as one particular way Black futures are being reconceived.

People of the African Diaspora are continuously creating culture and radically transforming visions of the future. And, certainly, Black people's futurist cultural productions offer a variety of futures—from portrayals that are optimistic, pessimistic, progressive, dystopian, or utopian. However, despite the variations in content, these visions are necessarily transgressive and subversive in relation to dominant discourse.[2] To be Black and not only envision yourself in the future but at the center of the future—to be the agent and subject of the future, and not relegated to the primeval past, used as props or pawns, or disappeared altogether—is an act of resistance and liberation, particularly in a present plagued by white supremacy and imperialism. And because Black women exist at the intersections of multiplicative oppressions yet remain producers of (often coopted) culture, their futurist imaginings of art, literature, film, and music are often ignored, dismissed, or diminished, but nevertheless remain fundamental to any complete understanding of futurity.

This essay begins by outlining Afrofuturism as an aesthetic and epistemology that thrives in the hostile white supremacist dystopia that is contemporary life. I then make the case that Afrofuturism and Black feminism are symbiotic modes of thought and provide a method for understanding Black women's futurist cultural productions. Thereafter, using Jewelle Gomez's 1991 novel *The Gilda Stories* as a foundational text, I both respond to Alexander's questions and argue that Black women's Afrofuturist feminist cultural productions challenge hegemonic notions of progress and futurity in favor of a truly transgressive feminist future. I contend that *The Gilda Stories*, like other examples of Afrofuturist feminist cultural production, such as Octavia Butler's writing, Janelle Monáe's music, and Wangechi Mutu's art, exposes the potentially radical ways of (re)envisioning embodiment and identity in regards to race, gender, and sexuality that is at the heart of Afrofuturist feminism. My essay illuminates the ways in which *The Gilda Stories* presents a Black feminist future in which Black women survive, thrive, and combat white supremacy as powerful vampires; it also participates in the larger critical conversation on *The Gilda Stories* by uncovering the ways in which the novel upends dominant futurist discourse to provide a transgressive Afrofuturist feminist vision of the future. My intervention in the field of Afrofuturism and Black feminism foregrounds the significance of Black women's visions of the future, even as we consider increasingly "post-racial" and "post-human" identities in the contemporary cultural landscape.

## Fear of a Black Planet

I understand Afrofuturism as an aesthetic, an epistemology, and as what Kodwo Eshun has called a "tool kit" that reflects an interrogative engagement with race, space, time, technology, and the arts in Black cultural productions.[3] And, as Ytasha Womack argues, "whether through literature, visual arts, music, or grassroots organizing, Afrofuturists redefine culture and notions of blackness for today and the future. Both an artistic aesthetic and a framework for critical theory, Afrofuturism combines elements of science fiction, historical fiction, speculative fiction, fantasy, Afrocentricity, and magical realism with non-Western beliefs."[4] Afrofuturism is a way of knowing, understanding, and creating in the world that transgresses the bounds of Western notions of progress, identity, and futurity. Indeed, "Afrofuturism insists that blacks fundamentally are the future and that Afrodiasporic cultural practices are vital to imagining the continuance of human society."[5] Afrofuturism is in the art and aesthetics of Octavia Butler, John Jennings, Janelle Monáe, Parliament Funkadelic, Nnedi Okorafor, Sun Ra, Ishmael Reed, and many other Black artists.

My use of the term *Afrofuturism* is particularly informed by Afrofuturist scholars, such as Mark Dery, Kodwo Eshun, Alondra Nelson, Ytasha Womack, and Lisa Yaszek, among others, who have written foundational analyses of the field. Dery, for example, coined the term *Afrofuturism* in the early 1990s to "describe African-American culture's appropriation of technology and SF imagery."[6] The combination of "afro" and "futurism" highlights the important connection between race and futurism. Alondra Nelson is another pioneer in the field of Afrofuturism; the Afrofuturism listserv she founded and the special issue of *Social Text* she edited in 2002 are foundational texts in Afrofuturist discourse. Literary scholar Lisa Yaszek's work has uncovered Afrofuturist themes in African American literature from the early twentieth century to the present. Ytasha Womack's recent monograph *Afrofuturism: The World of Black Sci-Fi and Fantasy Culture* is a groundbreaking primer and historiography of Afrofuturism. Unsurprisingly, Afrofuturism also has a vibrant presence online, with dozens of websites, Facebook groups, and special organizations devoted to the subject peppering the web. Clearly, Afrofuturism is a dynamic movement that spans several genres and offers up potentially transgressive possibilities for art, technology, and society.

A productive epistemological space opens when we consider Afrofuturism and Black feminism together because much of Afrofuturism's potentially transgressive politics align with the fundamental tenets of Black feminism.

Just as Afrofuturism fundamentally aligns Blackness with the future, so Black feminism argues for the validity and centrality of Black people—and Black women's—lived experience. However, linking feminism and futurism is more than wishful thinking or utopian progressivism. Futurist interventions connected to feminism can be seen in genres spanning literature, film, art, fashion, and more. In light of such a tradition, I see Afrofuturism and Black feminism as symbiotic modes of thought and practice in many ways, and argue that "coupling Afrofuturism with feminism expands the former's capacity to transgress normative boundaries of not only race, but of gender, sexuality, ability, and other subject positions; this coupling also catalyzes the latter's capacity for reimagining the past, present, and future."[7] The linking of Afrofuturism and feminism does another important thing—it illuminates what Alexander calls "the black interior": "an inner space in which black artists have found selves that go far, far beyond the limited expectations and definitions of what black is, isn't, or should be."[8] Black women's Afrofuturist feminism is one of many ways in which this Black interior space is created, expanded, and celebrated.

Afrofuturist feminism is manifested in a variety of ways in Black women's cultural production—whether through fine art, music, fashion, literature, or other genres. However, there are particular defining, recurrent features of Afrofuturist feminism that are important to note: the creation of a parallel feminist universe; the remixing of dominant futurist discourse; and futurist scenarios in which Black women are centered as agents, but not as martyrs. Parallel feminist universes are fully realized alternate futurist worlds. These alternate realities are not necessarily feminist utopias, however. Rather, these are worlds that are heavily influenced and shaped by feminist principles and actions. Take, for example, Octavia Butler's short story "The Book of Martha," which features a Black woman saving the world through her own wit and feminist ingenuity. The text critiques normative notions of power and agency and offers up transgressive futurist visions in their place, without simply resorting to heavy-handed moralizing or a simplistic utopia. Remixing, in the context of Afrofuturist feminism, refers to the pattern of disruption, pushing back, upending, and reassembling of futurist discourse that occurs in these pieces. Artist Wangechi Mutu's mixed-media collages embody this notion of remix. Much of her work takes found objects and pieces them together to form an entirely new work, frequently depicting raw, abrasive, unsettling, and grotesque images of Black women as monstrous hybrids of flesh and technology that trouble simplistic notions of futurism and progress. Mutu's Afrofuturist feminist art suggests that "we eroticize or create the same things we destroy."[9] Another particularly striking feature of Afrofuturist feminism in Black women's cultural production is the portrayal of Black women as agents of the future, charting their own singular and communal paths to humanity's destiny. Janelle Monáe's music is a major part of the Afrofuturist feminist soundtrack with concept albums called *Metropolis*, *Arch-Android*, and *Electric Ladies*. Monáe's albums reference Ray Kurzweil's notions of singularity as they map the life of Cindy Mayweather, an android on the run because of an illicit relationship with a human being. Monáe's concept albums, then, are futurist narratives that imagine a perhaps not-so-distant future where the intersections of racism, classism, and sexism collide with what it means to be fundamentally human in ways that mirror our own fractured and fractious social hierarchies. Octavia Butler, Janelle Monáe, and Wangechi Mutu are just a few members of a thriving cohort of Afrofuturist feminists whose work is actively reconfiguring the contours of futurist discourse.

Parallel feminist universes, remixed futurist discourses, and powerful Black women as agents of change occur in the works of the aforementioned women, but also in the work of Nnedi Okorafor, Jean Grae, Tanana-rive Due, Kara Walker, Nettrice Gaskins, Jewelle Gomez, and many others. I am not suggesting that all of these elements must be present for a work to be engaged in Afrofuturist feminism; neither am I insisting that these are the only ways to participate in Afrofuturist feminism. What I am suggesting is that Black women's cultural productions' engagement with Afrofuturist feminism frequently uses these methods to expand the possibilities for Black women's understandings of themselves and their places in the world and the future.

It is important to note that despite its nature to transgress and subvert,

Afrofuturist feminism is not fundamentally reactionary. Rather, Afrofuturist feminism is in the business of creating both counter-pasts and counter-futures and alternative and parallel universes that center Blackness, without constantly referencing whiteness.[10] Nevertheless, Afrofuturism has been created and currently exists in a world where futurist visions of Blackness are far from benign and are actually understood as dangerous, for as Alondra Nelson insists, "the racialized digital divide narrative that circulates in the public sphere and the bodiless, color-blind mythotopias of cybertheory and commercial advertising have become unacknowledged frames of reference for understanding race in the digital age. In these frameworks, the technologically enabled future is by its very nature unmoored from the past and from people of color."[11] Thus, Afrofuturism and Afrofuturist feminism must ultimately be understood within a historical context in which Blackness is constantly under surveillance and attack.

Indeed, Afrofuturist feminism is currently thriving in a dystopian America that is rife with apocalyptic fervor. In the summer of 2015, gunman Dylann Roof entered a Wednesday night Bible study meeting at a predominantly Black church and killed nine parishioners. His desire was to start a race war; he believed that Black people were "raping [white] women and taking over the country."[12] One might be quick to dismiss Roof's ravings as those of a madman. But his act of extreme violence makes sense in the larger context of white supremacy where Blacks experience state-sanctioned violence that aims to police and control. Too often public discourse around social problems often resorts to using thinly veiled references to the looming specter of Black and Brown bodies here and abroad, "taking over" as it were, as evidence of the rapid decay of society—despite the fact that this civilization, as we know it, depends largely upon the unpaid and underpaid labor of Black and Brown folk.

To be clear, much of this fear-soaked doomsdayism and apocalyptic fervor has very little to do with actual violence committed by Black and Brown people, and more to do with the terror of being unable to adequately contain, police, and repress people of color. Instead, the current American anxiety about the future is absolutely connected to fear of Black and Brown bodies and what the potential of our increased agency and autonomy might mean for the enduring power of white supremacy. Because Afrofuturism and Afrofuturist feminism are not simply historical phenomena but a contemporary set of beliefs and practices, these current events are important to note. In this contemporary moment Afrofuturist feminism is best understood alongside the quotidian anti-Blackness of daily life, as it responds to the fear of Blackness and misogynoir with the promise of more unapologetic Black womanhood.[13] Thus, the visions of the future that Black women writers and artists create are of vital importance. These works, such as Jewelle Gomez's *The Gilda Stories*, create and cultivate generative space that challenges the fear-driven script of a Black planet.

## The End of the World as We Know It

Jewelle Gomez's 1991 novel *The Gilda Stories* embodies the most salient aspects of Afrofuturist feminism: it creates a feminist parallel universe, remixes dominant cultural discourses (about vampires), and ends with powerful Black women restructuring society. These aspects of the novel also exemplify Alexander's notions of the Black interior by privileging Black women's meaning-making in a new world order. Blackness is often understood as abject, repulsive, even monstrous, but is rarely seen as the seductive predator that represents dangerous, yet delicious evil—the very characteristics vampires often embody in the West. However, Gomez remixes vampire mythology with distinctly Afrofuturist feminist sensibilities.

*The Gilda Stories* traces the over two-hundred-year lifespan of the titular heroine, who is an anomaly in the vampire genre. Gilda is an African American lesbian who becomes a vampire after her escape from slavery in 1850; and, perhaps most odd, she rarely kills humans, but feeds on them in a manner Gomez calls an "exchange," whereby a vampire feeds on a human donor and, in turn, leaves the donor with something—usually affirming thoughts or even advice. While Gilda and her vampire peers can and do sometimes kill humans, they are more interested in living peacefully rather than inflicting violence or amassing power and privilege—a striking fact, especially as the novel takes place in extremely hostile dystopian and eventually apocalyptic landscapes from the nineteenth to the twenty-first centuries.

In order to understand the contribution that *The Gilda Stories* makes in the Afrofuturist feminist canon, I would like to first place the text in context with the traditional vampire fiction that it remixes. *The Gilda Stories* has received a fair amount of critical attention in the decades since its publication, and this criticism has by and large focused on the novel's rendering of queer sexuality and its revision of vampire mythology.[14] For example, Lynda Hall's "Passion(ate) Plays: Wherever We Found Space" is a comparative study of Audre Lorde's *Zami* and Gomez's *The Gilda Stories* and analyzes lesbian representation in both texts, arguing that they "queer the 'master narrative' of 'normal' traditional white, heterosexual, male power and redefine the boundaries through taking the agency of writing their own and other's experiences into reality and visibility."[15] Sabine Meyer has argued that *The Gilda Stories* is another version of a passing narrative, one that calls normative identity into question with its queer depiction of "perverted" vampires passing for mortal. Similarly, Shannon Winnubst identifies *The Gilda Stories* as a queer counter-narrative to the dominant vampire trope. While these pieces, alongside the other scholarship that engages *The Gilda Stories*, have created a vibrant and robust critical conversation in the study of the novel, *The Gilda Stories* has not primarily been understood as an Afrofuturist text in literary criticism.[16] Thus, my analysis of the novel is a critical intervention that underscores the novel's place as a transgressive futurist reimagining that is part of a larger tradition of Afrofuturist feminist cultural production and meaning-making.

The vampire mythology at the heart of *The Gilda Stories* completely upends traditional depictions of these supernatural creatures, creating an alternate feminist universe.[17] In *Our Vampires, Ourselves*, her seminal text on vampires in literature and culture, Nina Auerbach proposes that American vampires at the end of the twentieth century "embody seditious urbanity rather than dangerous intimacy" and "began to die."[18] She suggests that "intimidated by ideological reaction and the AIDS epidemic, they mutated as a species, into unprecedented mortality, lacking the tenacity of the Victorian theatrical phantoms they resembled. The best of them took on the holy isolation of angels, inspiring awe in a humanity they could no longer govern."[19] Auerbach places *The Gilda Stories* in this last category, citing the novel's "anesthetized" vampires who are "inhibited by their self-righteous decade, whose protests dissipate in piety" and who are "so clannish and self-enclosed that they present no threat" to larger systems of dominance.[20] While Auerbach makes several persuasive connections between vampire lore and the politics it arises from, her negligence in discussing issues of race in conjunction with the role of gender exposes her dismissal of *The Gilda Stories* as a failure to recognize how understanding interlocking oppressions might enrich our understanding of Gomez's futuristic vampire tale. So, while the vampires in *The Gilda Stories* are perhaps more "defanged" than some of the book's predecessors or contemporaries, that fact is not simply a by-product inspired from the "defensive prudence" born out of the Reagan era. Rather, I would argue that Gomez has a fundamentally different project than, say, what her contemporary Anne Rice sets out to do in her *Vampire Chronicles*—a project that rejects traditional narratives of power and progress or contemporary fears about contagion and difference eroding white supremacy's future.[21]

Indeed, in "Recasting the Mythology: Writing Vampire Fiction," Gomez contends that in *The Gilda Stories* "the challenge . . . was to create a new mythology, to strip away the dogma that has shaped the vampire figure within the rather narrow Western, Caucasian expectation, and to recreate a heroic figure within a broader, more ancient frame of reference."[22] Gomez rejects the historically constricted Western vampire lore that identifies vampires as ruthless killers bent on destroying white, middle-class, heterosexual victims (as in the titular Count of Bram Stoker's *Dracula*, for example) or as tormented victims condemned to an eternity of anguish (as in Louis in Anne Rice's *The Vampire Chronicles*, for example). Instead, Gomez scales new territory in the depictions of black interiority and opts to ground her vampires in the legends of people of color with a distinctly queer sensibility. Gomez's Gilda retains only the most basic references of vampire lore: she is sensitive to sunlight and running water; she is preternaturally strong and swift; and she abhors most food and drink, subsisting primarily on human blood.[23] However, Gilda and the vampires she calls family are also markedly different from their undead literary predecessors for, as Kathy Davis Patterson notes, for them "vampirism is not a curse but a gift."[24] Vampirism provides the gift of immortality and allows those duly gifted to live and learn throughout several lifetimes until they decide to pursue the "true death."[25]

The text also positively remixes vampirism by creating a strict code of vampire ethics that has at its center a profound reverence for life of all forms and a deep appreciation of reciprocity—concepts seemingly at odds with the commonplace vampire-as-predator trope. These vampires constitute a threat to the social order because they reject the violence and tyranny that is the foundation of the dystopias they live within, not because they prey upon humans. The first Gilda, a three-hundred-year-old European vampire who transforms the Girl and subsequently gives the Girl her name, remarks: "In our life, we who live by sharing the life blood of others have no need to kill. It is through our connection with life, not death, that we live."[26] These vampires are life-affirming immortals who share and uphold life, rather than undead parasites devouring human resources.[27] Those vampires who refuse the ethics of the exchange and insist upon killing indiscriminately and with sadistic pleasure are denounced within the novel's generally progressive coven; as Gilda concludes, "betraying our shared life, our shared humanity makes one unworthy of sharing, unworthy of life."[28] *The Gilda Stories*, then, illuminates an Afrofuturist feminist vision of the future, whereby multiple humanoid species—humans and vampires—can coexist in relative harmony.[29] Blood ceases simply to symbolize "violence, pollution, and corruption," but comes to "represent communion and exchange."[30]

Nevertheless, despite the novel's emphasis on community and reciprocity, the episodes within *The Gilda Stories* feature several apocalyptic past and future landscapes, with human beings portrayed as the primary threat to social order.[31] The notion that humans, and not vampires, are fundamentally inhumane is a culminating theme of *The Gilda Stories*, but is also present in the earliest episodes of the novel that continuously reveal human beings as the persistent and pervasive catalysts for worldwide dystopia and eventual apocalypse. Not surprisingly, while the earlier episodes of the novel, which

take place in 1850, 1890, 1921, 1955, 1971, and 1981, respectively, do not feature the explicit delineations of apocalypse and dystopia seen in the episodes
that take place in 2020 and 2050, they too are characterized by misery and
oppression and feature societies teetering on the edge of self-destruction—
all the characteristics of apocalypse and dystopia. In Gomez's rendering,
dystopia is sharp and acute for much of the population—enslaved and free
Blacks, Indigenous Americans, poor whites, women, gays, and lesbians—
and is a seemingly unceasing situation. The novel engages an Afrofuturist
feminist project that recovers a counter-history of nineteenth-century New
Orleans as a dystopia for those who are not straight, slave-owning white
males. Likewise, the other time periods, similarly ravaged by war, poverty,
disease, oppression, and so on are similar dystopias.[32] In Gomez's version of
a Black feminist future, Black women vampires move from the margins to
the center as the world of *The Gilda Stories* becomes more apocalyptic. The
novel's final chapters take place in 2020 and 2050, respectively, and feature
a ravaged, dying planet and a population that is living "off-world" (that is,
outside of Earth), hunting vampires (who have been discovered as more than
myth) in order to enslave them for their powers of immortality, or rapidly
becoming extinct. The rabid inhumanity of white supremacist society had
already been foreshadowed early in the novel: when the Girl is enslaved on
a Mississippi plantation, her mother remarks that their white masters "ain't
been here long 'nough. They just barely human. Maybe not even. They suck
up the world, don't taste it."[33] The Girl's mother rejects the notion that she,
an African, is inferior to her white enslavers, denouncing Enlightenment
notions of European superiority, and calls into question their humanity in a
manner that evokes traditional descriptions of vampire-like "blood suckers."
Blacks are simply more human, in her assessment. Black women vampires,
therefore, become not only more than human but perhaps most human in
their understanding of power, reciprocity, and community. By 2050, human
communities in *The Gilda Stories* have lost the ability to be humane and it is
vampires who hold the key to the future, for Gilda and her family "would
plan a future much different from the one envisioned by the Government"
which has allowed the wealthiest to leave the ravaged planet behind in space-

ships, leaving the rest of the inhabitants on their own.[34] Gilda and her lover, Ermis, join the rest of her vampire family in the ruins of Machu Picchu in South America, forming an all-vampire enclave shut out from the human world. The destruction of human culture—and the impending demise of the human race on Earth—gives rise to an isolated vampire society based on the exchange, one that can finally flourish without negative influence or human interference.[35] The novel depicts Gilda and her vampire family ushering in a new era of humanity—a queer vampire utopia. Transgressive kinship is now only possible among vampires. Based in the ruins of the Incas, Gomez casts Gilda's progressive coven of queer vampires as the postdiluvian answer to human destruction.

The Gilda Stories ends as a cautionary tale of the high price of white supremacy and patriarchy: it implies that human beings will die out or become increasingly irrelevant and that vampires are the next step of social awareness and perhaps even evolutionary development. The ethics of the exchange that they adhere to enables them to recreate a more humane society, ironically, without humans. The novel illustrates that human life and culture will perish without a radical restructuring of power. To that end, vampires become most suited to survive the apocalypse and its aftermath: not only are their physical needs more capable for enduring the dystopian conditions, but their notions of identity, intimacy, family, and community also promote a self-preservation that is not predicated upon the subjugation and/or annihilation of other species, unlike humans in the world of the novel. Vampires in The Gilda Stories instead are archetypal shepherds of the land, prepared to nurture the Afrofuturist feminist Eden of their choosing.

While The Gilda Stories does not offer any sustained discussion of the structural or systemic changes necessary to stem the tide of the oncoming apocalypse, I challenge the claims that "it is not politics but family bonding that is most important to Gilda" and that ultimately "The Gilda Stories argues that communities are most important for interpersonal bonding and sharing of an alternative history. Such sharing is political in its resistance to individualist norms and history-erasing assimilationism, yet it emerges as ineffective as a force for more global cultural change."[36] For while it is true that Gilda chooses "family and individual happiness over a life dedicated to communal activism" in the traditional sense, as Helford suggests, Gilda's transgressive, non-normative queer family, in addition to the radical, homosocial friendship networks she cultivates throughout the centuries, is an intensely political enterprise—one that suggests the possibility of positive systemic change at the novel's end. Indeed, the novel illustrates the feminist adage that the "personal is political" and reflects Toni Cade Bambara's advice in her seminal essay "On the Issue of Roles": "We'd better take the time to fashion revolutionary selves, revolutionary lives, revolutionary relationships. . . . If your house ain't in order, you ain't in order. It is so much easier to be out there than right here."[37] Thus, while Gilda's political action is certainly localized, it is neither romantic nor ineffective. Rather, it promotes Bambara's notion that revolution, and, in particular, revolutionary relationships, begins at home. Those who leave their personal lives uninterrogated to go off and "save" others reify problematic structures and do not enact positive change.[38] In this way, the politics of family and identity in *The Gilda Stories* speaks directly to Elizabeth Alexander's query about what in our culture might survive post-nationalism and post-racial romance. These transgressive shifts the novel profiles are just one set of answers to the question of how we might (re)write the Black future we must imagine. *The Gilda Stories'* Afrofuturist feminist project underscores the centrality of Black women's personal lives, rejecting the notion that Black women must bear the weight of their communities to survive.

*The Gilda Stories* is a foundational Afrofuturist feminist tale of Black counter-pasts and counter-futures. The world the novel depicts is one where the hegemony of patriarchy and imperialism are challenged by Black women's visions of a society without normative divisions of power.

# Notes

1. Elizabeth Alexander, *The Black Interior* (St. Paul: Graywolf Press, 2004), x–xi; emphasis mine.

2. In the context of this essay, *transgressive* means whatever "violates or challenges social, moral, or artistic conventions" (*Oxford English Dictionary*).

3. In "Further Considerations on Afrofuturism," Kodwo Eshun identifies Afrofutur-

ism as a "tool kit developed for and by Afrodiasporic intellectuals" (301). Kodwo Eshun, "Further Considerations on Afrofuturism," *CR: The New Centennial Review* 3, no. 2 (2003): 287–302.

4. Ytasha Womack, *Afrofuturism: The World of Black Sci-Fi and Fantasy Culture* (Chicago: Lawrence Hill Books, 2013), 9.

5. Susana M. Morris, "Black Girls Are from the Future: Afrofuturist Feminism in Octavia E. Butler's Fledgling," *WSQ: Women's Studies Quarterly* 40, nos. 3 & 4 (2012): 153.

6. Mark Dery, "Black to the Future: Afro-Futurism 1.0," in *Afro-Future Females: Black Writers Chart Science Fiction's Newest New-Wave Trajectory*, ed. Marleen S. Barr (Columbus: Ohio State University Press, 2008), 6–13, 6.

7. Morris, "Black Girls Are From the Future," 154. I have previously argued in favor of illuminating the explicit connections and possibilities between Afrofuturism and Black feminism as Afrofuturist feminism, noting that "Afrofuturist feminism is a reflection of paired central tenets of Afrofuturism and black feminist thought and reflects a literary tradition in which people of African descent and transgressive, feminist practices born of or from across the Afro-diaspora are key to a progressive future" (Morris 154).

8. Alexander, *Black Interior*, 5.

9. "We categorize what we're afraid of": http://db-artmag.de/en/59/feature/wangechi-mutu-between-beauty-and-horror.

10. Kodwo Eshun notes that "Afrofuturism may be characterized as a program for recovering the histories of counter-futures created in a century hostile to Afrodiasporic projection and as a space within which the critical work of manufacturing tools capable of intervention within the current political dispensation may be undertaken" (301).

11. Alondra Nelson, "Introduction: Future Texts," *Social Text* 20, no. 2 (2002): 6.

12. Katie Zavadski, "Everything Known About Charleston Church Shooting Suspect Dylann Roof," *The Daily Beast*, June 18, 2015, http://www.thedailybeast.com/articles/2015/06/18/everything-known-about-charleston-church-shooting-suspect-dylann-roof.html.

13. This term, coined by Moya Bailey, refers to the hatred of Black women.

14. For more on *The Gilda Stories*, see the following: Nina Auerbach, *Our Vampires, Ourselves* (Chicago, IL: University of Chicago Press, 1995); Ellen Brinks and Lee Talley, "Unfamiliar Ties: Lesbian Constructions of Home and Family in Jeannette Winterson's *Oranges Are Not the Only Fruit* and Jewelle Gomez's *The Gilda Stories*," in *Homemaking: Women Writers and the Politics and Poetics of Home*, ed. Catherine Wiley and Fiona R. Barnes (New York: Garland, 1996), 145–74; DoVeanna S. Fulton, *Speaking Power: Black Feminist Orality in Women's Narratives of Slavery* (Albany: SUNY Press, 2006); Cedric Gael Bryant, "'The Soul Has Bandaged Moments': Reading the African American Gothic in Wright's 'Big Boy Leaves Home,' Morrison's *Beloved*, and Gomez's *Gilda*," *African American Review* 39, no. 4 (2005): 541–53; Jewelle Gomez, "Recasting the Mythology: Writing Vampire Fiction," in *Blood Read: The Vampire as Metaphor in Contemporary Culture*, ed. Joan Gordon and Veronica Hollinger (Philadelphia: University of Pennsylvania Press, 1997), 85–92; Lynda Hall, "Passion(ate) Plays 'Wherever We Found Space': Lorde and Gomez Queer(y)ing Boundaries and Acting In," *Callaloo* 23, no. 1 (2000): 394–421; Lynda Hinkle, "Bloodsucking Structures: American Female Vampires as Class Structure Critique," *MP Journal* 2, no. 2 (2008): 19–26; Elyce Rae Helford, "The Future of Political Community: Race, Ethnicity, and Class Privilege in Novels by Piercy, Gomez, and Misha," *Utopian Studies* 12 (2001): 124–42; Jerry Rafiki Jenkins, "Race, Freedom, and the Black Vampire in Jewelle

Gomez's *The Gilda Stories*," *African American Review* 46, nos. 2–3 (2013): 313–28; Christopher S. Lewis, "Queering Personhood in the Neo-Slave Narrative: Jewelle Gomez's *The Gilda Stories*," *African American Review* 47, no. 4 (2014): 447–59; Sabine Meyer, "Passing Perverts, After All?: Vampirism, (In)Visibility, and the Horrors of the Normative in Jewelle Gomez's *The Gilda Stories*," *Femspec* 4, no. 1 (2002); Ingrid Thaler, *Black Atlantic Speculative Fictions: Octavia E. Butler, Jewelle Gomez and Nalo Hopkinson* (New York: Routledge, 2009); Kathy David Patterson, "'Haunting Back': Vampire Subjectivity in *The Gilda Stories*," *Femspec* 6, no. 1 (2005).

15. Hall, "Passion(ate) Plays," 395.

16. Helford's "Future of Political Community" does discuss *The Gilda Stories* as a futurist tale, though not in Afrofuturist terms.

17. In reconfiguring the vampire trope way, Gomez's text is aligned with, and indeed paves the way for, other vampire novels by Black women, such as Octavia Butler's *Fledgling*, Tananarive Due's "African Immortal" series, and L.A. Banks' "Vampire Huntress" series.

18. Auerbach, *Our Vampires, Ourselves*, 7.

19. Auerbach, *Our Vampires, Ourselves*, 7.

20. Auerbach, *Our Vampires, Ourselves*, 186.

21. Auerbach, *Our Vampires, Ourselves*, 185.

22. Jewelle Gomez, "Recasting the Mythology," 87–88; emphasis in original.

23. Gomez's vampires are able to consume alcohol and, in particular, champagne.

24. There are vampires in *The Gilda Stories* who do not practice the exchange or treat human (or vampire) life with any sort of reverence. Anthony calls those who pervert the exchange "ghouls" (67). Such vampires are a distinct minority in the text.

25. The "true death" is when a vampire allows their body to be destroyed by direct exposure to the sun.

26. At the start of the novel, Gilda is a three-hundred-year-old European vampire. When she decides to seek the "true death," she transforms the Girl, who thereafter takes on the name "Gilda." I use the phrase "the first Gilda" to distinguish between the original bearer of the name and the protagonist who subsequently bears it, whom I refer to simply as "Gilda."

27. Receiving blood is depicted as "sharing," for, as Gomez contends, "If people can donate a pint of blood to the Red Cross and live, they can give it to Gilda." Gomez, "Recasting Mythology," 91.

28. Gomez, *Gilda Stories*, 62.

29. Fulton identifies the exchange as a type of nourishing, corporeal "call and response," especially as it relates to transubstantiation, whereby the giver and *the receiver of blood are engaged in a life-giving dialogue of mutuality that results in the two becoming family (Speaking Power*, 120).

30. The novel's use of the phrase "the exchange" to describe a vampire's feeding exemplifies the reciprocity at the center of the vampire code of ethics: "There is a joy to the exchange we make. We draw life into ourselves, *yet we give life as well*. We give what's needed—energy, dreams, ideas. It's a fair exchange in a world full of cheaters" (45; emphasis added). Taking blood from humans is joyful not because of an exhilarating bloodlust, but because vampires can pass on positive thoughts to their donors, thus enacting a symbiotic, rather than parasitic, relationship. Shannon Winnubst notes, "These vampires feed

on—and feed—hope, not fear. And, in sucking the blood from mortal's bodies (an act that the mortal is never conscious of), they inspire greater hope and resolve for love in the world" (11). I would add to Winnubst's comments that Gomez's vampires do more than feed hope. The notion of "giving life"—as the first Gilda describes—illustrates vampires positively as a type of supernatural parent. Indeed, the novel abounds with positive imagery of vampires as nurturing figures, emphasizing that the vampire code of ethics is productive and affirming, rather than destructive. This depiction of vampire family enacts a type of "transgressive kinship," to use Sara Wasson's phrasing, which reconfigures intimacies and family in radical ways (130). Sara Wasson, "Love in the Time of Cloning: Science Fictions of Transgressive Kinship," Extrapolation 45, no. 2 (2004): 130–44; Shannon Winnubst, "Vampires, Anxieties, and Dreams: Race and Sex in the Contemporary United States," Hypatia 18, no. 3 (2003): 1–20.

31. When Gilda travels from Louisiana to California in 1890, disguised as a man, she admits that, "on the road I met many more beasts on two legs than on four. My fears were not wolves or mountain cats. They have an understanding of the reasoning of nature. I found it comforting to share that reasoning that needs no words. But with men there is no reasoning at all sometimes" (67). Gilda's travels reveal that wild animals, predators, even, have a more nuanced understanding of the exchange than "civilized" human beings, who often had a pronounced predilection toward brutal behavior. These declarations come more than a century before the apocalyptic unraveling of human communities seen at the end of the novel, yet there is much in common. In all cases, so-called human beings, not vampires, are the predators.

32. The Gilda Stories not only reflects the trope of social fragmentation reflected in other dystopic and apocalyptic texts, but also reflects similar discourse that links Gomez to prevalent thematic concerns within the larger canon of African American literature. Dystopian literature and apocalyptic literature, in particular, often feature severe social and psychic fragmentation as hallmarks of their respective genres and of the postmodern condition in general; however, this sort of fractured experience is not simply a feature of these speculative genres—scholars of African American literature have long recognized this trope in writing across the African Diaspora for several centuries. Cedric Gael Bryant has argued, "African American literature situated within gothic discourse opens up discursive spaces in which revisions of identity are possible and geographies of the imagination can be remapped" ("'Soul Has Bandaged Moments,'" 551). To that end, Gomez implicitly links the persecution of vampires to the history of persecution of other so-called minority groups. The first Gilda's notion that "There are only inadequate words to speak for who we are. The language is crude, the history is false" is an invocation to remember and recognize the ways in which other marginalized groups—Blacks, Indigenous people, LGBT folk, and others—have been slandered by dominant groups and ideologies and that vampire could also be another potentially marginalized identity (43). Gilda repeatedly rebukes the notion that she is a "ha'nt or spook as many thought her and her kind to be," affirming her corporeality even while recognizing her difference (56). Sabine Meyer suggests that Gomez's novel "actively foregrounds reductive categorization and social normativity as very 'real' horrors that spread across time and cultures insidiously, slowly (re)establishing the contexts for acts of violent terror, forced displacement, and other monstrosities associated with social Othering and oppression" ("Passing Perverts," 3). In other words, vampires on the hunt for blood are much less scary in this apocalyptic world than the horrors of slavery, colonialism, poverty, and the other social ills plaguing humanity.

33. Gomez, Gilda Stories, 11.

34. Gomez, Gilda Stories, 242.

35. Fulton suggests "Gomez infers that the earth's future and healing rests in the hands of the vampires of Machu Picchu. . . . Born of a history of oppression, this community of 'outcasts,' with their values of collectivity, nonviolence, and tolerance, is earth's salvation" (*Speaking Power*, 122).

36. Helford, "Future of Political Community," 135.

37. Toni Cade Bambara, "On the Issue of Roles," in *The Black Woman: An Anthology* (New York: Signet, 1970), 134–5.

38. Bambara gives a slew of examples of this in her essay (134): Running off to mimeograph a fuck-whitey leaflet, leaving your mate to brood, is not revolutionary. Hopping on a plane to rap to someone else's "community" while your son struggles alone with the Junior Scholastic assignment on "The Dark Continent" is not revolutionary. Sitting around murder-mouthing incorrect niggers while your father goes upside your mother's head is not revolutionary. Mapping out a building takeover when your term paper is overdue and your scholarship is under review is not revolutionary. Talking about moving against the Mafia while your nephew takes off old ladies at the subway stop is not revolutionary. These outwardly "revolutionary" acts are inadequate, according to Bambara, if one's personal affairs—relationship with family members and spouse—are fraught with discord and informed by patriarchy, white supremacy, and self-hatred.

# Acknowledgments

I am so thankful to be my mother's child. I was queer from birth, but you loved me through and into my Black Lesbianism. Thank you for giving me my first litany. I love you, devotedly.

I am so grateful for every writer included in *Mouths of Rain*. Your words are archived here, evidence of generations of genius. Love knows no limits. This book is proof.

In the introduction to *Mouths of Rain*, I write about feeling seen and being kept. Thank you, Griselda D. Thomas, Beverly Guy-Sheftall, Pero Dagbovie, Yomaira C. Figueroa, Xhercis Mendez, Tamara Butler, Terrion Williamson, Kristie Dotson, and Julie Enszer. You all have entrusted me with your name, provided resources in my times of need, helped bring my ideas to language, creating space and conditions for me to discover myself. Thank you for feeding, clothing, and nurturing, and teaching me. Your generosity has sustained my life through every ebb and flow. I am also extremely thankful for my community at Michigan State University: Cara Cilano, Zarena Aslami, Justus Nieland, Stephanie Nawyn, Bill Hart-Davidson, and Christopher Long. You all have given me a room of my own and resources. Both gifts have afforded me the time to do my work. Suban, Shewonda, Bria, Asif, Sarah, Co, Cameron, Danielle and Rebecca, thank you for accepting and loving me as I am, providing the community I needed to live and do my work. Many thanks to Vanessa Attah for your creative, assiduous work and support. Eugenia, Regina, and Arshay, our shared space has been my place of refuge. I evolved and you all loved me through every dimension. Thank you for gathering me and caring for me, from seed to blossom. Cheryl Clarke and Alexis Pauline Gumbs, my intergenerational dynamic duo. Thank you for being my first "yes." My eye is keen, I stand assured, and my world is illuminated because of you.

I am most thankful for my grandparents, Mordester Smith and General Jackson. My first fugitives. Left Mississippi and went north. I am your wildest dream.

And, to every person I have ever loved: thank you for loving me back.

# Biographies

**Shariananda Adamz, PhD (1946–),** is an oracle healer, educator, author, performer, and poet also known as SDiane Bogus. Adamz was born in Chicago, Illinois, and raised in Birmingham, Alabama. She earned a BA from Stillman College (1968), an MA from Syracuse University (1969), and PhDs from Miami University (1988) and American International University (1998). She has authored *Woman in the Moon: Poems* (1977); *Dyke Hands & Sutras Erotic & Lyric* (1988); *The Chant of the Women of Magdalena and the Magdalena Poems* (1990); *The New Age Reader: Readings for Education in the New Millennium* (editor, 1994); and *The Studenthood Reader and New Age Educational Tarot* (1995). In 2011, she founded the Church of True Hearts, a church service blending her view of the sanctity and healing capability of the body with the Christian faith. Adamz is also trained in massage therapy, pranic healing, reiki, and hypnosis. Currently, she lives in Copenhagen, Denmark, and is the director of Oracle Shariananda's Global Healing Therapies. Adamz's papers are located at the New York Public Library in Manhattan, New York. Further information about the author is available on her website, shariananda-dk.danaweb4.com.

**Sangodare Akinwale, MDiv (Julia Roxanne Wallace),** is a sweet space for transformation. Akinwale comes from a thick legacy of Black Baptist preachers and church leaders. As co-founder of the Black Feminist Film School (2012), Visiting Artist in Film at Lawrence University (2017–18), and Artist in Residence in the art department at the University of Minnesota, Twin Cities (2017–19), Akinwale brings a creative, evolutionary, and love-filled approach to filmmaking, composing, interactive design, and preaching. As co-founder of the Black Feminist Film School with Sista Docta Alexis Pauline Gumbs, Akinwale created Ritual Screening, a film-viewing technology that is interactive and grounded in Black feminist practice and our nonlinear reality. As co-founder, with Gumbs, of Mobile Homecoming, a national experiential archive project, Akinwale amplifies generations of Black LGBTQ brilliance. Further information about the author is available on their website, www.sangodare.com.

**M. Jacqui Alexander, PhD,** is an Afro-Caribbean writer, activist, transnational feminist, and theorist. Alexander is the author of *Pedagogies of Crossing: Meditations on Feminism, Sexual Politics, Memory, and the Sacred*, a decade-long project exploring themes of transnational feminism, queerness, and critical race theory. Alexander's politics are informed by the practices of decolonization, liberatory pedagogies and feminisms, and the "queering" of the state. She has taught and researched at Lang College and spent time at Spelman College teaching classes funded by the Social Sciences and Humanities Council of Canada. Alexander is a Professor Emerita at the University of Toronto in the Women and Gender Studies Department.

**Monica Arac de Nyeko (1979–)** is a Ugandan writer, essayist, and poet. She is most known for her Kenyan lesbian–themed short story, "Jambula Tree," for which she won the Caine Prize in 2007. This short story was later adapted into a film, *Rafiki*. She has a degree in education from Makerere University and a master's degree in humanitarian assistance from the University of Groningen (Netherlands). While a student at Makerere, she was an active member of a Ugandan women writers' association called FEMRITE. Arac de Nyeko is currently living in Nairobi, working on a novel.

**Red Jordan Arobateau (1943–)** is a trans* artist and writer of Honduran and African American descent from Chicago, Illinois. He has written several novels, collections of poetry, short stories, and plays. Between the years 1958 and 1978, Arobateau wrote over eight hundred poems, housed in the book *Collected Poems: Vol. 1*. His early adulthood was riddled with poverty, which encouraged him to escape into his art and writing. Writing books "took the edge off [his] pain" and allowed him to create characters he never saw on television, such as "dykes." His work largely deals with themes such as homelessness, queerness, racial identity, mental health, religion, and American imperialism. Arobateau currently lives in San Francisco with his wife and their lovely animals.

**Moya Bailey, PhD,** is an assistant professor in the Department of Cultures, Societies, and Global Studies and the Women's, Gender, and Sexuality Studies Program at Northeastern University. Her work focuses on Black women's use of digital media to promote social justice as acts of self-affirmation and health promotion. She is interested in how race, gender, and sexuality are represented in media and medicine. Bailey currently curates the #transformDH Tumblr initiative in Digital Humanities (DH). She is a monthly sustainer of the Allied Media Conference, through which she is able to bridge her passion for social justice and her work in DH. Bailey is a graduate of the Emory University Women's, Gender, and Sexuality Studies Department. She is the founder and co-conspirator of Quirky Black Girls, a network for strange and different Black girls, and now serves as the digital alchemist for the Octavia E. Butler Legacy Network. Bailey also coined the term *misogynoir*, which describes the unique anti-Black racist misogyny that Black women experience. Further information about the author is available on her website, www.moyabailey.com.

**Lucille Bogan (1897–1948),** also known as Bessie Jackson, was a singer-songwriter in the early twentieth century. She was one of the most prolific blues singers of her time, alongside Ma Rainey and Bessie Smith. Bogan was considered a "dirty blues" musician because her lyrics often dealt with sex and drugs, as exemplified in the popular songs "Sloppy Drunk Blues" and "Tricks Ain't Walkin' No More." Moreover, some of her songs also elucidated a queer identity. Bogan became the first African American blues singer to record a song outside the

Northeast with her song "Pawn Shop Blues," recorded in Atlanta, Georgia. She was a Mississippi native.

**Cheryl Boyce-Taylor** is a Trinidadian poet, curator, workshop facilitator, and teaching artist earning her MFA in creative writing from the University of Southern Maine. Boyce-Taylor has authored four collections of poetry: *Raw Air, Night When Moon Follows, Convincing the Body,* and *Arrival.* She was a finalist for the 2018 Paterson Poetry Prize for *Arrival* and a judge for the Maureen Egan 2018 Poetry Prize. Boyce-Taylor recently completed a memoir titled *Mama Phife Represents* in honor of her son Malik "Phife Dawg" Taylor. A Voices of Our Nation fellow, her work has been published in *Poetry, Prairie Schooner, Pluck, Mom Egg Review, Black Lesbians: We Are the Revolution, Adrienne,* and the *Killens Review of Arts & Letters.* Her poetry has been commissioned by the Joyce Theater and the National Endowment for the Arts for Ronald K. Brown's Evidence, A Dance Company (Brooklyn, New York). She is also the founder and curator of the Calypso Muse and the Glitter Pomegranate Performance Series. Her papers can be found at the Schomburg Center for Research in Black Culture in New York City. Further information about the author is available on her website, cherylboycetaylor .net.

**Dionne Brand (1953–)** is a Canadian poet, novelist, essayist, and documentarian from Guayaguayare, Trinidad and Tobago. She obtained a BA from the University of Toronto and an MA from the Ontario Institute for Studies in Education. Brand is the author of *Fore Day Morning: Poems, Earth Magic, No Language is Neutral, A Map to the Door of No Return: Notes to Belonging, Thirsty, The Blue Clerk,* and *Theory,* among others. Brand's latest novel, *Theory,* won the 2019 OCM BOCAS Prize for Caribbean Literature, and her most recent poetry collection, *The Blue Clerk,* was shortlisted for the Griffin Poetry Prize. Her collection *Ossuaries* was awarded the Griffin Poetry Prize in 2011, and from 2009–12, Brand served as Toronto's poet laureate. Brand resides in Toronto and is a professor in the School of English and Theatre Studies at the University of Guelph.

**Sharon Bridgforth (1958–),** a Doris Duke Performing Artist, is a writer that creates ritual/jazz theatre. A 2020–23 Playwrights' Center Core Member, Bridgforth is a New Dramatists alumna and has received support from Creative Capital, the MAP Fund, and the National Performance Network. Bridgforth has served as a dramaturg for the Urban Bush Women Choreographic Center Initiative's Choreographic Fellowship Program and has been in residence with the NoVo Foundation, Thousand Currents, Brown University's MFA Playwriting Program, the University of Iowa's MFA Playwrights Program, the Theatre School at DePaul University, the Texas-statewide QPOC organization allgo, and the Department of Performance Studies at Northwestern University. Widely published, Bridgforth is executive producer and host of the *Who Yo People Is* podcast series. Further information about the author is available on her website, www.sharonbridgforth.com.

**Charlene A. Carruthers (1985–)** is a political strategist, writer, and leading community organizer in today's movement for Black liberation. She is the founder of the Chicago Center for Leadership and Transformation and author of *Unapologetic: A Black, Queer, and Feminist Mandate for Radical Movements*, available in English and Spanish languages. Further information about the author is available on her website, www.charlenecarruthers.com.

**Cheryl Clarke, PhD (1947–),** is a Black lesbian feminist, poet, and author of *Narratives: Poems in the Tradition of Black Women* (1982), *Living as a Lesbian* (1986), *Humid Pitch* (1989), *Experimental Love* (1993), the critical study *After Mecca: Women Poets and the Black Arts Movement* (Rutgers Press, 2005), and *The Days of Good Looks: Prose and Poetry 1980–2005* (Carroll & Graf, 2006). Clarke has written many essays over the years relevant to the Black queer community, such as "Lesbianism:

An Act of Resistance," which first appeared in *This Bridge Called My Back: Writings By Radical Women of Color* (Anzaldúa and Moraga, eds., 1982), and "The Failure to Transform: Homophobia in the Black Community," which was published in *Home Girls: A Black Feminist Anthology* (Smith, ed., 1984). Clarke continues to write poetry and essays. Her latest manuscript, *By My Precise Haircut* (2016), was selected as one of two winners of the Hilary Tham Capital Competition, sponsored by the Word Works Press of Washington, DC, and judged by noted poet Kimiko Hahn. Most recently, Clarke published a chapbook titled *TARGETS*. Further information about the author is available on her website, www.cherylclarkepoet.com.

**Michelle Cliff (1946–2016)** was born in Kingston, Jamaica, and raised in New York City. Cliff earned her bachelor of arts at Wagner College and completed her graduate work at the University of London's Warburg Institute. Cliff wrote across prose, memoir, and history, addressing themes including homophobia, racism, identity, and landscape. Her most notable works include *Abeng, No Telephone to Heaven, Claiming an Identity They Taught Me to Despise*, and *From the Land of Look Behind*. Cliff served as an editor at W.W. Norton & Co. and was the Allan K. Smith Professor of English Language and Literature at Trinity College in Hartford, Connecticut. She was also the life partner of poet Adrienne Rich. Cliff died at her home in Santa Cruz, California, at the age of sixty-nine.

**Cathy J. Cohen, PhD (1962–),** is the David and Mary Winton Green Distinguished Service Professor of Political Science at the University of Chicago. Cohen is the author of two books, *The Boundaries of Blackness: AIDS and the Breakdown of Black Politics* (University of Chicago Press) and *Democracy Remixed: Black Youth and the Future of American Politics* (Oxford University Press). Her articles have been published in numerous journals and edited volumes, including the *American Political Science Review, NOMOS, GLQ, Social Text*, and the *DuBois Review*. Cohen created and oversees two major research and public-facing projects: the GenForward Survey and the Black Youth Project. Cohen is also the recipient of numerous awards including the Robert Wood Johnson Investigator's Award, the Robert Wood Johnson Scholars in Health Policy Research Fellowship, and two major research grants from the Ford Foundation for her work as principal investigator of the Black Youth Project and the Mobilization, Change, and Political and Civic Engagement Project. Professor Cohen can be found on Twitter at: @cathyjcohen.

**Anita Cornwell (1923–),** born in Greenwood, South Carolina, is best known for *Black Lesbian in White America* (1983), the first published collection of essays written by an African American lesbian. In this book, she provides sociocultural critical analyses of the experiences of Black lesbians in a racist, homophobic, and sexist society. Prior to writing this book, she graduated from Temple University in 1948 with a bachelor's degree in journalism and social sciences. From college onward, Cornwell became very active in Philadelphia's lesbian activist organizations. Her unabashed critique of an unequal society led her to be a journalist for several publications and newspapers, including the *Negro Digest, Los Angeles Free Press*, and the *Feminist Review*. Cornwell's work as an activist, both literary and otherwise, is crucial to understanding the historical LGBTQ+ liberation movements of the 1970s and 1980s in Philadelphia and the United States.

**doris diosa davenport, PhD (1949–),** is an educator, writer, literary and performance poet, and independent, non-traditional scholar born and raised in northeast Georgia, davenport's self-described "lifelong inspiration, obsession, and joy." davenport is a seventy-one-year-old Goddess-serving, Affrilachian lesbian-feminist bi-amorous visionary, working against all the -isms (and still job-searching). davenport received her bachelor of arts in English from Paine College, her master of arts from SUNY Buffalo, and her PhD in literature from the University of Southern California. She has published twelve books of poetry;

most recently, *rectify my soul* (2018) and *dancing in time* (2019). To contact the author, please email: zorahpoet7@gmail.com.

**Kai Davis** (she/her) is a Black queer writer, performer, and teaching artist from Philadelphia. Davis received her BA in both Africana studies and English with a concentration in creative writing from Temple University. Her work explores Blackness, queerness, womanhood, and the many ways these identities converge. She speaks on structural racism, misogyny, Black womanhood, ancestral trauma, mental health, intersectionality, queer love, Black love, and more. Davis has performed for TEDxPhilly, CNN, BET, PBS, and NPR, among others. She has given readings and speeches in many notable venues, including the San Francisco Opera House, Gramercy Theatre, the Kimmel Center, and the Nuyorican Poets Cafe, along with over fifty colleges across the country. Davis has delivered keynotes and facilitated workshops at several conferences, including IvyQ, the Diversity, Inclusion, and Fairness Conference at Georgia Southern University, and the Black Students Alliance Conference at Smith College. She is a two-time international grand slam champion, winning Brave New Voices in 2011 and the College Union Poetry Slam Invitational in 2016. In 2017, Davis received the Leeway Transformation Award for her years of work in art for social change in Philadelphia. Further information about the author is available on her website, www.kaidavispoetry.com.

**Alexis De Veaux, PhD (1948–),** is a poet, playwright, fiction writer, essayist, and biographer. De Veaux was born and raised in Harlem, the product of two merging streams of Black history in New York City—immigrants from the Caribbean on her mother's side and migrants from North Carolina on her father's side who settled in Harlem in the early decades of the twentieth century. The second of eight children, that history was embedded in her mother's view of life: "You got three strikes against you. You poor, you Black, and you female." But De Veaux was drawn to the world of words and books, and literature soon became the means by which she reimagined the world her mother understood. De Veaux's work is nationally and internationally known and published in five languages—English, Spanish, Dutch, Japanese, and Serbo-Croatian. Her work has appeared in numerous anthologies and publications, and she is the author of several books, including *Warrior Poet: A Biography of Audre Lorde* (2004), which was the recipient of several awards, including the Gustavus Myers Outstanding Book Award (2004), the Lambda Literary Award for Biography (2004), and the Hurston/Wright Foundation Legacy Award for nonfiction (2005). De Veaux's novella *Yabo* (RedBone Press, 2014) won the 2015 Lambda Literary Award for Lesbian Fiction. De Veaux was a faculty member of the State University of New York at Buffalo from 1992 to 2013. At present she resides in New Orleans, where she is at work on a new manuscript. Further information about the author is available on her website, www.alexisdeveaux.com.

**Alice Ruth Moore Dunbar-Nelson (1875–1935),** born in New Orleans, was a teacher, suffragist, clubwoman, journalist, and writer who published her first book, *Violets and Other Tales*, at the age of twenty. Her diary *Give Us Each Day* (1984), edited by literary critic Gloria T. Hull, is one of the only extant diaries by a nineteenth-century Black woman and reveals an active Black lesbian network, of which Dunbar-Nelson was a part during the 1920s. Her poem "You! Inez!" is queer in form and further expresses her same-sex desire. Dunbar-Nelson was an active political organizer and representative for the Woman's Committee of the Council of Defense (1918). She also campaigned for the passing of the Dyer Anti-Lynching Bill of 1924. Dunbar-Nelson died in Philadelphia and is remembered for the poetic way she portrayed the complexity of African American women and intellectuals, addressing themes like sexuality, racism, oppression, the nuclear family, work, and domestic spaces.

**Demita Frazier, JD,** is a Black feminist, social justice activist, thought leader, writer, and teacher who received her juris doctorate degree from

Northeastern University. A founding member of the Combahee River Collective, Frazier has remained a committed activist in Boston for over forty-four years. Frazier organized against the Vietnam War as a high school student in Chicago and has organized a myriad of movement initiatives like the Black Panther Party's Breakfast Program and the Jane Collective. Frazier has worked in coalition with organizations on the issues of reproductive rights, domestic violence, the care and protection of endangered children, urban sustainability issues affecting food access in poor and working-class communities, and a host of other important issues affecting communities of color. Frazier's activism is further outlined in Keeanga-Yamahtta Taylor's *How We Get Free: Black Feminism and the Combahee River Collective.*

**Jewelle Gomez (1948–)** is an author, poet, cultural critic, and playwright based on the West Coast. She is of African American and Ioway descent and has recently begun to explore her Native American heritage through her artistry. Prior to living on the West Coast, she lived in New York City for twenty-two years, immersed in the Black television and theater scene. During this time, Gomez worked at the Frank Silvera Writers' Workshop and as a stage manager for off-Broadway theater productions. While in NYC, she became involved with feminist and Black nationalist activism and the lesbian activist literary magazine *Conditions*. Gomez has authored seven books and is best known for her Lambda Literary award–winning Afrofuturist novel, *The Gilda Stories* (1991). Gomez has presented lectures and taught at numerous institutions of higher learning, including San Francisco State University, Hunter College, Rutgers University, New College of California, Grinnell College, San Diego City College, Ohio State University, and the University of Washington, Seattle. She is currently Playwright in Residence at the New Conservatory Theatre Center. Further information about the author is available on her website, www.jewellegomez.com.

**Angelina Weld Grimké (1880–1958)** was a poet, journalist, playwright, and activist born in Boston, Massachusetts, to mixed-race parents. Her biracial identity provided fertile ground on which she explored issues of sexuality, race, and activism. Coming of age in Washington, DC, Grimké became involved with poets of the Harlem Renaissance, like Countee Cullen and W.E.B Du Bois, many of whom considered her an inspiration. Her play *Rachel* was one of the first plays written by an African American woman and was publicly performed in 1916. Grimké is best known for her poetry, which expresses a sense of loneliness, a desire for love, and natural imagery. Her poems were featured in *Negro Poets and Their Poems* (1923) and *The Poetry of the Negro* (1949). After the death of her father in 1930, she moved to Brooklyn, New York, and never published again. Grimké is remembered as a foremother of Black lesbian literature and thought. Her papers are archived at the Moorland-Spingarn Research Center at Howard University.

**Alexis Pauline Gumbs, PhD (1982–),** is a queer Black troublemaker, Black feminist love evangelist, and an aspirational cousin to all sentient beings. Her work in this lifetime is to facilitate infinite, unstoppable ancestral love in practice. Her poetic work in response to the needs of her cherished communities has held space for multitudes in mourning and movement. Gumbs's co-edited volume *Revolutionary Mothering: Love on the Front Lines* (PM Press, 2016) has shifted the conversation on mothering, parenting, and queer transformation. Gumbs has transformed the scope of intellectual, creative, and oracular writing with her triptych of experimental works published by Duke University Press: *Spill: Scenes of Black Feminist Fugitivity* (2016), *M Archive: After the End of the World* (2018), and *Dub: Finding Ceremony* (2020). Gumbs's work has inspired artists across forms to create dance works, installation works, paintings, processionals, divination practices, operas, quilts, and more. Gumbs is currently in residence as a National Humanities Center Fellow, funded by the Founders' Award. During her residency she is writing *The Eternal Life of Audre Lorde: Biography as Ceremony* (forthcoming from Farrar, Straus and Giroux) and *Go There*, a book about the Black feminist transnational history of *Essence* magazine. Her book *Undrowned: Black Feminist Lessons from Marine Mammals*, a series of meditations based on the increasingly relevant lessons of marine mammals in a world with a rising ocean levels, was released in fall 2020 as part of adrienne maree brown's Emergent Strategy Series at AK Press. Further information about the author is available on her website, www.alexispauline.com.

**JP Howard, JD,** is an author, educator, literary activist, curator, and community builder. Her debut poetry collection, *SAY/MIRROR* (The Operating System), was a 2016 Lambda Literary Award finalist. She is also the author of *bury your love poems here* (Belladonna) and co-editor of *Sinister Wisdom*'s *Black Lesbians: We Are the Revolution!* Howard is a 2020 featured author in Lambda Literary's LGBTQ Writers in Schools Program and was a Split This Rock Freedom Plow Award for Poetry & Activism finalist. She is featured in the Lesbian Poet Trading Card Series from Headmistress Press and was the recipient of the Lambda Literary Judith A. Markowitz Emerging Writer Award. Howard has received fellowships and grants from Cave Canem, Voices of Our Nation, Lambda, Astraea, and the Brooklyn Arts Council. She curates the Women Writers in Bloom Poetry Salon, a New York–based forum offering writers a monthly venue in which to collaborate. The Salon celebrated its ninth year in 2020 and has a large LGBTQ POC membership that is open to all. Howard's poetry and/or essays have appeared in the Academy of American Poets' Poem-a-Day series, *Anomaly, Apogee Journal*, the *Feminist Wire, Split This Rock, Muzzle Magazine*, the *Best American Poetry* blog, *Nepantla: A Journal for Queer Poets of Color, Talking Writing, Connotation Press*, and others. Her poetry is widely anthologized. Howard holds a BA from Barnard College, an MFA in creative writing from The City College of New York, and a JD from Brooklyn Law School. Further information about the author is available on her website, www.jp-howard.com.

**Andrea Jenkins (1961–)** is an award-winning poet, writer, and performer. She has earned fellowships from the Bush Foundation, the Givens Foundation, and the Playwrights' Center, among others. Her poems have been published in journals, anthologies, and chapbooks. In 2015, Jenkins published a full-length poetry collection, *The T Is Not Silent*, and became the first oral historian for the Transgender Oral History Project of the Jean-Nickolaus Tretter Collection in GLBT Studies at the University of Minnesota. Jenkins also has more than twenty-five years of public service experience as a Hennepin County employment specialist and a Minneapolis City Council policy aide, nonprofit executive director, and consultant. On November 7, 2017, Jenkins made history as the first African American transgender woman to be elected to the city council of a major city. Further information about the author is available on her websites, andreajenkins.webs.com and andreajenkins-forward8.org.

**Terri Jewell (1954–1995)** was an African American lesbian, poet, and writer, from Louisville, Kentucky. Jewell was a prolific writer whose work was featured in more than three hundred publications, including *Sinister Wisdom*, *Woman of Power*, *Sojourner*, *Kuuma*, *A Lesbian of Color Anthology*, the *American Voice*, *Calyx*, and the *Black Scholar*. She was the editor of the *Black Woman's Gumbo Ya-Ya*, a collection of inspirational quotes by Black women around the world. She also authored *Our Names Are Many: The Black Woman's Book of Days*. Jewell attended Michigan State University, which houses her archival collection, the Terri Lynn Jewell Papers. She was an active member of the *Lesbian Review of Books* since its founding. At the time of her death, Jewell was working on *Dreadsisters: Lock-Sisters*, a collection of narratives from Black women with dreadlocks. Loved by many, she resided in Michigan.

**Janae Johnson** is a writer, performer, educator, and curator. Johnson is a Women of the World Poetry Slam Champion, National Poetry Slam Champion, and a Write Bloody Book Award finalist. Johnson is a founder of two nationally recognized poetry venues, and her work has appeared in outlets and on stages such as ESPN, PBS Newshour, *Lenny Says*, SFJazz, *Kinfolks: A Journal of Black Expression*, and Button Poetry.

**Barbara Jordan, JD (1936–1996),** was a lawyer and politician from Houston, Texas, widely recognized for being the first Black woman to deliver a keynote speech at the Democratic National Convention in 1976. Jordan was one of few African Americans in her program when she graduated from Boston University School of Law. She was also the first African American elected to the Texas Senate and the first Southern Black woman elected to Congress. A leader of the Civil Rights Movement, Jordan was notable for her powerful opening statements at the House Judiciary Committee during Richard Nixon's impeachment. Toward the end of her life, Jordan lived with her partner of twenty years, Nancy Earl, who became her primary caregiver when Jordan's health began to fail. Faithful to her Texan roots, they were living in Austin at the time of her passing.

**Audre Lorde (1934–1992)** was a renowned Black lesbian mother warrior poet, born in New York City to Caribbean immigrants from Barbados and Grenada. Lorde published her first poem in *Seventeen* magazine while attending Hunter High School. In 1954, Lorde spent a year at the National University of Mexico; this period was crucial for Lorde's personal and artistic journey into her lesbianism and life as a burgeoning poet. Lorde earned her bachelor's degree from Hunter College in 1959 and her master's degree in library science from Columbia University in 1961. Lorde is the author of over a dozen poetry collections, prose essays, and speeches, including *The First Cities* (1968), *Cables to Rage* (1970), *From a Land Where Other People Live* (1973), *New York Head Shop and Museum* (1974), *Coal* (1976), *The Black Unicorn* (1978), *The Cancer Journals* (1980), *Zami: A New Spelling of My Name* (1983), *Sister Outsider: Essay and Speeches* (1984), and *A Burst of Light* (1988), among many others. *From a Land Where Other People Live* was nominated for a National Book Award in 1973. Lorde was one of the founders of the Women's Coalition of St. Croix in 1981 and was part of a delegation of Black women writers invited to Cuba in 1985 to discuss revolution, racism, and the status of gays and lesbians in Cuba. She was also a visiting professor at the Free University of Berlin from 1984–92. Former Free University lecturer Dagmar Schultz released a documentary in 2012 entitled *Audre Lorde: The Berlin Years (1984–1992)*. This documentary chronicles their friendship and Lorde's experience in the Afro-German community as a professor, poet, and Black lesbian. Lorde's work bridges the gap between Black feminism and transnational feminism and activism. The largest archive of Lorde's work can be found at Spelman College's Women's Research and Resource Center in Atlanta, Georgia.

**Bettina Love, PhD,** is an award-winning author and professor of educational theory and practice at the University of Georgia. Dr. Love is one of the field's most esteemed researchers in the area of hip-hop education. Her research focuses on the ways in which urban youth negotiate hip-hop music and culture to form social, cultural, and political identities in order to create new and sustaining ways of thinking about urban education and intersectional social justice. Dr. Love's work is also concerned with how teachers and schools working with parents and communities can build communal, civically-engaged schools rooted in intersectional social justice for the goal of equitable classrooms. Dr. Love's work has appeared in numerous books and journals, including the *English Journal*, *Urban Education*, the *Urban Review*, and the *Journal of LGBT Youth*. She is the author of the award-winning book *We Want to Do More Than Survive: Abolitionist Teaching and the Pursuit of Educational Freedom*, as well as *Hip Hop's Lil Sistas Speak: Negotiating Hip Hop Identities and Politics in the New South*. Further information about the author is available on her website, bettinalove.com.

**Catherine E. McKinley** and **L. Joyce Delaney** are best known for co-editing *Afrekete: An Anthology of Black Lesbian Writing* (1995). A collection of fiction, nonfiction, and poetry by Black lesbian writers, *Afrekete* illuminates the richness of Black lesbianhood through a seamless interweaving of stories that center healing, romance, reproductive justice, and coming of age. Featured in this anthology are Audre Lorde, Alexis

De Veaux, Carolivia Herron, Jewelle Gomez, Jacqueline Woodson, and Jamika Ajalon, among others. McKinley and Delaney met at Sarah Lawrence College and eventually began collaborating for *Afrekete*. McKinley is a writer currently living in Brooklyn, New York, and Delaney is a screenwriter and independent film producer based in Los Angeles.

**Lisa C. Moore** is the founder and editor of RedBone Press, which publishes award-winning work celebrating the culture of Black lesbians and gay men and promoting understanding between Black gays and lesbians and the Black mainstream. Moore is the editor of *does your mama know?: An Anthology of Black Lesbian Coming Out Stories*, co-editor of *Spirited: Affirming the Soul and Black Gay/Lesbian Identity*, and co-editor, co-compiler, and co-publisher (with Vintage Entity Press) of *Carry the Word: A Bibliography of Black LGBTQ Books*. A former editor of the *Lambda Book Report*, Moore has judged numerous literary awards and speaks at conferences, colleges, and universities about Black gay/lesbian publishing. She is a former board member of the Money for Women Barbara Deming Memorial Fund.

**Susana Morris, PhD,** is a queer Jamaican-American writer based in Atlanta. She teaches at the Georgia Institute of Technology. Morris is the author of *Close Kin and Distant Relatives: The Paradox of Respectability in Black Women's Literature* (University of Virginia Press, 2014); co-editor, with Brittney C. Cooper and Robin M. Boylorn, of *The Crunk Feminist Collection* (Feminist Press, 2017); and co-author, with Brittney C. Cooper and Chanel Craft Tanner, of the forthcoming young-adult handbook, *Feminist AF: The Guide to Crushing Girlhood* (W.W. Norton & Co., 2021). She is passionate about Afrofuturism, Black feminism, and climate change. When she's not reading, writing, or teaching, she's probably baking somebody a cake.

**Pauli Murray, JD (1910–1985),** born in Baltimore, Maryland, was a significant figure in the emergence of the modern women's movement. She was a lawyer, professor, ordained priest, civil rights activist, femi-

nist, and writer. Murray was the only woman in her law school at Howard University, the first African American to earn a doctorate in juris-
prudence from Yale University Law School (1965), and the first Black
woman to be ordained an Episcopalian priest (1977). Murray coined the
term "Jane Crow" to describe how the law negatively and dispropor-
tionately affected African American women. Murray is remembered for
her broad vision of justice and human rights. Murray was believed to be
queer, and more of her life is outlined in Brittney Cooper's book *Beyond
Respectability: The Intellectual Thought of Race Women*.

**Pat Parker (1944–1989)** was a renowned African American, lesbian-
feminist poet and performer. She was the author of *Jonestown and Other
Madness* (1985), *Movement in Black* (1978), *Womanslaughter* (1978), *Pit
Stop* (1974), and *Child of Myself* (1972). Her poems appeared in numerous
journals, newspapers, and anthologies. With Judy Grahn, she recorded
the album *Where Would I Be Without You* (Olivia Records, 1976), and
one of her spoken poems appeared on the album *Lesbian Concentrate*.
Parker was born in Houston, Texas, in 1944 and moved to Los Angeles,
California, after graduating high school. She lived in the San Francisco
Bay Area from 1965 until her death from complications of cancer. She
was survived by her partner of nine years, Martha Dunham, and their
daughter, Anastasia Dunham-Parker-Brade, as well as Cassidy Brown,
whom she co-parented. *The Complete Works of Pat Parker* (A Midsummer Night's Press/Sinister Wisdom, 2016) is available in print, as well as
her letters with Audre Lorde in the collection *Sister Love*. In June 2019,
Parker was posthumously inaugurated as one of fifty American pioneers
advancing LGBTQ equality, as noted on the National LGBTQ Wall of
Honor in New York City's Stonewall Inn.

**Michelle Parkerson** is an award-winning independent filmmaker and
academic based in Washington, DC. Her work has been shown widely
on public television and at various film festivals. She is most known for
the documentaries *A Litany for Survival: The Life and Work of Audre Lorde*;
*But Then, She's Betty Carter*; and *Gotta Make This Journey: Sweet Honey in*

*the Rock.* Parkerson has received grants from the Independent Television Service, the Corporation for Public Broadcasting, and the American Film Institute, as well as a fellowship from the Rockefeller Foundation. Her work has premiered at the Sundance Film Festival, and she is most known for her feminist activism and political work concerning the LGBTQ+ community. Parkerson received the Audience and Best Biography Awards at the San Francisco International Film Festival and the Prix du Public at the Festival International de Créteil Films de Femmes.

**Ma Rainey (1899–1933)** is one of the most well-known blues singers of all time. Rainey was born Gertrude Pridgett and came from humble beginnings in Columbus, Georgia. Her ascent in the music industry began as a teenager when she performed at a talent show in Columbus. Rainey rose to fame and recorded songs such as "Jelly Bean Blues" and "See, See Rider" with Louis Armstrong. Although most of Rainey's songs were heterosexual in content, some songs had a clear queer presence, such as "Prove It on Me." Rainey is remembered as and affectionately called the "Mother of Blues."

**Kate Rushin (1951–)** is the author of *The Black Back-Ups.* Rushin's "The Bridge Poem" appears in *This Bridge Called My Back: Writings by Radical Women of Color,* a groundbreaking feminist anthology edited by Cherríe Moraga and Gloria E. Anzaldúa. A recipient of the Rose Low Rome Memorial Poetry Prize and the Grolier Poetry Prize, Rushin's work is widely anthologized. A Connecticut resident, Rushin has read at Hill-Stead Museum's Sunken Garden Poetry Festival, the Geraldine Dodge Poetry Festival, and the Smith College Poetry Center, and has led workshops for the Omega Institute for Holistic Studies and the Cave Canem Foundation. Rushin received her BA from Oberlin College and her MFA from Brown University. She is a former fellow of the Fine Arts Work Center in Provincetown and a graduate fellow of Cave Canem. Further information about the author is available on her website, katerushinpoet.com.

**Savannah Shange, PhD,** is a Black queer feminist and urban anthropologist. Shange researches abolition, blackness and antiblackness, social movements, late liberal statecraft, multiracial coalition, gentrification, anthropology of education, queer theory, femme gender, ethnographic ethics, California, and North America. She earned a PhD in Africana studies and education from the University of Pennsylvania, an MAT from Tufts University, and a BFA from Tisch School of the Arts at New York University. Shange is the author of *Progressive Dystopia: Abolition, Antiblackness, and Schooling in San Francisco* (2019) and assistant professor of anthropology at the University of California, Santa Cruz. Further information about the author can be found on her website, savannah-shange.com.

**Ann Allen Shockley (1927–),** a native of Louisville, Kentucky, is an author and journalist widely known for writing *Loving Her* (1974), the first novel written by an African American that explicitly addresses lesbianism. Shockley's work addresses issues concerning racism and oppression in America, as well as interracial relationships—romantic, platonic, and otherwise.

Shockley graduated from Fisk University in 1948 and received her master's degree in library science from Case Western Reserve University in 1959. She worked at Delaware State College and the University of Maryland Eastern Shore as a librarian before obtaining a position as a professor of library science and university archivist in the Special Negro Collection at Fisk University. Shockley founded the Black Oral History Program before retiring in 1998. She is the author of over thirty novels, short stories, and articles that address the myriad issues of homophobia and racism in America.

**Barbara Smith (1946–)** is a socialist, organizer, and Black feminist famous for her irreverent work in sustaining Black feminist politics in the United States. Her legacy as an activist began to concretize while attending the all-girls Mount Holyoke College, which she helped desegregate in 1965. This activism was heavily informed by the larger freedom struggles happening during this time, such as the Black Power and women's rights movements. As a young adult, these social struggles worked to shape her political consciousness. In 1973, Smith attended a meeting in New York City led by the National Black Feminist Organization (NBFO). This led her, her twin Beverly, and Demita Frazier to found a Boston chapter of the NBFO. This chapter proved to be substantially more radical than the national chapter, leading them to break off and form a new organization in 1975: The Combahee River Collective. The Combahee River Collective was a socialist Black feminist organization; the collective concretized their tenets in the Combahee River Collective Statement, published in 1977. The Combahee River Collective is also featured in Keeanga-Yamahtta Taylor's *How We Get Free: Black Feminism and the Combahee River Collective*. For her substantial and priceless contributions to collective liberation, Smith can be supported in her journey as an elder through the Barbara Smith Donor Caring Circle at smithcaringcircle.com.

**Beverly Smith (1946–)** is an organizer, health advocate, writer, academic, and twin sister to Barbara Smith. She was co-founder of Kitchen Table: Women of Color Press in 1980, a feminist publishing press that sought to publish women writers of color in response to their exclusion from larger presses. Smith is best known for writing the Combahee River Collective Statement, along with Barbara Smith and Demita Frazier, which delineated a framework for Black feminist organizing and sexual politics. Smith has written many essays and conducted extensive research on Black women's health. Her contributions appear in the anthology *But Some of Us Are Brave: Black Women's Studies*, titled "Black Women's Health: Notes for a Course," and *How We Get Free: Black Feminism and the Combahee River Collective*, edited by Keeanga-Yamahtta Taylor. Smith has also taught women's health at the Schomburg Center for Research in Black Culture at Emerson College and the University of Massachusetts, Boston.

**Shawn(ta) Smith-Cruz** is an archivist at the Lesbian Herstory Archives, an assistant curator, and Associate Dean for Teaching, Learning, and Engagement at the New York University Division of Libraries. She is a co-chair for the board of CLAGS: The Center for LGBTQ Studies at the Graduate Center, CUNY, and chair of the Archives committee. Smith-Cruz has a BS in queer women's studies from the CUNY Baccalaureate Program, an MFA in creative writing/fiction, and an MLS with a focus on archiving and records management from Queens College. She is the 2020 recipient of the WGSS Award for Significant Achievement—sponsored by Duke University Press and administered by the Association of College and Research Libraries, a division of the American Libraries Association—for her work archiving and exhibiting the Salsa Soul Sisters, the first lesbian of color organization in the country. Further information about the author is available on her website, shawntasmithcruz.com.

**Pamela Sneed** is a New York–based poet, writer, visual artist, and performer. She earned her BA from Eugene Lang College and her MFA from Long Island University. Sneed is the author of the books *Imagine Being More Afraid of Freedom than Slavery* (1998) and *Kong and Other Works* (2009), as well as the chapbooks *Lincoln* (2014), *Gift* (2015), and *Sweet Dreams* (2018). Her poetry has appeared in *100 Best African American Poems* (edited by Nikki Giovanni, 2010), *Best Monologues from Best American Short Plays* (edited by William Demastes, 2013), and Zoe Leonard's *Transcript of a Rally* (2016). Sneed's writing has appeared widely in magazines such as *Artforum*, *Hyperallergic*, and the *New York Times Magazine*.

**Kaila Story, PhD (1980–),** is an associate professor of women's, gender, and sexuality studies with a joint appointment in the Department of Pan-African Studies at the University of Louisville. She holds the Audre Lorde Chair in Race, Class, Gender, and Sexuality Studies. Story was also an honoree of NBC's inaugural #Pride30, which featured LGBTQ community leaders and changemakers. She co-hosts an award-winning podcast with longtime Louisville activist Jaison Gardner called *Strange Fruit: Musings on Politics, Pop Culture, and Black Gay Life* on WFPL, the Louisville affiliate of NPR. You can find current and past episodes here: strangefruitpod.org.

**Mecca Jamilah Sullivan, PhD,** is the author of the short story collection *Blue Talk and Love*, winner of the Judith Markowitz Award from Lambda Literary. She holds a PhD in English literature from the University of Pennsylvania, an MA in English and creative writing from Temple University, and a BA in Afro-American studies from Smith College. In her fiction, Sullivan explores the intellectual, emotional, and bodily lives of young Black women through voice, music, and hip-hop-inflected magical realist techniques. Sullivan's short stories have appeared in *Best New Writing*; *American Fiction: Best New Stories by Emerging Writers*; *Prairie Schooner*; *Callaloo*; *Crab Orchard Review*; *Robert Olen Butler Fiction Prize Stories*; *BLOOM: Queer Fiction, Art, Poetry and More*; *TriQuarterly*; *Feminist Studies*; *All About Skin: Short Stories by Award-Winning Women Writers of Color*; *Baobab: South African Journal of New Writing*; and many others. Sullivan is an assistant professor of English at Bryn Mawr College, where she teaches courses in African American poetry and poetics, Black feminist literature, and creative writing. Her forthcoming book, *The Poetics of Difference: Queer Feminist Forms in the African Diaspora*, explores the politics of experiment in Black queer and feminist literary cultures. She is currently completing a novel. Further information about the author is available on her website, www.meccajamilahsullivan.com.

**Alice Walker (1944–),** born in Eatonton, Georgia, is an award-winning essayist, novelist, and poet. Walker is best known for writing *The Color Purple* (1982), a novel that was a pioneer for its time because of its unabashed critique of the sexism and sexual assault permeating the lives of young Black girls and women. *The Color Purple* also illuminates the potentiality of lifesaving relationships between Black women. The novel won the Pulitzer Prize and the National Book Award in 1983. Walker carried on this legacy with her nonfiction book *In Search of Our Mother's Gardens* (1983), in which she coins and constructs "womanism." Walker's work offers vital insights about African American culture and life.

**Arisa White,** a Cave Canem graduate fellow, received her MFA from the University of Massachusetts, Amherst, and is the author of *Perfect on Accident, You're the Most Beautiful Thing That Happened, Black Pearl, Post Pardon, A Penny Saved,* and *Hurrah's Nest.* White's poetry has been nominated for a Lambda Literary Award, NAACP Image Award, California Book Award, and Wheatley Book Award. Her chapbook *"Fish Walking" & Other Bedtime Stories for My Wife* won the inaugural Per Diem Poetry Prize. White is the co-author of *Biddy Mason Speaks Up,* the second book in the Fighting for Justice Series for young readers. A native New Yorker living in central Maine, White is an assistant professor of creative writing at Colby College and serves on the board of directors for Foglifter and Nomadic Press. She is currently co-editing, with Miah Jeffra and Monique Mero, the anthology *Home is Where You Queer Your Heart,* which will be published by Foglifter Press in 2021. Her poetic memoir *Who's Your Daddy* is forthcoming from Augury Books in March 2021. Further information about the author is available on her website, arisawhite.com

# Selections

*Every effort has been made to find the owners of copyright for the works included in this anthology. The editor gratefully acknowledges the following permissions and sources for the works and apologizes for any that may have been missed inadvertently.*

## Part I: Uses of the Erotic, 1909–2020

Alice Walker, "Can It Be?" Copyright © 2020 by Alice Walker. Used with permission.

Audre Lorde, "Love Poem." Copyright © 1975 by Audre Lorde, "Woman." Copyright © 1978 by Audre Lorde, from *The Collected Poems of Audre Lorde* by Audre Lorde. Used by permission of W.W. Norton & Company, Inc. "Uses of the Erotic": from *Sister Outsider* by Audre Lorde, Copyright © 1984, 2007 by Audre Lorde. Used herein by permission of the Charlotte Sheedy Literary Agency.

Cheryl Clarke, "Kittatinny." *Living as a Lesbian.* Sinister Wisdom: A Midsummer Night's Press. Copyright © 2014 by Cheryl Clarke. Used with permission.

Michelle Parkerson, "Finer with Time." Copyright © 2020 by Michelle Parkerson.

Monica Arac de Nyeko, "Jambula Tree." *Jambula Tree and Other Stories.* Oxford: New Internationalist. Copyright © 2008 by Monica Arac de Nyeko. Used with permission.

Pat Parker, "Metamorphosis," "My Lover Is a Woman," "Sunshine." *Movement in Black.* Baltimore: Diana Press, 1978. Copyright © 2020 by Anastasia Dunham-Parker-Brady. All rights reserved. Used with permission.

Terri Jewell, "Celebrant." *Succulent Heretic.* Lansing: Opal Tortuga Press, 1994.

## Part II: Interlocking Oppressions and Identity Politics, 1980–2020

Anita Cornwell, "Three for the Price of One: Notes from a Gay, Black Feminist." *Black Lesbian in White America.* Tallahassee: Naiad Press. Copyright © 1983 by Anita Cornwell. Reprinted by permission of Anita Cornwell.

Ann Allen Shockley, "A Meeting of the Sapphic Daughters." *The Black and White of It.* Tallahassee: Naiad Press. Copyright © 1987 by Ann Allen Shockley. Used with permission.

Dawn Lundy-Martin, "To be an orphan inside of 'blackness.'" *Good Stock, Strange Blood.* Minneapolis: Coffee House Press. Copyright © 2017 by Dawn Lundy-Martin. Used with permission of Dawn Lundy-Martin.

Kai Davis, "Ain't I a Woman." *Ain't I.* San Francisco: Blurb. Copyright © 2019 by Kai Davis. Used with permission.

Kaila Story, "Not Feminine as in Straight, but Femme as in Queer #AF: The Queer & Black Roots of My Femme Expression/Experience." Copyright © 2020 by Kaila Story.

Mecca Jamilah Sullivan, "Wolfpack." *Blue Talk and Love*. Bronx: Riverdale Avenue Books. Published with permission from Riverdale Avenue Books. Copyright © 2015.

Pamela Sneed, "We Are Here." *Sinister Wisdom* 107: *Black Lesbians—We are the Revolution!* Copyright © 2019 by Pamela Sneed. Used with permission.

## Part III: Coming Out and Stepping Into, 1978–2020

Lisa C. Moore, *does your mama know?: An Anthology of Black Lesbian Coming Out Stories.* Copyright © 1997, 2009 by Lisa C. Moore. Reprinted by permission of RedBone Press.

Beverly Smith, "The Wedding." *HomeGirls: A Black Feminist Anthology*, ed. Barbara Smith. Kitchen Table: Women of Color Press. Copyright © 1983 by Beverly Smith. Used with permission.

Dionne Brand, Poem from *No Language Is Neutral* by Dionne Brand. Copyright © 1990. Used by permission of The Wylie Agency LLC.

Akasha Gloria Hull, "Angelina Weld Grimké: 1880–1958." Originally published in *Color, Sex, and Poetry: Three Women Writers of the Harlem Renaissance*. Indiana UP. Copyright © 1987. Reprinted with permission of Indiana University Press.

JP Howard, "aubade, in pieces, for my ex-lovers." Copyright © 2020 by JP Howard. Used with permission.

Janae Johnson, "Black Butch Woman." Copyright © 2020 by Janae Johnson. Used with permission.

Jewelle Gomez, "Curtain 1983." Copyright © 2020 by Jewelle Gomez. Used with permission.

Michelle Cliff, "Notes on Speechlessness." *Sinister Wisdom* 5, no. 1: 5–10. Copyright © 2020 by The Estate of Michelle Cliff. Used with permission.

Moya Bailey, "Living Single." Crunk Feminist Collective Blog. Copyright © 2011 by Moya Bailey. Used with permission.

Pat Parker, "funny." *Movement in Black*, 1978. Baltimore: Diana Press. Copyright © 2020 by Anastasia Dunham-Parker-Brady. All rights reserved. Used with permission.

## Part IV: The Sacred, 1970–2020

Alexis De Veaux, "Inter**species**." Copyright © 2019 by Alexis De Veaux. Used with permission.

Alexis Pauline Gumbs, "her relationship to Africa lives in the part of her that is eight years." Excerpt originally published in *M Archive: After the End of the World*. Duke UP. Copyright © 2018 by Alexis Pauline Gumbs. Used with permission.

Arisa White, "Black Pearl: A poetic drama for four voices." *Black Pearl*. Nomadic Press. Copyright © 2016 by Arisa White. Used with permission.

Cheryl Boyce-Taylor, "How to Make Art." Copyright © 2020 by Cheryl Boyce-Taylor. Used with permission.

doris diosa davenport, "Erzulie- Oshun (Georgia Style)." *Voodoo Chile: Slight Return Poems*. Soque Street Press. Copyright © 1991 by doris diosa davenport. Used with permission.

Pauli Murray, "Without Name." Copyright © 1948 by the Pauli Murray Foundation, from *Dark Testament and Other Poems* by Pauli Murray. Used by permission of Liveright Publishing Corporation.

Shariananda Adamz, "Fighting Racism: An Approach Through Ritual." *Lesbian Contradiction*. Copyright © 1984, 2020 by Shariananda Adamz. Used with permission.

Sangodare Akinwale, "Anew." Copyright © 2019 by Julia Wallace.

Sharon Bridgforth, Excerpt from *love conjure/blues*. *love conjure/blues*, by Sharon Bridgforth. Copyright © 2004 by Lisa C. Moore. Reprinted by permission of RedBone Press.

## Part V: Radical Futurities, 1976–2020

Charlene A. Carruthers, Epigraph from "The Mandate." *Unapologetic: A Black, Queer, and Feminist Mandate for Radical Movements*. Copyright © 2018 by Charlene Carruthers. Reprinted by permission of Beacon Press, Boston.

Alexis Pauline Gumbs, "The Shape of My Impact." *Feminist Wire*. Copyright © 2012 by Alexis Pauline Gumbs. Used with permission.

Audre Lorde, "I Am Your Sister": from *Burst of Light* by Audre Lorde, Copyright © 1988, 2017 by Audre Lorde. Used herein by permission of the Charlotte Sheedy Literary Agency.

Barbara Smith, "Toward a Black Feminist Criticism." *Conditions* 1, no. 2: 25–44. Copyright ©1977 by Barbara Smith. Used with permission.

Bettina Love, "A Ratchet Lens: Black Queer Youth, Agency, Hip-Hop, and the Black Ratchet Imagination." *Educational Researcher* 46, no. 9: 539–47. Copyright © 2017 by *Educational Researcher*. Used with permission.

Cathy J. Cohen, "Deviance as Resistance: A New Research Agenda for the Study of Black Politics." *DuBois Review* 1, no. 1: 27–45. Copyright © 2004 by DuBois Review: Social Science Research on Race. Used with permission.

doris diosa davenport, "Never Mind the Misery/Where's the Magic?" Copyright © 1981, 2020 by doris diosa davenport. Used with permission.

Kate Rushin, "At Another Crossroads." Copyright © 2020 by Kate Rushin. Used with permission.

Shariananda Adamz, "The Myth and Tradition of the Black Bulldagger." *Black Lace*. Copyright© 1988, 2020 by Shariananda Adamz. Used with permission.

Savannah Shange, "Play Aunties and Dyke Bitches: Gender, Generation, and the Ethics of Black Queer Kinship." *The Black Scholar* 49, no. 1: 40–54. Copyright © 2019 by *The Black Scholar*. Used with permission.

Shawn(ta) Smith-Cruz, "Archiving Black Lesbians in Practice: The Salsa Soul Sisters Archival Collection." *The City Amplified: Oral Histories and Radical Archives*. Copyright © 2018 by Shawn(ta) Smith-Cruz. Used with permission.

Susana Morris, "More Than Human: Black Feminisms of the Future in Jewelle Gomez's *The Gilda Stories*." *The Black Scholar* 46, no. 2: 33–45. Copyright © 2016 by *The Black Scholar*. Used with permission.

This page constitutes an extension of the copyright page.

# About the Editor

**Briona Simone Jones** is a doctoral candidate and scholar of Black Feminist Thought and Queer Studies in the Department of English at Michigan State University. She is a Black Lesbian Feminist of Jamaican and African American descent, born and raised in Rochester, New York.

# Publishing in the Public Interest

Thank you for reading this book published by The New Press. The New Press is a nonprofit, public interest publisher. New Press books and authors play a crucial role in sparking conversations about the key political and social issues of our day.

We hope you enjoyed this book and that you will stay in touch with The New Press. Here are a few ways to stay up to date with our books, events, and the issues we cover:

- Sign up at www.thenewpress.com/subscribe to receive updates on New Press authors and issues and to be notified about local events
- Like us on Facebook: www.facebook.com/newpressbooks
- Follow us on Twitter: www.twitter.com/thenewpress
- Follow us on Instagram: www.instagram.com/thenewpress

Please consider buying New Press books for yourself; for friends and family; or to donate to schools, libraries, community centers, prison libraries, and other organizations involved with the issues our authors write about.

The New Press is a 501(c)(3) nonprofit organization. You can also support our work with a tax-deductible gift by visiting www.thenewpress .com/donate.

*Write about our people: tell their story.*

—Lorraine Hansberry